GW00455567

The Lyotard Dic

The Lyotard Dictionary

Edited by Stuart Sim

Edinburgh University Press

© editorial matter and organisation, Stuart Sim 2011
© in the individual contributions is retained by the authors

Edinburgh University Press Ltd
22 George Square, Edinburgh

www.euppublishing.com

Typeset in 11/13 Ehrhardt
by Servis Filmsetting Ltd, Stockport, Cheshire, and
printed and bound in Great Britain by
CPI Antony Rowe, Chippenham and Eastbourne

A CIP record for this book is available from the British Library

ISBN 978 0 7486 4005 8 (hardback)
ISBN 978 0 7486 4006 5 (paperback)

The right of the contributors
to be identified as author of this work
has been asserted in accordance with
the Copyright, Designs and Patents Act 1988.

Contents

Acknowledgements

I would like to thank all the contributors to this volume, many of whom also suggested additional entries in the project's planning stages, which were gratefully received. My editor, Carol MacDonald, has been immensely supportive throughout the writing process, as have EUP staff in general, as always.

Special thanks go to Dr Helene Brandon for yet again helping me successfully negotiate the various problems that any book project inevitably involves.

Abbreviations

Introduction

Stuart Sim

Postmodernism and poststructuralism have already turned into historical phenomena, with many of the leading lights of the movements now gone and their legacies under assessment. Jean-François Lyotard (1924–98) will no doubt always be identified with the former movement, and he was indeed one of the most powerful and persuasive commentators on postmodernism – if perhaps not always classifiable as a postmodernist as such himself. He tended to present himself as an observer of postmodernism and could be critical of what it involved on occasion (only too able as he put it, 'to embrace . . . conflicting perspectives');[1] but so influential was he in his observations in works like *The Postmodern Condition* that he has become one of postmodernism's definitive voices.[2] For many, postmodernism is above all else, adopting Lyotard's terminology, a campaign of resistance against oppressive grand narratives/metanarratives that seek to dominate our lives and keep us in a state of socio-political subjection. His intellectual career reveals someone who grows progressively more hostile to the grand narrative ethos, especially after the 1968 *événements* in Paris, and who takes on great symbolic import for the post-Marxist left in consequence. More than any of his contemporaries, Lyotard wrestles with what it means to have to reinvent one's politics on the left as the theories on which these were based in modern times lose their credibility and any semblance of mass public support.

Lyotard is the most political of philosophers, always concerned to relate his work to the wider public sphere. His left orientation is unmistakable from the beginnings of his writing career, as is his mistrust of universal theories claiming to possess the complete answer to all of humanity's problems. His dialogue with Marxism is never less than tortuous, culminating in his spectacularly vicious attack on it in *Libidinal Economy*: that 'evil book' as he saw it from a later perspective.[3] It is certainly a bad-tempered piece of work, suggesting someone at the end of his tether politically; there is not even the pretence of observing the decorums of intellectual debate in its pages which castigate not just Marx and Marxists but intellectuals as a class in general: 'Why, political intellectuals, do you *incline towards* the proletariat? In commiseration for what?', as he acidly remarks at one point.[4] The problem Lyotard is facing up to in this book is how to continue politically without an organisation such as communism to fall back on: the left has traditionally laid great store by solidarity, and lone thinkers who have rejected the very notion of affiliation tend to be looked on with suspicion. Many thinkers have fallen out of love with Marxism over the years, but they have generally adopted some other form of political creed to sustain themselves, whether from the left, right or centre. Lyotard never finds such comfort, and he cuts a rather isolated figure in that respect: a radical with no proper base. In this respect he becomes representative of a whole generation in France who could no longer turn a blind eye to the totalitarianism of the communist movement, nor to the excesses committed in its name over the course of the twentieth century, and who could find almost nothing within the Marxist tradition on which to build a future radical politics. Even as early as the 1950s in his writings on Algeria for *Socialisme ou barbarie* Lyotard began to suspect this was the case, and with characteristic honesty went ahead and said so, even though it could only create enemies for him on the left.[5] Those enemies were to multiply substantially after the publication of *Libidinal Economy*.

LYOTARDIAN PHILOSOPHY

To survey Lyotard's writing career is to find recurrent themes and concerns, which may seem to go against the grain of his antipathy to anything that smacks of essentialism – a trait he shares with most of the postmodernist movement, for whom Gilles Deleuze and Felix Guattari's nomadism becomes all but second nature.[6] Yet there is all the same a distinctively Lyotardian philosophical position that knows what it finds unacceptable, and is not afraid to court unpopularity in the way it articulates this. Few thinkers of his generation in France can be as withering about intellectuals as Lyotard, who can seem oblivious to the reaction of his peers, dismissing them as being little better than dupes of the dominant ideology:

For a long time in the West, philosophers have been exposed to the temptation of the role of the intellectual, they have been tempted to turn themselves into the representatives of an authority. And there are not many, since Plato, over the past twenty-five hundred years, who have not succumbed to this temptation.[7]

It is a temptation that Lyotard always does his best to resist. There is in fact a strong negative element in his thought, and we can easily enough compile a list of what Lyotard is against: for starters, absolutist theories, determinist thinking, overbearing authority, the injustice done in the name of grand narrative, the injustice done to minority groups throughout history, Holocaust deniers. What he will not do is wheel in the standard leftist solutions to these problems: instead, each of them has to be painstakingly thought through without recourse to a grand narrative line, which is a daunting task for a thinker of Lyotard's persuasion but one that to his considerable credit he never shirks away from.

At the heart of Lyotard's work is the commitment to the little narrative, which for him is the only honest way to conduct political life, acting to restrict its inherently totalising tendencies. Little narratives come and go and should have no interest in converting themselves into centres of power that then proceed to oppress their fellows. They are designed for the short-term rather than the long, to be fluid and flexible rather than ideologically consistent and correct, and there is no doubt that if they were adopted as a model they would effect a radical change on the way we conduct, and conceive of, politics. It remains a loose end in Lyotard's oeuvre, however, that it is never entirely clear how we can bring about that state of affairs. Grand narratives have in that respect proved to be more resilient than Lyotard was implying when he wrote works like *The Postmodern Condition* – as in the case of religious fundamentalism. A similar problem arises in the work of the influential post-Marxist theorists Ernesto Laclau and Chantal Mouffe, whose call for a shift to a 'radical democratic' politics is similarly lacking in practical detail.[8] That is part of the penalty that left-wing thinkers face when they move away from the mainstream, however, as they can no longer call on traditional methods for bringing about political change.

Lyotard's move involves 'drifting' from Karl Marx towards Sigmund Freud, that is, from rational and systematic analysis to desire. In common with many other thinkers of his generation in France (most notably Deleuze and Guattari in their highly controversial *Anti-Oedipus*)[9] Lyotard begins to see desire, and in his case specifically libidinal desire, as a more powerful factor in human affairs than theories like Marxism were prepared to admit. This does not make him an irrationalist, as critical voices such as Jürgen Habermas have accused French poststructuralist thinkers in general of being, but rather someone who no longer believes that reason is the dominant force in our existence, that we have overestimated its power.[10] Another way of seeing this shift in perspective is as a drift from theory to experience. In one sense Lyotard is always a phenomenologist, more interested in our actual experience of events than in any theoretical reading of them. Desire had effectively been marginalised by theories like Marxism, which was unhappy with anything it could not control – and control totally. Lyotard is never at ease with the totalising imperative, and from his days in the Socialisme ou Barbarie group onwards he becomes more and more critical of how this works in terms of politics. His reporting on the Algerian revolution against French rule for *Socialisme ou Barbarie's* journal, reveals someone increasingly irritated by interpretations of events which are failing to acknowledge the differences between cultures as well as the diversity of the individual experiences involved. Marxist theorists simply closed these off in the name of theoretical purity: class struggle was the only scenario they would allow themselves to countenance for Algeria, despite the many anomalies that Lyotard kept drawing attention to, such as the lack of anything approaching a proletariat in what was still largely a pre-industrial society.

Algeria clearly had a profound effect on Lyotard's intellectual development, but the events of May '68 pushed this on to a different level altogether. Official Marxism in the form of the French Communist Party (PCF) revealed itself to be not just narrow in its socio-political analyses but also deceitful, siding with the de Gaulle government in bringing down the revolt led by an alliance of students and workers. The *événements* left deep scars on French life, and certainly encouraged the drift from Marxism to Freud in Lyotard's case, culminating in the almost hysterical denunciation of Marxism that we are to find in *Libidinal Economy*, where Lyotard unashamedly aligned himself with the forces of desire. Totalising philosophy was being rejected with a vengeance and Lyotard's commitment to little narrative was to become ever stronger, constituting the backbone of his social philosophy as he was to go on to underline in *The Postmodern Condition*.

Another issue to have a profound effect on Lyotard's development, as will soon become evident when going through this volume's entries, is the Holocaust. Indeed, the Holocaust, Auschwitz, the Jews and Judaism loom large over his later writings, becoming representative of everything that he thinks is wrong with grand narratives as cultural projects. The Jews have remained a race apart in European culture, never quite culturally assimilable, always representative of an Other that Western society strove to efface from its history, always recognisably different. The Holocaust becomes one last desperate attempt to eliminate this difference, thus leaving the grand narrative of European culture apparently intact. Grand narratives invariably work to achieve cultural homogeneity, and the Holocaust represents this drive taken to its extreme, the extreme where difference and diversity are simply not tolerated. Lyotard repeatedly returns to this topic (most notably in *The Differend* and *Heidegger and "the jews"*, for example)[11] emphasising its cultural significance, and treating the fate of the Jews as a terrible warning of what can happen when we allow ourselves to be taken in by grand narratives – to the point of conveniently 'forgetting' that such a shameful event as the Holocaust had in fact ever happened at all.[12] The Jews have a history of being excluded from mainstream European culture,

Supporters of Grand Narratives like Hitlers Fascism Stalins Party Communism and the Christian Church with the Inquisition all define the other or the Enemy to be exterminated

This led to the Holocaust of the Jews

but grand narratives are capable of acting this way against any group they deem to be significantly different enough from the norm. If we forget the historical injustice the Jews have suffered then we are in effect colluding with grand narrative and its campaign against difference and diversity – and those are properties that Lyotard is tireless in his support for.

LYOTARD'S LEGACY

What sort of a legacy does Lyotard leave to philosophy and social theory? It is likely, as I have indicated above, that he will always be identified in some form with postmodernism, the legacy of which is hard to determine at this stage.[13] As I write, we are entering a period of considerable uncertainty, both economically and environmentally, which many commentators feel signals severe underlying problems and contradictions in a cultural system which, postmodernism notwithstanding, is still largely based on the principles of modernity that have grown out of the Enlightenment project.[14] Whether postmodernism can respond creatively, whether its concepts still have any purchase, must remain open questions. The term post–postmodernism has emerged of late, often used rather mockingly to imply that postmodernism was merely a passing phase in cultural history. The concept of the 'altermodern' has also been floated as a way of moving past the modernism–postmodernism impasse, despite the general success of postmodernism as an aesthetic.[15]

Lyotard refers in his introduction to *The Inhuman* to what 'I have always tried, under diverse headings – work, figural, heterogeneity, dissensus, event, thing – to reserve: the unharmonizable', and it is in that abiding concern with the unharmonisable where his greatest value as a philosopher most likely lies.[16] Lyotard never takes the easy option of aligning himself with some system or other, but remains stubbornly outside, in the very best tradition of scepticism, of which he remains one of the most creditable and dedicated of latter-day exponents. David Hume could be so overcome by the 'philosophical melancholy and delirium' generated by his sceptical enquiries on occasion that he felt compelled to give up, leave his study and throw himself back into the social round;[17] but Lyotard continued to worry away at the unfortunate implications of scepticism, always seeking to find ways of justifying resistance to authoritarianism and totalitarianism. Relativism plainly did not mean 'anything goes' politically to this thinker, even if he felt himself forced to admit that 'I judge. But if I am asked by what criteria do I judge, I will have no answer to give'.[18] That is very much the postmodernist philosophical dilemma, but for Lyotard it cannot absolve us from taking sides and taking positions politically. In his refusal to back away from the problem, Lyotard can be said to have transcended postmodernism.

APPROACHING LYOTARD

The archipelago is an image to which Lyotard is very much drawn, suggesting as it does both relationship and separateness. He tends to conceive of discourses, narratives and phrase regimens in this way, each having its own unique identity but being reachable from each other in the manner that a chain of islands is. Michael Naas has made the interesting suggestion that we can treat Lyotard's work itself as a substantial archipelago, where we can sail from island to island discovering how each port of call can alter one's perception of the archipelago as an entity. He enjoins us to acknowledge 'the absolute singularity' of each 'passage' that we undertake around that archipelago, which means that we can never arrive at any definitive understanding of it, that it is always in a process of change and re-creation.[19] It is a nice idea, and it might be thought that a dictionary runs counter to its spirit, that it is engaged instead in trying to pin down Lyotard's themes and concepts to give an overall vision of his life's work. But the entries do not stand alone; all of them inevitably offer the prospect of passages opening up to other entries, and so in each case throughout the dictionary some such will be denominated – without in any way claiming that these are definitive either, or the only ones that could be made, but rather to start the process of making such cross-connections in the reader's mind. Lyotard is a complex and highly creative thinker and if this dictionary helps to stimulate such mental passages, which will of course differ significantly from reader to reader, then it will have achieved its main aim.

STRUCTURE AND FORMATTING

The dictionary consists of 116 main entries (ranging from 500 to 1,000 words in length), compiled by a team of Lyotard specialists drawn from around the world, and from a variety of academic disciplines as befits the interdisciplinary impact Lyotard unmistakably has had (contributor biographies can be found at the end of the book). Interspersed with these is a series of 'Linking Entries', indicating where in the main entries there are references to related figures and topics. Immanuel Kant, for example, turns up in 21 main entries over the course of the volume, the 'Holocaust' in 14, and those linking entries itemise these so that the reader can see yet other networks that emerge from Lyotard's work. As stated above, there will also be a list of keywords after each entry suggesting 'passages' that can be made to elsewhere in the volume, although these will be restricted to 6 for any one entry. Since 'postmodernism', 'postmodern/postmodernity' and 'grand narrative' are central preoccupations of Lyotard that permeate every aspect of his work it would seem repetitive to include them in each entry, so readers should assume their silent 'presence' there instead.

A word of explanation is called for on the entry for 'Martin Heidegger'. Lyotard was in dialogue with the major figures in the history of Western philosophy throughout his writings, as even the most cursory glance at *The Differend* alone would show, but only Heidegger has been given an entry on his own. The reason for this decision is that he turns into a specific topic in Lyotard's work in connection with his involvement with Nazism. As such, Heidegger becomes a route into the debate about one of the defining events of our time – the Holocaust. It is not just Heidegger's philosophy with which Lyotard is in dialogue therefore but his public role, of which Lyotard is scathing. The so-called 'Heidegger Affair' of the later 1980s, when French intellectual life was riven by disputes over Heidegger's political beliefs, brings this to a head, spurring Lyotard on to write *Heidegger and "the jews"*.[20] Heidegger displays some of the traits that Lyotard most despises in the grand narrative ethos, and takes on considerable symbolic significance in consequence, hence his status as an entry. Lyotard's dialogue with other major philosophical figures such as Kant and Aristotle can be traced through the relevant Linking Entries.

The first mention of any Lyotard text in an entry will give the date of the first French edition in brackets, followed by the date of the English edition (note that in one case, *Peregrinations*, the English version preceded the French by two years). Quotations will give the initials of the book – *PC* for *The Postmodern Condition*, for example – and the page number in brackets (see list of abbreviations below). Readers can check the texts in the author's bibliography at the end of the volume where full publication details of Lyotard's main works and their English translations will be provided in chronological sequence. A subsequent bibliography lists the major critical works on Lyotard for purposes of further reading. Reference will also be made to other authors' works in various entries and full details of these can be found in the last of the bibliographies. English titles will be used for Lyotard's works throughout the entries, except in the case of untranslated texts, where French will be used. Since *grand récit* is variously translated into English as 'grand narrative' and 'metanarrative', both forms will be found throughout the book, depending on the preference of the individual contributor. As one of Lyotard's most important concepts, *le différend* has for some time now been anglicised to 'differend', and so it will appear in the entries in this volume, except where the French has been used in some quoted material.

NOTES

1. Lyotard [1986b] 1992: 41.
2. Lyotard [1979] 1984b.
3. Lyotard 1988b [1990]: 13.
4. Lyotard [1974] 1993a: 115.
5. See Lyotard 1993b: Part V, 'Algerians', pp. 165–326.
6. See Deleuze and Guattari [1980] 1988.
7. Lyotard 1993b: 95.
8. Laclau and Mouffe 1985.
9. Deleuze and Guattari [1972] 1983.
10. See, for example, Habermas 1981.
11. Lyotard [1983] 1988a; and [1988b] 1990b.
12. Lyotard [1988b] 1990b: 3.
13. I discuss what some of postmodernism's legacy might be in my book *The End of Modernity* (2010).
14. As witness the steady stream of books that global warning has generated, and then the rush of analyses that followed the recent credit crunch. The titles of books such as Fred Pearce's *The Last Generation: How Nature Will Take Its Revenge for Climate Change* (2006), or Gillian Tett's *Fool's Gold: How Unrestrained Greed Corrupted a Dream, Shattered Global Markets and Unleashed a Catastrophe* (2009), signal the growing doubts about the sustainability of our modern, economic progress-based lifestyle.
15. See Bourriaud 2009.
16. Lyotard [1988c] 1991a: 4.
17. Hume [1739–40] 1962: 318.
18. Lyotard and Thébaud [1979] 1985: 15.
19. Naas 2007: 196.
20. The controversy was sparked off by the publication of Victor Farías's book *Heidegger and Nazism* [1987] 1991.

A

ADDRESSEE, ADDRESSOR/SENDER

Lloyd Spencer

An addressee is simply anyone to whom something is addressed. That something could be thought of as a word or sign, a phrase or sentence, an instruction, exhortation, question or other form of communication. Lyotard usually talks of phrases thus encouraging us to think not of signs or words in isolation but linked, connected: 'to whom something is addressed'. Addressed by whom? By an addressor. The addressor is the subject of the verb 'to address'. The addressor is the person, or persons, who author or utter a phrase.

Phrases can imply an addressee – for example 'Nobody loves me!' is not a bald statement of fact. It is more likely to be a plea, or complaint addressed more or less unambiguously to one or more addressees. This light-hearted example is not found in Lyotard's writings. He examines instead some of the most resonant and widely accepted phrases – phrases with the most universal appeal or address – and asks us to question who is being addressed and who is doing the addressing. So, for example, the Declaration of the Rights of Man in the French Revolution implies that we are all being addressed. It also claims to be authorised by . . . well, the question is by whom? It is signed by individuals, the Nation is invoked as authorising the proclamation. Lyotard asks us to pay attention to what is being obscured in this process. He asks us to be suspicious of the universal gesture by asking who exactly is its addressor.

For many readers, Lyotard's references to an addressee and addressor (or sender) evoke echoes of the S–M–R (Sender-Message-Receiver) model of communication as transmission developed by Claude E. Shannon and Warren Weaver at the Bell Laboratories as a result of developments during the Second World War. That model of communication seems by comparison to Lyotard's treatment rather reductive and linear. The aim of such a model – that of maximising the efficiency of communications – could be seen as symptomatic of the 'condition of knowledge' which Lyotard sets out to diagnose in *The Postmodern Condition* ([1979] 1984b); that is, the drive in recent history to turn knowledge into information which can then be used to further the power of such as the techno-scientific establishment: 'Knowledge is and will be produced in order to be sold, it is and will be consumed in order to be valorized in a new production: in both cases, the goal is exchange. Knowledge ceases to be an end in itself, it loses its "use-value"' (*PC*, 4–5). That is certainly not what Lyotard sees himself as doing in addressing the public as a philosopher, arguing in the Preface to *The Differend* ([1983] 1988a), for example, that he 'had the feeling that his sole addressee was the *Is it happening?*', and that 'he will never know whether or not the phrases happen to arrive at their destination' (*D*, xvi). The notion of a model of communication in which the addressor controls the addressee's response remains alien to Lyotard, for whom phrasing and linking will always be unpredictable activities which in any large-scale sense cannot be regimented or controlled by interested parties.

Passages

Is It Happening?
Knowledge
Links, Linkage
Philosophy
Phrase, Phrasing
Pragmatics

ADORNO, THEODOR W. (1903–69) – see 'Auschwitz', 'Enlightenment', 'music', 'posthumanism' and 'postmodernism'

AESTHETICS

Bella Adams

Aesthetics is often understood in two ways: a theory of art; and a more general theory of perception and sentiment vis-à-vis the categories of the beautiful and the sublime in art and nature, or philosophical aesthetics. Philosophers have debated these categories typically in terms of their relationship to epistemology and ethics, most notably, for Lyotard, Immanuel

Kant, G. W. F Hegel and, more recently, Jürgen Habermas. Modern and postmodern aesthetic theories, understood, in this instance, through the work of Habermas and Lyotard respectively, turn on a question of particular concern to Kant. In *Critique of Judgement* ([1790] 2000) and in the context of modernity that 'cannot exist without a shattering of belief' and, adds Lyotard, 'without discovery of the "lack of reality" of reality' (*PC*, 77), Kant considers whether aesthetics fulfils a unifying and legitimating role with respect to this modern crisis. Can the feelings associated with aesthetic experiences provide a reliable basis for knowledge and justice, and in the process 'open the way to a unity of experience' (*PC*, 72)?

This unity troubles Lyotard, as he explains in, for example, the Appendix to *The Postmodern Condition* ([1979] 1984b), 'Answering the Question: What Is Postmodernism?', which begins by listing his main detractors, principally Habermas. Lyotard and Habermas charge each other with conservatism, despite some points of agreement. They both criticise advanced capitalism for contributing to the modern crisis by evaluating life and art according to criteria of saleability and efficiency. Both also argue that art has a function beyond its commodification that enables progress to occur. Crucially, however, progress takes two different forms, which arguably tally with Habermas's and Lyotard's different aesthetic theories: 'one corresponds to a new move . . . within the established rules', whereas the other, explains Lyotard, corresponds 'to the invention of new rules' or 'a change to a new game' (*PC*, 43).

Habermas's modern aesthetics requires 'the arts and the experiences they provide . . . to bridge the gap between cognitive, ethical and political discourses' for the purposes of 'sociocultural unity' and 'communicational consensus' (*PC*, 72, 73). Such unity appeals in its beauty and pleasure, if only up to a point. Modern aesthetics may be progressive in supplying meaning to reality shattered under capitalism, but this therapeutic function is consistent with established metanarratives of speculation and emancipation. Modern aesthetics is nostalgic and conservative. It also risks terror. As Lyotard states and as 'Kant also knew . . . the price to pay for such an illusion [of unity] is terror' (*PC*, 81). For Lyotard, totalising discourses see their most terrifying articulation in totalitarian political regimes (Nazism and Stalinism). Hence he asserts: 'Let us wage war on totality' (*PC*, 82), with art and aesthetics proving increasingly fundamental to his anti-totalitarian critique.

Following a totalising logic, Habermas's modern aesthetics subordinates art to the demands of the social system by bypassing the reality of the sublime and subordinating this category to the beautiful. In contrast, Lyotard's postmodern aesthetics bears witness to the fact that the sublime constitutes a limit that is profoundly dislocating, and beyond which lies the unpresentable, or 'the incommensurability of reality to concept which is implied in the Kantian philosophy of the sublime' (*PC*, 79). Unlike the feeling of pleasure associated with beauty, sublime sentiment combines pleasure *and* pain: 'the pleasure that reason should exceed presentation, the pain that imagination or sensibility should not equal the concept' (*PC*, 81).

Although the sublime is beyond form and sense, it is possible none the less to make 'an allusion to the unpresentable by means of visible presentations' (*PC*, 78). For example, the biblical commandment 'Thou shalt not make graven images' is a presentation that in its prohibition of presentation alludes to the unpresentable. Lyotard argues that a similar command informs avant-garde art by, for example, Paul Cézanne, Marcel Duchamp and Kasimir Malevitch. In the literature of Marcel Proust and James Joyce, he also observes allusions 'to something which does not allow itself to be made present' (*PC*, 80).

Avant-garde art forms offer visible presentations that in their inventiveness prove incommensurable with presentation and by extension socio-cultural and commercial demands. On this latter count, the avant-garde enables progress to occur in its anti-totalitarian sense. More radical in its understanding of art and progress than Habermas's, Lyotard's postmodern aesthetic theory is not simply a new move but a new game that bears witness to the sublime rather than bypasses it. Indeed, Lyotard makes it his and 'our business not to supply reality but to invent allusions to the conceivable which cannot be presented' (*PC*, 81), thereby ensuring that art and aesthetics function properly to open the way to experiences in their differences.

Passages

Art
Modernism
Music
Sublime
Totality, Totalisation
Writing

AGONISTICS

Roy Sellars

Lyotard loves trouble. He is both troublemaker and trouble finder, and the trouble he finds can be called agonistics. For Lyotard, agonistics is not a philosophical doctrine or a social theory to be applied, but first and fore-most a practice. What makes it so disquieting is that we always already find ourselves *in* agonistics. We find ourselves called not only to witness and judge but also to participate, and in this daily struggle there is no admissible alibi. Agonistics calls for responsibility without end – and indeed without plan. If life is what happens to you while you're busy making other plans, agonistics is also a name for the ineluctable tension between life and those plans. Agonistics defies planning, in the name of the event. Even writing a sentence (like this one), and making it look as if it naturally follows on from a previous sentence, becomes a risky business, asking for trouble. To pretend otherwise and eschew trouble, for Lyotard, is to be dishonest or unjust.

In *The Postmodern Condition* ([1979] 1984b), introducing the concept of language games, Lyotard announces a first methodological principle: 'to speak is to fight, in the sense of playing, and speech acts fall within the domain of a general agonistics' (*PC*, 10). This makes him sound like the Harold Bloom of *Agon* (1982); but while they both focus on conflict, pleasure and the potential for events in literature, Lyotard is equally concerned with everyday speech acts – and with the social relation as such. Lyotard emphasises both pleasure and conflict, as if the one could not be separated from the other. Instead of accepting consensus as a goal, he argues for exercising a strong, agonistic difference; he engages in agon in the dialogues translated as *Just Gaming* ([1979] 1985), and in different ways throughout his work. So what is agon?

As the *Oxford English Dictionary* etymology makes clear, the Greek *agōn* (from *agein*, 'to lead, bring with one') denotes 'a gathering or assembly', especially for public games; from here it acquires the more general sense, 'any contest or struggle'. If we allow ourselves to be led by H. G. Liddell and R. Scott (1995), we see further that *agein* in the sense of leading is used 'of living creatures' (sense I) and that the verb has a rich field of reference, including 'conduct' (II.3), 'refer' (II.4) and 'educate' (II.5). An *agōn*, then, is an assembly for the games, a contest, a struggle, a battle, a trial, a speech 'delivered in court or before an assembly or ruler' or the 'main argument' of a speech (III.4). The power that is *agōn* is not easily delimited; as process, it seems already to have begun, and even as spectators or third parties we are not external to it.

Concerning agonistics, we are referred to Heraclitus and the Sophists, among others, and then to an essay by Friedrich Nietzsche, 'Homer's Contest' (*PC*, 88 n. 35), helping us see that with which Lyotard is fighting, pleading or playing (on Heraclitus, see also *PC*, 59; on Lyotard and the Sophists, see Crome 2004). Fredric Jameson, in his Foreword to *The Postmodern Condition*, gets it exactly wrong: agonistics is not 'quasi-heroic'

(*PC*, xix). Lyotard *agōnistēs* might say: we don't need another hero. Agonistics does not concern the struggle of a subject as such; subjectivity may be a product or waste product of agon, but agon matters because it is a figure of the social as difference. Lyotard develops this figure in *The Differend* ([1983] 1988a) where, analysing rhetoric and regulation in Plato, he asserts: 'We readers [i.e., those not privileged to participate in Socratic dialogue] . . . believe in agonistics' (*D*, 25–6; see Geoffrey Bennington 1988: 141–54; and Rodolphe Gasché 2000: 136–9). He glosses agonistics as 'three-way games' (*D*, 26), games exceeding and dislocating the pseudo-consensual dialogue that has become hegemonic.

Agonistics must be contrasted with the competition institutionalised by so-called free-market capitalism, the quasi-natural game seeking either to incorporate or to delegitimate other games. Let us end this *agōnologia* ('laborious discussion') with reference to Simon Cowell's *The X Factor*, the remarkably profitable, popular and influential TV talent competition – and parody of agonistics – in which the UK viewing public is set up as *agōnodikēs*, 'judge of the contest', while Cowell as *agōnarchēs*, 'organizer of contest' (see Liddell and Scott 1995: Supplement), retains power beyond that of a mere judge on the live panel. The model has been widely imitated and exported. Lyotard had celebrated the experimentation of pop music, claiming that its ocean-like audience 'does not have its own stable sound-filtering system' (*JG*, 13). Much has changed since then, and the Cowellism of the music industry may now seem irresistible; but the metalepsis of the third party (see *D*, 25–6), turning unknowable ocean into colluding partner, remains unstable. Lyotard rages not only against but also within the machine, such that 'machine' becomes not only the name for series as such but also a term in a series. If Lyotard has the X factor, this is not because, as subject, he can sway a crowd or programme the profitable rediscovery of the known, but, on the contrary, because through agonistics he maintains 'the desire for the unknown' (*PC*, 67, the book's final phrase).

Passages

Difference
Dissensus
Language Games
Music
Subject
Unknown

ALGERIA

Eleanor Byrne and Stuart Sim

After graduation from the Sorbonne Lyotard taught philosophy at a Lycée in Constantine, in French-occupied East Algeria, from 1950 to 1952. The Algerian War of Independence from France lasted from 1954 to 1962 with Algerian independence being proclaimed on 3 July 1962. During this time, Lyotard was writing regularly for the publication *Socialisme ou Barbarie* as its Algerian specialist. He comments in his preface to his collected writings on Algeria (*La Guerre des Algériens*, 1988a):

> When the group Socialism or Barbarism gave me responsibility for the Algerian section in 1955, Algeria did not name a 'question' of revolutionary politics for me, it was also the name of a debt. I owed and I owe my awakening, *tout court*, to Constantine. (*PW*, 170)

The situation in Algeria at the time, on the cusp of revolution, radicalises Lyotard politically, hence his notion of being in 'debt' to the country for playing such a critical part in his development as a thinker (a debt he feels he can never really pay off). While in Constantine he is able to witness the effects of colonial oppression at close hand, and what he sees, to his dismay (and also no doubt his embarrassment and awkwardness, as a representative of the colonial power) is 'a great civilization, wronged, humiliated, denied their identity' (*PW*, 170). It is a classic instance of what he would later dub a 'differend', with the indigenous population being unable to articulate their grievances within what is to them an alien socio–political system. He describes putting together his Algerian writings for later publication as 'a quite singular anamnesis' (*PW*, 169); anamnesis in Lyotard's writing being understood as the task of not forgetting.

His essays on Algeria trace the unfolding of events in this uprising and follow its developments closely: (1956) 'The Situation in North Africa', (1957) 'The North African Bourgeoisie', (1957) 'A New Phase in the Algerian Question', (1958) 'Algerian Contradiction Exposed', (1958) 'The "Counterrevolutionary" War, Colonial Society, and de Gaulle', (1959) 'The Social Content of the Algerian Struggle', (1960) 'The State and Politics in the France of 1960', (1961) 'Gaullism and Algeria', (1962) 'Algeria: Seven Years After', (1963) 'Algeria Evacuated'. These essays offer detailed analysis on the connections between political repression, terror (including state terror), capitalism and colonialism, while communicating a growing disenchantment with Marxist thought on the part of the author, who increasingly feels moved to question the validity of Marxist categories in general.

The first essay reflects on the events in Tunisia in January 1952, Morocco in December 1952, Indochina in 1954 and North Vietnam in 1955, as well as the uprising in Algeria 1954. Lyotard feels that collectively these events signal the imminent collapse of the French imperialist project, remarking approvingly that as far as North Africa in particular is concerned the political system instituted by the colonisers has now effectively broken down anyway. He expresses worries that the nationalist leaders may turn out to be as exploitative of the local masses in their turn once the French colonisers are defeated, but in terms of French intellectual support for anti-colonial struggle he nevertheless feels compelled to conclude that,'[w]e in France can do nothing other than support this struggle in its extreme consequences. Contrary to the totality of the "left" our concern is in no way the preservation of the "French presence in the Maghreb"' (*PW*, 175). First and foremost, imperialism must be banished.

His late essay 'Algeria Evacuated', written in 1963 after Independence, however, comments wryly on the unforeseeable results of the war and the subsequent French withdrawal:

They expected a revolution; they got a country in collapse. In the political vacuum that was established along with independence, the FLN [Algerian National Liberation Front] leadership exploded into pieces. Joy at the end of the war and the ferment of liberation faded away: the masses were immobilized. (*PW*, 294)

It is as if his worst fears, voiced repeatedly throughout the sequence of essays, have been confirmed. Algeria will continue to suffer, his analysis concludes, until 'a model of new social relations' (*PW*, 326) is introduced – but there is little sign of that on the horizon, unfortunately enough.

As various commentators have noted, Algeria becomes a site where Lyotard can work through his critical understanding of Marxism. The revolution there 'failed' in that while independence was achieved there was no successful uprising of the peasant or working class. Instead, a new grand narrative had been instituted and the various little narratives that made up the Algerian population were still being kept in a state of subjection, unable to make their needs known. As a theory, Marxism had been found badly wanting in this instance, with its insistence that a European-oriented metanarrative could be imposed on an underdeveloped nation with a very different kind of cultural history: 'It is in a completely *abstract* way, that is, exclusively *economistic*, that one can speak of *a* proletariat, *a* middle class, *a* bourgeosie in Algeria' (*PW*, 210). The Algerian experience overall leaves Lyotard at odds with Marxism, and it will not be long before its totalising pretensions provoke a differend with it on his part.

Passages

Anamnesis
Differend
Little Narrative
Marxism
Postcolonialism
Socialisme ou Barbarie

ALTHUSSER, LOUIS (1918–90) – see 'figure', 'Marxism', 'posthu-manism', 'post-Marxism' and 'terror'

ANAMNESIS

Neal Curtis

Anamnesis literally means without forgetting, or non-forgetting, but for Lyotard the work of anamnesis is quite distinct from that of memory. Rather it is directly linked to that which cannot be remembered, in the sense of being recovered, namely the immemorial. For Lyotard responsibility, obligation and hence the moral law stem from a time prior to any capacity to remember. The law is anterior to the thinking, remembering subject. Not only does the immemorial signal a temporal dislocation but also it testifies to the fact that any memory always includes a forgetting, an exclusion of the non-graspable, that which is in excess of thought and representation. But for Lyotard this is not related to an absentmindedness, or an inability to retain everything, it is an *active* forgetting that permits our politics to function.

In *Heidegger and "the jews"* ([1988b] 1990b), Lyotard discusses this active forgetting and argues that Nazi Germany's genocide was not simply a programme to exterminate a people but was also the mark of a more pervasive and consistent murder: the attempt to rid Western thought of the unrepresentable and unincludable. This is suggested by Lyotard writing "jews" in the lower case. The lower-case "jews", then, is neither a political, religious nor philosophical subject, but stands for the ghettoising of the Other by 'the same'. 'The jews' is a testament to the excluded and unfinished, the sign of something incommensurate, a reminder of that which remains, and a call to fight to remember that one forgets. By being sensitive to our debt to the immemorial Lyotard does not offer us a new totality inclusive of the Other, but asks us not to forget, or to remember that we do forget, that which is otherwise to our philosophy of representation. This process of exclusion is likened by Lyotard to Sigmund Freud's idea of the 'protective shield'. In *Beyond the Pleasure Principle* (Freud 1953–74: vol. 18), Freud adds the economic to the other two components of metapsychology in order to consider how consciousness yields pleasure rather than pain. His conclusion is that there must be a protective shield between consciousness and perception that diverts, or removes that which is painful to another scene, thus saving the subject from trauma and the collapse that such trauma might threaten. When the traumatic event is in turn remembered it returns in a sublimated and edified form.

On Remembrance Sunday, for example, the day in the UK set aside for the memory of those who died in the two World Wars, the nation remembers and the nation mourns, but the protective shield is in place because there is honour in death. The violence and seeming meaninglessness of war is replaced by notions of heroism, sacrifice and community. This does not mean that remembrance is converted into a pleasurable experience, it simply means that something is gleaned from the memory to lessen the pain, a pain that remains potentially devastating. The practice of non–forgetting or anamnesis is, then, a remembering where the 'rules' of memory and of re-presentation are at stake. It is also a remembering that something is always forgotten. Perhaps most significantly for questions of politics it intimates the permanence of an outside and an excluded remainder that directly challenges the historiography and memorial practices of the closed and bounded communities which fuel the most violent chauvinisms.

Passages

Forgetting
Heidegger, Martin
History, Historians
Jews, Judaism
Obligation

ANTIFOUNDATIONALISM

Stuart Sim

Challenging the grounds on which the theories of one's opponents are constructed is an integral part of the sceptical tradition within Western philosophy, and it has become a central concern of poststructuralism too.

Sceptics from classical times onwards have persistently pointed out that the foundations of theories of truth can be called into question because they themselves lack foundations, being based on nothing stronger than ungrounded assumptions. This raises the spectre of an infinite regress, which for sceptics undermines the claims of any theory: relativism becomes the only acceptable position to adopt under the circumstances. Poststructuralists use this technique to attack not just structuralism but eventually, in the case of Jacques Derrida and Lyotard in particular, the entire edifice of Western philosophy. There is a strong current of anti-foundationalism in poststructuralist and postmodernist thought which is designed to demolish the authority assumed by philosophical and cultural theories, and to make us realise that no theory can be universal in its application.

Western philosophy is full of attempts to find foundations for discourse that would lie beyond all possible doubt as self-evidently true, with René Descartes providing one of the most famous of these right at the beginnings of modern philosophy in his *Meditations on First Philosophy* (Descartes [1641] 1970). He bemoaned the fact that his senses could mislead him and saw the need for something stronger on which to test his knowledge of the world around him. This turned out to be the famous proposition *cogito ergo sum*, which asserted that the one thing Descartes could never call into doubt was that he was thinking. Using that as a starting point, he felt able to construct a theory of knowledge (although this subsequently has been subjected to much criticism within the philosophical world).

Lyotard's critique of the concept of metanarrative clearly demonstrates the determinedly antifoundationalist cast of his thought. Metanarratives like Marxism cannot be verified, Lyotard insists, since no transcendental signifier exists that could perform the task. In Marxist terms of reference, these constitute such principles as history being the history of class strug-gle, and the concept of dialectical materialism, by which human history is said to be evolving towards a utopian state where class struggle is finally overcome. For Marxists these are natural laws, and we should conduct our political lives according to their demands, but thinkers like Lyotard reject that line of argument. Without legitimation of this kind (God offer-ing the same guarantee in the religious sphere) no theory can ever claim precedence over any of the others, making a mockery of the notion that there could ever be a metanarrative meriting our unconditional support. Lyotard's preference is for short-term little narratives with specific objec-tives, such as campaigning on environmental issues.

Consistently throughout his writings Lyotard argues against the pos-sibility of there being universally legitimating foundations for discourse. The postmodern is the condition where we come to realise, as most philosophers and creative artists already do, that there are no rules to be followed:

[T]he text he writes, the work he produces are not in principle governed by pre-established rules, and they cannot be judged according to a determining judge-ment, by applying familiar categories to the text or to the work. Those rules and categories are what the work of art itself is looking for. (*PC*, 81)

Lyotard emphasises the creative aspect of thought and artistic work, which changes the landscape around it, being in the nature of an event, with at least a measure of unpredictability about it. We enter uncharted territory every time we confront a problem or start a work of art, and no theory can dictate how we should proceed, or be an acceptable judge of the outcome.

It has to be admitted, however, that many obvious problems arise if one takes an antifoundationalist line, and Lyotard does not escape these. Relativism is an awkward position to adopt because it offers no way of veri-fying one's own claims: in the absence of a valid theory of truth, the rela-tivist's judgements have to be as open to doubt as anyone else's. Lyotard rather neatly sums up the dilemma faced by the relativist in his flippant comment in *Just Gaming* ([1979] 1985) that, 'I have a criterion (the absence of criteria) to classify various sorts of discourse here and there' (*JG* 18). Lyotard is in fact pressed hard about this issue by his interviewer in *Just Gaming*, Jean-Loup Thébaud, who is very much exercised by the quandary relativism leaves us in as regards justice: 'What do we do with a thesis like "it is unjust; I rebel"? How is one to say this if one does not know what is just and what is unjust? If the determination of the just is the object of perpetual sophistic debate?' (*JG*, 66). And as Thébaud goes on to point out, people do develop a strong sense of what is unjust socially and politically, and they do rebel in protest. Injustice to Lyotard turns out to be imposing one's will on others so that they cannot enter into that perpetual debate; but Thébaud does not find such a pragmatic solution very convincing and is clearly looking for something more traditional and harder-edged in order to justify taking action (hence his concern about what 'warrants' our judge-ments, or gives us the 'right' to make them). Relativism, however, pre-cludes providing this, and Lyotard can only complain that 'you are making me talk beyond what I am capable of articulating' (*JG*, 71) when pushed on the topic: there simply is, from his perspective, no transcendental signifier to which we can appeal for justification of our actions.

The positive side of antifoundationalism is that it leads us to ques-tion authority, and Lyotard is certainly in the vanguard of that trend in recent philosophical discourse. Antifoundationalism is not to be regarded as purely negative, therefore; it does inspire debate about the grounds of authority, which is a healthy thing to be happening in any society. In the hands of postmodernists like Lyotard, antifoundationalism is not just a philosophical concern, it has far-reaching political implications as well.

Passages

Justice
Legitimation
Little Narrative
Rules
Poststructuralism
Scepticism

ARCHIPELAGO

Stuart Sim

The archipelago is a figure that Lyotard uses at various points throughout his work to suggest both relationship and separateness. An archipelago is made up of various islands, any of which can be reached from the others; but they can be very different from their neighbours, with their own individual customs and even languages. The rules and conventions that apply in one territory may not do so in another, which, to use Lyotard's terminology, will have its own separate phrase regimen. We might think of the archipelago as being like a group of little narratives, each with its own unique identity, and although communication can take place between them, and they stand in some kind of recognisable relationship, they never amount to a unity. Little narratives are in fact marked by difference, and that must always be respected. Narratives in general, as well as language-games, function as archipelagos.

Lyotard uses the notion of archipelago to explicate what is going on in Immanuel Kant's *Critique of Judgement* (Kant [1790] 2000). Kant sought in this work to find the bridge between the faculties of human reason and human judgement such that our judgements could be seen to have a grounding in necessity rather than mere arbitrariness (as, e.g., many would contend is largely so in aesthetic judgements); that is, he wanted our judgements to proceed from a categorical imperative such that they became universal. But Lyotard did not believe that Kant was successful in his project, with the sublime in particular constituting a massive obstacle. The existence of the sublime meant that our concepts fell short and we were forced to acknowledge limits to our understanding: reason and experience could never match in the case of something like infinity, for example.

Lyotard conceived of the faculty of judgement as a way of moving between genres of discourse, with each genre being 'like an island' (*D* 130). The faculty of judgement was to be considered

like an admiral or like a provisioner of ships who would launch expeditions from one island to the next, intended to present to one island what was found (or invented, in the archaic sense of the word) in the other, and which might serve the former as an 'as-if intuition' with which to validate it. (*D*, 131)

There can be inter-island commerce therefore, but that does not mean they constitute a unified entity, or that the faculty of judgement can bring this condition about. Instead, the faculty merely 'ensures the passages' (*D*, 131) from island to island. It is another instance of the ineradicability of difference on which Lyotard insists, with any attempt to create a whole out of the disparate elements involved being doomed at source. We have to accept that the sheer separateness of these elements just cannot be overcome, with the faculty of judgement being no more than a go-between for the purpose of establishing and facilitating relationships. Lyotard even goes so far as to question whether the 'faculty of judgement is a faculty' (*D*, 130), in Kant's sense of the term, at all.

Passages

Judgement
Little Narrative
Narrative
Phrase, Phrasing
Sublime

ARENDT, HANNAH (1906–75) – see 'event'

ARISTOTLE (384–322 BC) – see 'judgement', 'paralogy' and 'probity'

ART

Stuart Sim

Art held a lifelong fascination for Lyotard, and his writings on the topic are fairly extensive, running from exhibition catalogues through to book chapters and full-length book studies. Much of the time his interest seems to lie in artists more generally defined as modernist rather than postmodernist, although those labels can often be imprecise and over the course of the last few decades many artists formerly thought of as the former have been appropriated to their cause by theorists of the latter position. Lyotard insists that the postmodern 'is undoubtedly a part of the modern' anyway, and praises modern art (Pablo Picasso and Georges Braque, for example) for its 'invention of new rules of the game' (*PC*, 79, 80) – something he is always keen to promote to frustrate the build-up of any metanarrative consciousness. Not surprisingly, Lyotard takes his own philosophical and political preoccupations into his engagement with art, and he is particularly drawn to work, such as that of Marcel Duchamp, which is difficult to pin down in terms of meaning, to the point of even seeming to have been designed in order to resist critical interpretation. In general, one could say that Lyotard prefers art which is calling into question aesthetic rules and conventions, as his blanket criticism of aesthetic 'isms' in *Soundproof Room* ([1998a] 2001) would indicate; there, they are witheringly described as 'military schools where one practiced attack strategies against whatever came up by way of response to questions about painting, writing, putting to music or dance, staging' (*SR*, 62).

Lyotard's distinction between modern and postmodern art is based on their respective relationship to the unpresentable. Both modernists and postmodernists are aware that they cannot reach a total understanding of the world, as their forebears believed was possible, and that aspects of it must always elude them. There is, in other words, an unpresentable to be acknowledged, and modern art is in consequence motivated by an aesthetic of the sublime; but whereas postmodern artists are generally unfazed by this (indeed, can even embrace it with enthusiasm), modern artists evince a sense of nostalgia for a lost totality. The concern of modern art, Lyotard argues, is 'to present the fact that the unpresentable exists. To make visible that there is something which can be conceived and which can neither be seen nor made visible: this is what is at stake in modern painting' (*PC*, 78). The aesthetic of the sublime involves proceeding 'negatively' (*PC*, 78), meaning that it moves away from realism and even representation itself. Lyotard cites Kasimir Malevitch's all-white paintings (such as *White Square on a White Ground*) as a prime example of such negative 'presentation' (Ad Reinhardt's later all-black canvasses might be regarded as an even more extreme expression of that aesthetic).

Duchamp's art resonates with Lyotard because of what he feels is its 'pointlessness' (*DT*, 69): it has no grand vision of the world to present, no set narrative of any kind for the viewer to relate to, and is plainly not in the service of any metanarrative. For Lyotard, its effect is to confound interpretation, and the appropriate response to a work like *The Bride Stripped Bare by Her Bachelors*, he suggests, 'would be not to try to understand and to show what you've understood, but rather the opposite, to try not to understand and to show that you haven't understood' (*DT*, 12). Duchamp's art seems to bear out Lyotard's contention that postmodernism is modernism 'in the nascent state' (*PC*, 79); that is, in process of emerging rather than being identifiable as part of an aesthetic creed operating according to agreed ground rules by which artworks could then be judged. We could say that *The Bride Stripped Bare* is constantly in a state of 'becoming' rather than 'being', to contextualise this view of art within another long-running philosophical debate (and the poststructuralist movement is generally on the side of 'becoming'). Overall, what Duchamp is challenging is the ethos that 'says one must make a painting' (*PC*, 79); in Lyotard's terms of reference he is setting himself up as a little narrative in response to the entire metanarrative of Western art, in which painting, and the construction of fixed artworks with their own particular message to communicate to the viewer, holds pride of place.

Barnett Baruch Newman is another artist that Lyotard particularly admires, and devotes two essays to in *The Inhuman* ([1988c] 1991a). Newman's abstract expressionism also avoids representation, often taking the form of large blocks of colour, which Lyotard argues have no 'message' to proclaim. The work '"speaks" of nothing', and makes no attempt 'to show us something' (*I*, 81). Rather it presents only the 'instant', having no reference at all to anything outside, to any 'history which is situated on the other side' (*I*, 82) of that instant. A Newman painting does not 'recount' events, it has no 'purpose other than to be a visual event in itself' (*I*, 83). We can read nothing into Newman, nor use his work to reinforce any scheme of thought or metanarrative. Like Duchamp, Newman's art is proof against interpretation.

There should be no 'nostalgia for the unattainable' (*PC*, 81) in artistic practice, therefore, but rather a desire to keep challenging established norms and notions of totality, as Lyotard believes postmodernism is equipped to do. He wants the creative act to be free from socio-political imperatives and for artists to work 'without rules' (*PC*, 81). It is a vision of art based on the notion of the little narrative, which conceives of art as a series of disruptive events preventing metanarratives from settling down and establishing domination over us. As such it fits in with Lyotard's overall political vision. Whether postmodern art in a general sense has proved to live up to Lyotard's ideals is more debatable. The double-coding notion has encouraged a rather formulaic practice in much of the artistic community in recent times, and a postmodern 'style' has certainly evolved, along with an aesthetic to judge it by – an 'ism' in other words, and Lyotard will always be deeply suspicious of the motives behind those.

Passages

Aesthetics
Event
Little Narrative
Modernism
Sublime
Unpresentable

AUSCHWITZ

Stuart Sim

The fate of the Jewish race in Europe, particularly in the twentieth century with the dreadful event of the Holocaust, is a topic that nags away at Lyotard throughout his writing career, and Auschwitz comes to stand for him, as it had for Theodor W. Adorno earlier, as a shorthand for that entire experience. Lyotard is appalled by the fact that what had happened in camps like Auschwitz is denied by some (a school of Holocaust-denial historians had developed by the closing decades of the twentieth century in several European countries, including France), and 'forgotten' by others (most of German society, and in particular such significant cultural figures as the eminent philosopher Martin Heidegger). Neither of these responses is at all acceptable to Lyotard, who rails against them in a series of books such as *Heidegger and "the jews"* ([1988b] 1990b) and *The Differend* ([1983] 1988a). Auschwitz is a stain on modern culture that Lyotard is determined we must bear witness to such that those who suffered are not forgotten, and that we realise the horrors that can be committed in the name of grand narrative.

Nazism is for Lyotard a particularly ruthless form of grand narrative which sets out systematically to eliminate all evidence of difference and diversity within its domain in its quest for total ideological domination. For the greater part of its recorded history the Jewish race has been marked out by its difference in the various host cultures in which it has settled; thus Europe, as Lyotard notes, 'does not know what to do with' (*Hj*, 3) the Jews in its midst. Nazism's 'final solution' is to be seen within the context of this centuries-old persecution of the Jewish race for its divergence from the cultural norm, even when its members have chosen to try to assimilate themselves within their host culture – as many have over the years, as in modern Germany prior to the Nazi takeover. Even worse, Nazism tries to hide the truth of its policy and to make it appear as if the Jews had never actually existed in European society, to efface not just every trace of their physical being but the very memory of their existence from the public consciousness. It becomes the worst example in modern history of the grand narrative principle at work: the different are not to be marginalised, they are to be eradicated altogether, including any evidence of a differend between the respective parties. 'Nazism', as Lyotard observes, 'requires nothing from what is not "Aryan," except for the cessation of its appearing to exist' (*D*, 103). Grand narrative can go no further in the pursuit of its objectives than this.

The final insult of Auschwitz is that so many are willing to go along with such a horrific programme and quietly to 'forget' that it ever took place. There is, as Lyotard emphasises, 'a politics of forgetting' (*Hj*, 3) that must be brought out into the open, and one of its worst exponents is Martin Heidegger, who in the aftermath of the Second World War and Germany's defeat maintains 'a leaden silence' (*Hj*, 52) over the entire episode, an attitude which Lyotard clearly finds despicable.

Lyotard engages directly with Adorno's conception of Auschwitz in *Heidegger and "the jews"*, sympathising with how he wrestles to interpret the meaning of an event which seems to go beyond any rational explanation. There is a very strong sense in Adorno of Auschwitz marking a watershed in human history, a point after which things would never be the same again: 'Auschwitz', he maintained, 'demonstrated irrefutably that culture has failed', despite that culture's pride in its 'traditions of philosophy, of art, and of the enlightening sciences' (Adorno [1966] 1983: 355). Adorno had queried the status of art after Auschwitz, and here Lyotard feels there is an important insight, that it is no longer possible to produce 'beautiful art' once one becomes fully aware of the presence of the sublime within human affairs, that any such effort will merely come out as 'kitsch':

It is important, very important, to remember that no one can – by writing, by painting, by anything – pretend to be witness and truthful reporter of, be 'equal' to the sublime affection, without being rendered guilty of falsification and imposture through this very pretension. (*Hj*, 45)

The sublime lies beyond our power to understand, as Auschwitz must also be considered to do, and Lyotard feels the need to make this far more explicit than Adorno ever does. Auschwitz must be seen to resist explanation, and for his own part Lyotard is adamant that 'I will not explain it anymore than anyone else' (*Hj*, 81).

Passages

Event
Forgetting
Heidegger, Martin
Jews, Judaism
Reason, Rationality
Sublime

B

BADIOU, ALAIN (1937–) – see 'event' and 'poststructuralism'

BARTHES, ROLAND (1915–80) – see 'language games', 'poststructuralism' and 'thought'

BAUDRILLARD, JEAN (1929–2007) – see 'event', 'Marxism' and 'poststructuralism'

BEARING WITNESS

Stuart Sim

Lyotard ends his short essay 'Answering the Question: What Is Postmodernism?' (the 'Appendix' to the *The Postmodern Condition* ([1979] 1984b) in its English version) with the following injunction: 'Let us wage a war on totality; let us be witnesses to the unpresentable; let us activate the differences and save the honor of the name' (*PC*, 82). This very neatly sums up his philosophical mission with its consistent opposition to grand narratives and absolutist theories of any description, and unfailing commitment to the cause of difference – precisely what grand narratives and absolutist theories are always determined to efface. The unpresentable constitutes everything that lies beyond our knowledge and power to affect, and again grand narratives do their level best to pretend otherwise, encouraging us to 'forget' that such things, which threaten their claims to authority and assumed right to legitimate the discourses of our world, actually exist. Lyotard repeatedly calls on us to resist the temptation to forget in this way and instead to bear witness to what the dominant ideology is desperately striving to hide from us. To bear witness is to refuse to give in to grand narrative and to frustrate its purposes.

Bearing witness has something of the force of a moral principle in Lyotard (although he is never a moralist in any traditional sense), in that it requires us to be vigilant against all attempts to 'whitewash' history – and dominant ideologies are only too skilled in such practices as we know. The most shameful example of that in modern times is the Nazi treatment of the Jews, whose 'slaughter pretends to be without memory, without trace' (*Hj*, 23) as Lyotard damningly observes in *Heidegger and "the jews"* ([1988b] 1990b). He is harsh on those who allow themselves to be drawn into such ideological deceptions, and even more so on those who continue to propagate them well after the event, as in the case of the Holocaust deniers of the later twentieth century; thus his reference in the same text to 'the debt that is our only lot – the lot of forgetting neither that there is the Forgotten nor what horror the spirit is capable of in its headlong madness to make us forget that fact' (*Hj*, 93). To acknowledge such a debt is to bear witness to what has actually happened as opposed to what those in political power, and their apologists (all too often the 'intellectuals' that Lyotard so despises), would prefer to have us believe.

Returning to the phrase with which the entry began, grand narratives will always try to deny the existence of the unpresentable and efface difference in order to protect their totalising aspirations. To follow Lyotard's injunction and bear witness to these phenomena is to take a stance, therefore, against everything that the grand narrative project in general stands for. It is to refuse to be deceived, thus a politically loaded act. We could say that the recognition of the need to bear witness at all times is an integral part of the postmodern consciousness, the first step in any campaign of resistance to entrenched power.

Passages

Difference
Forgetting
Intellectuals
Jews, Judaism
Totality, Totalisation
Unpresentable

BODY

Stuart Sim

The Inhuman's ([1988c] 1991a) subtitle tells us that the book consists of *Reflections on Time*, but it could also have been called *Reflections on the Body*, given its determination to defend the body against the inhuman schemes of the techno-scientific establishment. Lyotard postulates a future in which techno-science will steadily move away from the human body to put its faith in computer systems as the most efficient way to survive the death of the sun. It is a far-fetched scenario, but it does fore-ground some of Lyotard's most pressing concerns about the direction in which our culture seems to be heading. It is a plea to rein in the overt com-mercialisation of our lives in the name of technological efficiency, on the grounds that these threaten our humanity. The spectre of Artificial Life and Artificial Intelligence hovers around Lyotard's reflections on what the body means to us, and why we must strive to prevent it from being down-graded in importance.

These concerns are brought to a head in the extraordinary essay in *The Inhuman*, 'Can thought go on without a body?', to which the answer, in a firm rebuttal of the philosophical tradition of mind-body dualism, is a resounding no. The essay is cast as a dialogue between He and She, who questions whether computer programs can even count as thought: 'If you think you're describing thought when you describe a selecting and tabulating of data, you're silencing truth. Because data aren't given, but givable, and selection isn't choice' (*I* 18). She insists that thinking can be a painful activity, and that unless we can devise machines capable of such suffering then thought must remain a human experience only. The more general point being made is that thought involves emotion, and machines of course neither have nor need emotions to perform their tasks. There is also the factor of gender difference to be borne in mind, something else that distinguishes the human from computing systems, which again have no need of such an attribute. Ultimately, the conclusion drawn is that '[t]hought is inseparable from the phenomenological body' (*I*, 23).

Whether that condition of inseparability will always remain true in the future as Artificial Intelligence and Artificial Life are developed further (and more to the point, develop *themselves* further, as they are increasingly able to do) is, however, a more problematical issue. We may indeed one day have to face up to the existence of bodiless thought obeying an agenda of its own, perhaps even competing with us for resources. We may also find ourselves having to face the progressive cyborgisation of the human race, with much greater interaction (possibly highly invasive in character) between our bodies and technology, which might require us to alter quite radically our conception of what the body is – or could become. While such a prospect may excite theorists like Donna Haraway (see Haraway 1991), for Lyotard the body as we know it and the human are inextricably linked: a defence of one is a defence of the other, and it is a defence we are under an obligation to make if we want to see the inhuman kept at bay.

Passages

Inhuman
Techno-Science
Thought
Thought Without a Body

CAPITALISM

Stuart Sim

Lyotard has an intriguingly ambivalent attitude towards capitalism. As a left-wing thinker with at least some kind of Marxist past, one would expect him to be critical of a system which in one sense could be described as a grand narrative – and a grand narrative that in the form of neoliberal economics and globalisation has been very exploitative of large swathes of the world's population in recent times. Lyotard does equate capitalism with modernity, and in that guise he considers it to be '[t]he problem that overshadows all others' (*PW*, 25) in contemporary society. The rise of techno-science has brought this to a head, given that its main concerns are to increase efficiency and refine performativity such that the vast majority of the working population is subordinated to its demands. Lyotard's line is that capitalism-led techno-science's quest for an 'endless optimalization of the cost/benefit (input/output) ratio' (*PW*, 25) is moving us into the realm of the 'inhuman', where machines and computers are to be preferred to human beings because of their far greater efficiency and reliability in following through pre-set programmes. Lyotard is very worried about the threat posed by the growth of the multinationals, the basis of techno-science as a system, warning that their 'economic powers have reached the point of imperilling the stability of the State through new forms of the circulation of capital' (*PC*, 5). Crucially, this gives the multinationals potential control over the dissemination of knowledge, the key to the new world order as Lyotard sees it. As he pointedly asks, if firms like IBM are allowed to launch their own communications satellites with data bank facilities: 'Who will have access to them? Who will determine which channels or data are forbidden?' (*PC*, 6).

In contrast, Lyotard is very much alive to the disruptive qualities of capitalism, its well-attested ability to initiate rapid and unforeseen change in such a way that it undermines the grand narrative behind otherwise apparently entrenched social and political systems, observing that it 'inherently possesses the power to derealise familiar objects, social roles, and institutions' (*PC*, 74). Lyotard is no great supporter of the modern nation state after all, and capitalism as a system can often throw this entity into some considerable disarray since its agenda transcends the merely national – and in fact has no real interest in this. Capitalism escapes the controlling imperative behind such grand narratives, their wish to subsume all aspects of human existence within their own tightly monitored storyline: 'capital's superiority over the speculative genre resides at least in its not seeking to have the last word, to totalize after the fact all the phrases that have taken place in all the genres of discourse (whatever their finality might be) but rather in seeking to have the next word' (*D*, 138). That is, capitalism is more akin to an open-ended system than a totalising grand narrative, and it can in consequence generate 'the most unheard of occurrences' (*D*, 139) – much in the manner of a 'libidinal system' (1993b: 65). Although there is always the proviso to be made that behind capitalism's restless search for new phrases and linkages there does lie a driving force – 'profitability' (*D*, 138).

Capitalism helps to break down the certainties of belief-systems, therefore, as does science, and Lyotard is very much in favour of that, speaking of how the sheer energy capitalism releases proceeds to undermine, and eventually even exhaust, pre-capitalist institutions such that new kinds of social formation are enabled to emerge. It is to be thought of as a 'figure' (*PW*, 25) in this respect, and Lyotard is always attracted by figures and the destabilising effect they can have within settled discourses. 'Capitalism does not love order; the state loves it' (*PW*, 25–6), as he pithily describes what happens in this particular, epic, encounter between figure and discourse. When capitalism and science combine in the form of technoscience, however, we find ourselves confronted by a formidable new enemy that gives us substantial cause to worry about our ability to go on constructing little narratives to express our individual needs and differences. Profitability is an end in itself, and human beings, as Marx too had complained at length in *Capital* (1976, 1978, 1981 [1867, 1885, 1894]), are viewed essentially as a means to that end in a capitalist system; but techno-science is developing to the point where human beings are possibly expendable, and any support Lyotard may have felt moved to extend towards capitalism as an iconoclastic, figural force within our midst drains away faced with such a desperate prospect as that.

Passages

Figure
Inhuman
Knowledge
Links, Linkages
Modern, Modernity
Techno-Science

CASTORIADIS, CORNELIUS (1922–97) – see 'Socialisme ou Barbarie'

CATASTROPHE THEORY AND CHAOS THEORY

Stuart Sim

Both catastrophe and chaos theory fit in very neatly with Lyotard's overall world picture, in that they point out the limits of human power and suggest that a vast unknown lies past the reach of human understanding. These theories clearly inform Lyotard's view of recent science, since he considers that this is more productive of the unknown than the known; indeed, that is how he explicitly characterises what he calls 'postmodern science', which would include quantum physics as well as catastrophe and chaos. And the next generation of the latter two theories, complexity, is just as compatible with Lyotard's outlook and concerns.

Catastrophe theory emphasises the underlying continuity to systems, such that breakdowns and collapses are seen to be part of the overall development of the system. For the mathematician René Thom, what we were ultimately dealing with in catastrophe theory was 'the ceaseless creation, evolution, and destruction of forms' (Thom [1972] 1975: 1) that go to make up the physical world. Chaos theory emphasises the dependence of systems on their initial conditions, which can be magnified out of all recognition as the system develops; thus the famous example of the 'butterfly effect', where the beating of a butterfly's wings could in theory be expanded up to a major storm in another part of the globe. What is critical in both theories is that it is the internal dynamics of the system that dictate what happens, irrespective of human input. Complexity theory builds on such ideas to give us a world where systems are capable of self-organisation – again, a question of internal dynamics driving the process rather than any human planning. Such ideas resonated throughout the poststructuralist community, although their appropriation by thinkers like Lyotard did draw criticism – notably from the physicists Alan Sokal and Jean Bricmont in their highly combative book *Intellectual Impostures* (1998), which argued that there was a profound misunderstanding of the science being shown by poststructuralist theorists in most cases.

Lyotard specifically refers to catastrophe theory and chaos theory in *The Postmodern Condition* ([1979] 1984b), when he is putting forward his concept of postmodern science. One of the most thought-provoking observations he makes using these theories is that greater knowledge of systems does not necessarily give us more power over them: 'It is not true that uncertainty (lack of control) decreases as accuracy goes up: it goes up as well' (*PC*, 56). Even something as apparently simple as measuring a stretch of coastline, as Benoit Mandelbrot had shown, lies beyond our powers to do precisely, as no matter how far down we go to microscopic levels we can never reach the end. The point becomes that there is always an unknown, and ultimately unknowable, realm that is lying beyond us. We may think we have cracked the secret of the workings of a natural system, and that we can predict on the basis of that knowledge, but something in it will always elude us.

Chaos theory's interest lies in non-linear systems, those whose development cannot be predicted with accuracy, and which, paradoxically enough, can simultaneously feature chance and deterministic factors in their workings. Chaotic systems include such everyday examples as clouds, with the weather in general following a non-linear trajectory that creates considerable difficulty, as we all know from experience, for forecasters. Systems like this are held to be controlled by a strange attractor, a mysterious force which directs their course but whose character is hidden from us. We can never detect any pattern in such systems that makes sense to us, and have to adapt to whatever events flow from them. For Lyotard, that is true of events in general of course: they are unpredictable and demand that we adapt ourselves to them. He cannot accept that there is any determinable pattern to human existence (as Marxists believed there was in the form of a historical dialectic), and suggests that it is a waste of time looking for one. From Lyotard's perspective, life is a non-linear system, and that is all the more reason to steer well clear of metanarratives since they are based on the premise that this is not so, that we can engineer life to our advantage (monotheistic religions are excellent examples of such a linear vision, with human existence being contained within a universal scheme presided over by an omnipotent being with a master plan). Language is similarly non-linear to this thinker: a series of unpredictable linkages of phrases, by a host of individuals, whose trajectory is unmappable.

It is not hard to see why Lyotard would be attracted to the theories of such as Thom and Mandelbrot, although Sokal and Bricmont's criticisms do need to be borne in mind. Catastrophe and chaos may not provide the reinforcement Lyotard believes they do, but on the other hand that does not invalidate his own theories of how narratives function.

Passages

Fractals
Links, Linkage
Phrase, Phrasing
Postmodern Science
Unknown

CÉZANNE, PAUL (1839–1906) – see 'aesthetics', 'May '68, *événements*' and 'touch'

CHAOS THEORY see CATASTROPHE THEORY AND CHAOS THEORY

CHRISTIANITY

Daniel Whistler

Lyotard's most typical intervention on the issue of Christianity is his characterisation of it as a grand narrative. Christianity is 'the oldest and most "comprehensive" of the great Western narratives' (*PF*, 70). It is a primary example (along with Marxism and the Enlightenment) of a form of thought which determines all future phrases. Lyotard even suggests Christianity is the grand narrative *par excellence* whose success is owing not only to its 'invention' of an eschatological mode of thought (*PF*, 96–7) but also to the ethical obligation it imposed to 'love'-making linkages (*D*,

159–60). Lyotard's early invocation of 'the pagan', in contrast, must be seen in the light of his resistance to the grand narrative of Christianity.

However, Lyotard's most significant engagement with the Christian tradition is to be found in his posthumously published work, *The Confession of Augustine* ([1998b] 2000). While Augustine's name frequently appears throughout Lyotard's corpus from *Libidinal Economy* ([1974] 1993a) onwards, *The Confession* is his only detailed engagement with his work. In these incomplete fragments, Lyotard begins to think through the legacy Patristic theology – in the form of Augustine's *Confessions* – has bequeathed our own structures of thought, and he does so both by reading Augustine through the lens of his own usual armoury of concepts and by using Augustine's own ideas to stimulate new ways of thinking.

Augustine's *Confessions* exemplifies many of the motifs of Lyotard's late thought. The encounter with God is likened to the coming of the event. 'The shattering visit of the Other' (*CA*, 17) exceeds all our finite structures of thought and perception: it is a sublime *quod* to which no concept is adequate. Sin is envisaged as the temptation to *represent* the event and subsume it back into the platitudes of conventional ways of thinking. Such is Augustinian *distentio*: 'the accursed time in which the encounter with the absolute is incessantly put off' (*CA*, 12). The self in its everyday distended existence is unable to realise the power and significance of the Other. Thus, Lyotard speaks of a differend that emerges between the everyday existence of the self and the advent of the Other.

Engagement with Augustine also leads Lyotard back to some of the themes of his very earliest work. He writes (in a manner that recalls *Libidinal Economy*) of the 'libidinal-ontological constitution of temporality' (*CA*, 19). He also makes much of Augustine's influence on the phenomenological tradition (out of which Lyotard's own thought developed): '[In the *Confessions*] the prose of the world gives place to the poem of memory, or more exactly the phenomenology of internal time. The whole of modern, existential thought on temporality ensues from this meditation: Husserl, Heidegger, Sartre' (*CA*, 73).

However, this 'theological turn' at the end of Lyotard's life does more than merely confirm pre-existent concepts; it gives rise to new avenues of philosophical inquiry. Indeed, the minute scrutiny Lyotard gives to the texture of the *Confessions* reveals a side of Lyotard – Lyotard *as literary critic* – rarely seen in his other works.

Passages

Enlightenment
Event

CLOUDS

Stuart Sim

Clouds constitute one of the more poetic images in Lyotard's work, used by him to symbolise the nature of thought: 'Thoughts are not the fruits of the earth. They are not registered by areas, except out of human commodity. Thoughts are clouds. The periphery of thoughts is as immeasurable as the fractal lines of Benoit Mandelbrot . . . Thoughts never stop changing their location one with the other' (*P*, 5). The image captures the amorphous quality of thought, its lack of precise boundaries, that Lyotard considers to be necessary to philosophy, indicative of the flexibility he feels philosophers should exhibit in their approach to the world and its problems. Everything is to be considered as in a state of flux, with the possibility of new states of affairs always tantalisingly present. Lyotard's anti-totalising bias is very much in evidence here again, with the Mandelbrot reference signalling how we never can come to have full knowledge of any phenomenon, how there is always something beyond our reach (Mandelbrot had pointed out that we could never measure anything absolutely accurately, the coastline being a cited example, because there were always fractal levels further down within the surface we were measuring).

In *Peregrinations* (1988b [1990]) Lyotard describes the narrative of his own life as being a rather random process, much like the behaviour of clouds. Lyotard firmly believes in the openness of the future and there is no sense in which anyone's life falls into a neat narrative pattern that can be projected forward with confidence. It is impossible to programme one's life given the presence of so many variables in the world, and the same point applies to grand narratives: the degree to which they can exert control over their environment is far more limited than they ever claim, events continually disrupting any plan that might be put forward.

Clouds provide an appropriate metaphor for such a worldview, since neither do they have any definite substance we can manipulate nor are they predictable in their development. If thought is of a similar nature then no one individual can claim mastery over it as it is in a constant process of change; ideally, all of us should be as adaptable as we can be to the shifts that naturally keep occurring, Lyotard encouraging us to cultivate 'an ability to be responsive to slight changes affecting both the shape of the clouds you are trying to explore and the path by which you approach them' (*P*, 8). That responsiveness is a trait which ought to be endemic to the practice of philosophy; an example of svelteness in action. The less intellectual baggage we are carrying the better. Thinkers should be particularly sensitive to unfolding events, to the 'I don't know what' that always lies ahead of us, refusing to assume that this will fit any predetermined pattern – a fault of which intellectuals are consistently guilty in Lyotard's view. The acceptance or otherwise of the 'I don't know what' thus becomes an index to the integrity of one's thought.

Passages

Fractals
I Don't Know What
Intellectuals
Philosophy
Svelteness
Thought

COMMUNISM – see 'incredulity', 'law', 'literature', 'Marxism', 'May '68, *événements*', 'narrative of emancipation', 'pluralism', 'Socialisme ou Barbarie' and 'totality, totalisation'

COMPLEXITY THEORY – see 'catastrophe theory and chaos theory', 'postmodern science' and 'reason, rationality'

COMPUTERS – see 'body', 'capitalism', 'development', 'inhuman', 'knowledge', 'little narrative', 'narrative' and 'time'

D

DE GAULLE, PRESIDENT CHARLES (1890–1970) – see 'Algeria', 'intellectuals', 'literature', 'Marxism' and 'May '68, *événements*'

DEBORD, GUY (1931–94) – see 'event'

DECONSTRUCTION

Stuart Sim

Although he does have certain reservations about deconstruction as a philosophical technique (such as its tendency to treat almost everything as textual), there is nevertheless a fair amount of commonality between the overall projects of Lyotard and Jacques Derrida – not surprisingly for two thinkers whose work is categorisable under the heading of poststructuralism. As we have come to expect from poststructuralists, both figures are concerned to draw attention to the limits of human reason and the many aspects of existence that lie beyond our control, to reject the claims of universal theories, as well as to emphasise the openness of the future. In philosophical terms of reference, both can be described as anti-determinists, and it is characteristic that each views writing as an activity the course of which cannot be predicted: for Lyotard it 'marches to its own beat and has no debts' (*P*, 8); for Derrida 'writing is *inaugural* . . . It does not know where it is going' (Derrida [1967b] 1978: 11).

Deconstruction was one of the more widely publicised and adopted forms of poststructuralist thought, having a considerable influence within the academy. It is at base a theory of language and meaning that makes great play of the ambiguities and slippage that discourse inevitably contains. Derrida argued that meaning was never wholly present in the sense that it always hinted at other contexts, permanently carrying traces of other words at any one point of utterance (including writing). He devised the notion of *différance* to describe this condition, countering the belief in what he called the 'metaphysics of presence' (that meanings were fully present in the mind of the speaker/writer whenever uttered, and could be received in that same form by hearers/readers) that he saw as the underlying assumption of all discourse in Western culture. According to Derrida *différance* worked away persistently within language to prevent the full union of signifier and signified, and the sign was to be considered an incomplete entity in a state of transition (half 'not there' and half 'not-that' at any one stage, as his translator Gayatri Chakravorty Spivak succinctly summarised it (Preface, Derrida [1967a] 1976: xvii)). Structuralism had sought to find a unity in human discourse whereby it could be reduced to a series of grammars representing underlying deep structures, whereas Derrida wants to stress the factor of difference instead – as do all the main figures in the poststructuralist movement, including Lyotard.

The main difference between Lyotard and Derrida is that the former is far more overtly political in his writing, the latter being somewhat notorious for refusing most of time to make any very specific political commitments (although that has not stopped many of his followers from finding political implications in deconstruction). Lyotard speaks of figure working within discourse such that the latter can never be grasped in its entirety, so there are some parallels to be made with the effect of *dif-férance* (although figure is the more elusive concept), and also insists that the links applying within any particular phrase regimen cannot be transferred into another phrase regimen. But he sees a political significance to such phenomena: that grand narratives can never control discourse, and thus our lives, as they have always assumed they had the power to do. Lyotard also keeps returning in his later work to the notion of the sublime (as in *The Postmodern Condition* ([1979] 1984b)) and *Lessons on the Analytic of the Sublime* ([1991b] 1994), which as a condition lying beyond human comprehension ensures that we can only ever have a partial understanding of how our world works. Again, he interprets this politically to the detriment of grand narrative, which is seen to have far less control over events than it believes: the sublime is uncapturable in this respect.

Passages

Difference
Figure
Politics
Poststructuralism
Sublime
Writing

DEICTICS

Stuart Sim

Deictics are words that are dependent on their context for their meaning, as in Lyotard's description: 'Deictics relate the instances of the universe presented by the phrase in which they are placed back to a "current" spatio-temporal origin so named "I-here-now." These deictics are designators of reality. They designate their object as an extra-linguistic permanence, as a "given"' (*D*, 33). But since that 'given' is specific to the phrase universe in which it occurs, that means it appears and disappears with it, with Lyotard insisting that deictics can have 'no import' (*D*, 46) at all outside that particular context.

Although deictics are part of language, they cannot be pinned down in terms of their value as structural linguistics – with its emphasis on language as a system – would indicate. Rather, for Lyotard, 'they open language onto an experience which language cannot stock in its inventory since it is the experience of a *hic et nunc*, of an ego, i.e. precisely of sense-certainty' (Geoffrey Bennington 1988: 63). We cannot define 'I', for example, in the straightforward way that we could a word like, say, 'whale', which can be recognised instantly as an acquatic mammal, whereas 'I' requires a more technical description such as 'first person pronoun'. The meaning of a deictic term, as Lyotard rather dramatically puts it, 'is not, it can only *exist*' (Bennington 1988: 63). Unlike 'whale', the 'I' is context-dependent and can never signify as unproblematically as the former does. The implication, as commentators like Bennington have pointed out, is that a deictic does not really signify at all (see Bennington 1988).

Lyotard's poststructuralist credentials come through strongly at such points, in his insistence that language is not the closed system that structuralists believe it to be, that some things escape its reach. Poststructuralist thinkers are always concerned to identify such gaps, which put the notion of universal explanation under stress. Taken to its extreme, structuralism claims to offer the prospect of attaining a total understanding of systems through a detailed knowledge of the grammar involved in each case; but if language, the theory's model for systems in general, has gaps in terms of its operations then the theory loses much of its power. Deictics effectively undermine the assumption of unity in structuralist thought: 'the deictic is not a simple value inside the system, but an element which from the inside refers to the outside; it is not thinkable *in* the system, but *through* it' (Bennington 1988: 64). The existence of such an 'outside' is precisely what structuralism excludes; as a theory it is committed to making everything within the system relate to the working of it as a whole, to have a specifiable internal function. In such a theory there can be no extraneous, or rogue, elements, so everything is made to combine together somehow or other, every function made to conform to an overall pattern. Jacques Derrida is particularly scathing of this 'tidying up' approach in *Writing and Difference* ([1967b] 1978), and Lyotard suggests a similar dislike in works like *Discourse, Figure* ([1971] 2010).

For deictics to have no import outside their particular phrase universe is for Lyotard to strike yet another blow against the metanarrative consciousness. To be dependent on context means that we cannot make assumptions about the future or maintain any notions about being able to exercise control over events. Deictics are yet more evidence of the openness, thus unpredictability, of the future that Lyotard keeps insisting we have to acknowledge.

Passages

Event
Language Games
Phrase, Phrasing
Poststructuralism
Totality, Totalisation

DELEUZE, GILLES (1925–75) **AND GUATTARI, FELIX** (1930–92) – see 'desire', '*dispositif*', 'ethics', 'event', 'libidinal economy', 'Marxism', 'philosophy', 'post-Marxism' and 'poststructuralism'

DERRIDA, JACQUES (1930–2004) – see 'antifoundationalism', 'deconstruction', 'deictics', 'difference', 'event', 'Jews, Judaism', 'legitimation', 'Marxism', 'philosophy', 'poststructuralism', 'thought', 'totality, totalisation' and 'writing'

DESCARTES, RENÉ (1596–1650) – see 'antifoundationalism', 'ethics', 'phenomenology', 'postmodernism', 'reason, rationality' and 'subject'

DESCRIPTIVES AND PRESCRIPTIVES

Stuart Sim

One of our great failings, according to Lyotard, is our seemingly ingrained disposition to construct prescriptives out of descriptives – a move that we are never justified in making in his view. Descriptions of states of affairs in the world do not, he contends, ever signal clear-cut courses of action as to how to deal with them, nor what they mean in the larger scheme of things. This is Lyotard's version of the is–ought debate, and he is adamant that the former does not entail the latter: 'though I start from a description, I do not draw prescriptions from it because one cannot derive prescriptions from descriptions' (*JG*, 59). He concedes that there must be prescriptions in our lives: decisions do have to be made constantly about a multiplicity of things, whether mundane or serious in nature, and these will be backed up by reasons which we find personally meaningful and persuasive. But Lyotard holds that such decisions should be constructed on a 'case-by-case' basis rather than on the assumption of some transcendental principle that lays down irrefutable guidelines on how we ought to respond.

What we should be doing with descriptions instead is trying 'to extend, or maximize, as much as possible, what one believes to be contained in the description' (*JG*, 59) in order to see what might be the most productive way to proceed. Different phrase regimens apply in each instance, and phrase regimens should not be applied outside their own territory. A pagan society is one where prescriptions are reached in this 'case-by-case' fashion and not from some pre-existing scheme claiming universal validity (as with religion, or socio-political theories like Marxism); one in which prescriptions are left, as Lyotard rather intriguingly puts it, 'hanging' (*JG*, 59). As an example of how one maximises descriptions, he cites the situation of the French intelligentsia in the later twentieth century when its collective belief in metanarratives such as Marxism had gone into sharp decline – the post-1968 effect which led to works such as Lyotard's own *Libidinal Economy* ([1974] 1993a) with its vicious attack on the Marxist tradition of thought and political action. From this particular situation we can conclude that little narratives are growing in popularity, and then, further, that it is desirable to increase the number of these rather than continue with a discredited metanarrative. No transcendental prescription is involved in this assessment.

Lyotard's antipathy towards universally applicable ethical theories creates problems for a thinker who is so incensed by injustice, and he has to indulge in some tortuous reasoning as to why we should oppose phenomena such as fascism. We should do so because fascism does not just suppress little narratives, but in the case of Judaism tries to obliterate it altogether from the historical record. Fascism manifestly does not allow us to bear witness to the injustices committed in its name, and Lyotard takes that to be a fundamental obligation that we have to one another (which some might construe as a prescriptive). Metanarratives of the fascist type are therefore the antithesis to paganism, with its active encouragement of little narratives.

Paganism would, however, be too pragmatic for most societies, which tend to be uncomfortable with open-ended systems like the 'case-by-case' method with its lack of universalisable principles of good and evil. The criticism of Lyotard's interviewer in *Just Gaming* ([1979] 1985), Jean-Loup Thébaud, still carries considerable weight in this respect: 'Why draw up instructions whose validity is limited to one move? They can no longer be called "instructions," I should think. They could be called reveries, remarks, opinions, but not instructions' (*JG*, 55). In other words, it is simply unrealistic to expect us to construct ethics anew for each event that requires such a decision; few societies could contemplate such an unwieldy system without any concept of prescriptives that extended past the local. Lyotard's claim that instructions 'are always local' (*JG*, 55) can certainly be questioned: we may not have a total picture of what is happening in the world, but few of us are incapable of seeing a wider context than the local – especially in an age so saturated by information as our own.

It is possible to argue that universal prescriptives have a positive side; that their existence does help to keep human behaviour within reasonable bounds much of the time. Whether a pagan society would be any less prone to injustice has to remain a moot point. Bearing witness can seem a very weak basis for ethics, or at least a very idealistic one, overly dependent on the assumed goodwill of individuals. Maximising descriptions can feel similarly vague. However, if Lyotard has done no more than make us examine our prescriptions in a bit more detail rather than simply following them by reflex, then his enquiries into how ethics are implemented can nevertheless be considered of value.

Passages

Ethics
Jews, Judaism
Little Narrative
Marxism
Paganism
Phrase, Phrasing

DESIRE

Tony Purvis

It is in *Libidinal Economy* ([1974] 1993a) and in *Discourse, Figure* ([1971] 2010) that Lyotard writes in detail about desire, though all his writings have desire as one of their major or minor thematic undercurrents. Desire is framed by Lyotard in an esoteric, meditative language. Nevertheless, his meditations on art, aesthetics and painting also speculate on the ethical dimensions of desire, pleasure and human action. Indeed, Lyotard is arguably one of the key theorists of desire after Jacques Lacan. Although he departs from Freudian-Lacanian traditions, betraying as a consequence an indebtedness to the work of Gilles Deleuze on the way, this is not to be read as a rejection of either the work of Sigmund Freud and Lacan or of psychoanalysis more generally.

Desire as formulated in Lyotard's *Libidinal Economy* is an elusive and attractive concept, even if its definitional status remains perplexing. It is at once a 'great ephemeral skin', a 'tensor' and something 'named Marx' – a 'Libidinal Marx' (*LE*, 95) – 'Every political economy is libidinal' (*LE*, 108), he argues. If Lyotard's account puzzles and confuses, then this is intentional, part of his desire to experiment with desire's very language. Desire is phrased in terms of the physicality of 'the so-called body', and it is also a desire which is linked to the skin's very real surfaces, folds, scars, as well as the body's 'great variety of planes' (*LE*, 108). Desire, is about its contours and so Lyotard stays with a lexical range which alludes all the time to the psychoanalytic dimensions of desire. But it is *in* and *on* the body, too, with all its materiality, that desire takes shape. Internal/external and inside/outside, as traditional binary pairs used for understanding desire in Western metaphysics, are melded and brought together in Lyotard's work. Akin to a Möbius strip, desire is without an upper/lower or under/over dimension but, following the route of metonymy, desire always changes its aim and object.

Before he deconstructs the language of desire, Lyotard returns to Freud and Karl Marx. Indeed, across the pages of *Libidinal Economy*, an indebtedness to both these figures is writ large. This is in part because of Lyotard's critique of modernity. Freud, proto-analyst of modern civilisation's discontent subjects, theorises a way of understanding modernity and everyday life via neuroses, or the outward demonstration of *repressed* desires. Dreams and fantasies, crucial to Freud's concept of desire, remain central in Lyotard's formulation. Karl Marx is important to Lyotard because of his fascination with desire by way of his critique of material life under capitalism. 'We must come to take Marx as if he were a writer, an author full of affects, take his text as a madness and not a theory' (*LE*, 95).

Desire, Lyotard acknowledges, is a force which has often been theorised in terms of a moment of lack and a moment of satisfaction. This deficit model, where desire comes about on the basis of a lack, is one which Lyotard incorporates into his own theory of the libidinal. However, he combines this model, where lack functions around the fantasy of a lost object or person, with a model of desire conceived as force, intensity and productivity. Desire, in Lyotard, is productive and creative, and comparable to abstract art, where figures and lines criss-cross interminably. There is no end to desire in that sense, in part because there is no inherent or specific truth which the satisfaction of desire unfolds. Rather, it is something which is inseparable from all activities in culture, at once sublime and mundane, transgressive as much as it is adaptive. Psychoanalytic theory has often implied that contemporary societal relations place a hold on desire. Lyotard argues the opposite: desire intersects all aspects of daily life. *Libidinal Economy*'s analysis of the history of capitalism sees desire everywhere.

Lyotard commends the figure of the Möbius band (a strip where the boundaries upper/lower and inside/outside are blurred) as a way of conceiving the operations of desire. Following psychoanalysis, he situates desire on the axis of metonymy and not metaphor; and as soon as one desire is satiated another emerges in the ever-new language games of postmodern culture. But the Möbius band is also suggestive of another aspect of desire upon which Lyotard draws. The Möbius band, along with the many allusions to the 'great ephemeral skin' throughout *Libidinal Economy*, draws attention to a *topographical* notion of desire rather than one which relies on notions of inner drives or instincts. It is figure, form and image – and the language of art and aesthetics more generally – which Lyotard makes central in his accounts of desire. The playful dimensions of his writings on desire are intentional, and they underline Lyotard's own desire to question the binary oppositions which have traditionally structured how desire is conceived in Western philosophy.

Passages

Body
Figure
Great Ephemeral Skin
Libidinal Economy
Marxism
Tensor

DEVELOPMENT

Stuart Sim

Development is Lyotard's term for modernity in its most progress-oriented mode – effectively the late capitalist, techno-science dominated culture that we now live in, characterised by the ceaseless search for new markets and ever more efficient methods of exploiting the world's resources for corporate profit. Globalisation is the public face of this project, and it has succeeded in transforming the world in just a few decades into one gigantic market operating under the principles of neoliberal economic theory, which demands constant expansion and economic growth.

Lyotard is particularly critical of development in *The Inhuman* ([1988c] 1991a), where he treats it as part of a sinister programme to bypass the human in favour of computers, creating a world of the inhuman in which technology would totally rule our lives – perhaps eventually dispensing with the human altogether. Development regards human beings as mere means to an end, and has become a self-sustaining project which is only interested in maximising efficiency and performativity in pursuit of its goals: 'Development imposes the saving of time. To go fast is to forget fast, to retain only the information that is useful afterwards' (*I*, 3). The result is a society in which the human dimension is progressively being diminished, making resistance to the system significantly harder to sustain. Development is the enemy of difference and the little narrative, 'the very thing which takes away the hope of an alternative to the system from both analysis and practice' (*I*, 7), and Lyotard urges us to oppose its relentless drive towards controlling all aspects of our world and instituting a realm of the inhuman.

The financial crisis that broke in 2007 has made us realise just how reckless development has become in its search for greater profits, and how dangerous that can be for our culture in terms of the risks taken. Lyotard's criticisms of the development model seem all the more justified in the light of the collapse of much of the global banking system, which has only survived thanks to massive injections of public money by governments throughout the world's major economies. Champions of neoliberal economics regard the market as a law unto itself, the workings of which should be kept completely free from human intervention. We are to assume that the market is regulated by an 'invisible hand' (Adam Smith's notion) that must be left to its own mysterious devices. The implication is that we are mere servants of the market, which brings to mind quite forcefully Lyotard's warnings about the turn to the inhuman in our culture and how this may render humanity largely irrelevant.

Lyotard had theorised that, although development had no more of an end than 'accelerating and extending itself according to its internal dynamic alone' (*I*, 7), its scope for expansion was nevertheless limited by the lifetime of the sun. But the system could well fail far earlier than that would suggest, as resources dry up and the contradictions of its 'internal dynamic' become ever more evident, generating even more dramatic collapses than we have just witnessed.

Passages

Difference
Inhuman

DIALECTICS

Gary Browning

Dialectics is a method of linking concepts together that is associated primarily with G. W. F. Hegel and his successors, notably Karl Marx. Hegel
considered that concepts are linked to one another in that their specifica-
tion of thought implies other thoughts, and the movement constituted by
the demand for a further more complete concept to rectify the partiality of
a concept is what dialectics consists in. As Hegel maintains that thought
captures reality, in that reality can only be specified in conceptual terms,
the upshot is that reality itself, for Hegel, is dialectical. Hence for Hegel,
individuals presuppose the more inclusive concept of social relations,
and individual rights presuppose civil society and the state. Likewise the
present presupposes the past and the historical development of present
experience. Marx abrogates Hegel's idealism but he retains dialectics
in that he makes a great play of the dialectical inter-relations between
aspects of production and the dependence of political and moral relations on productive ones. Again, he sees the present as emerging out of
the past to which it is dialectically connected. History, for both Hegel
and Marx, constitutes a unity whereby the meaning of particular forms
of society is revealed by their subsequent development into other forms
of society. History is a dialectical narrative in which its various components are seen to relate to one another and to reveal an ultimate shape or
directionality.

Lyotard is fiercely opposed to dialectics, because he is opposed to
holism and the attempt to bridge differences so that distinct perspectives
are integrated within a more general position. *The Differend* ([1983] 1988a)
highlights how there is a sheer difference between perspectives rather than
possibilities of uniting them. There is no common language into which the
various ways in which standpoints are formulated can be assimilated. In
The Postmodern Condition ([1979] 1984b) Lyotard imagines society as consisting in so many diverse and discrete language games. These language
games are not to be assimilated to one another via dialectical speculation
and the postmodern perspective is one that celebrates their differences.
The dialectical urge to connect them together is seen as part and parcel of

the modern urge to invent grand narratives that supersede smaller-scale particular narratives. Lyotard imagines dialectics to constitute a putative master or metalanguage, which obfuscates the differences between forms of activity and thinking. Dialectics for Lyotard is emblematic of a modernity that looks for certainties, objectivity and the mastering of the dissonant and the divergent. Lyotard's critique of dialectics is connected to what he takes to be an illicit modernist supplanting of the limits of philosophy that is intimated by Immanuel Kant. Lyotard's sympathetic reading of Kant in *Lessons on the Analytic of the Sublime* ([1991b] 1994) and *The Differend* is linked to his critique of dialectics. Kant was critical of attempts to explain the nature of the world in metaphysical terms, maintaining that metaphysical speculation breaks down into dialectical readings that allow for opposing qualities to be maintained. In contrast, Kant highlights the limits within which knowledge operates and suggests that experience is not be interpreted as a whole. Lyotard takes Kant's careful designation of the differing characters of aesthetics, science and morals to be indicative of his own project of specifying differences rather than looking for dialectical unities between forms of experience.

The strength of Lyotard's objection to dialectics is presented in his denial of grand narratives in *The Postmodern Condition*. He takes Hegel and Marx to be the prime exponents of grand narratives because they provide holistic dialectical accounts of history, whereas Lyotard denies that there is an overriding dialectical unity to history.

In *Libidinal Economy* ([1974] 1993a) Lyotard breaks with his former Marxist allegiances by rejecting the claims for a Marxist scientific dialectical account of capital and instead observing the libidinous engagement of Marx with his object of study, his never-ending fascination with capital. Lyotard's critique of dialectics represents a particular reading of dialectical reasoning and a corrigible interpretation of Hegel and Marx. Non-metaphysical readings of Hegel and a sympathetic postmodern take on Marx would play down the alleged absolutism of Hegel and the linear account of social change ascribed to Marx. Moreover, a case can be made for seeing difference relationally so that different practices are seen as being defined in part by their relations with one another, hence a dialectical unity in diversity might be seen as possessing more explanatory potential than a reliance on mere difference. None the less Lyotard's rejection of dialectics challenges supporters of dialectical reasoning to construe its operations to be inclusive of difference rather than dismissive of it and to see it as something different from a metalanguage that merely subsumes difference within its own distinct and absolutising logic.

Passages

DIFFERENCE

Stuart Sim

If there is one thing that sums up poststructuralism as a movement it is the strength of its members' commitment to difference. As cases in point, Jacques Derrida devises a special concept, *différance*, to deal with the issue (see *Of Grammatology* ([1976] 1967a)); difference feminists like Luce Irigaray reconstruct feminism on the basis of it, taking it to hold the key to gender relations. Structuralism sought to identify similarities and commonalities across systems, but poststructuralists put difference at the centre of their worldview instead, rejecting the idea that there is any underlying deep structure that directs and controls the operation of systems. Lyotard proves no less committed to the cause of difference, and his entire philosophy is informed by the notion. When he is criticising the communist movement for its interpretation of the Algerian war of independence in the 1950s and 1960s, for example, it is because he feels it is failing to take difference properly into account, forcing Algeria to conform to a theoretical model of what it thinks revolutionary struggle should be. For Lyotard, in contrast, '[n]o consciousness can span the whole of society so as to pose the question of what that society wants for itself' (*PW*, 302), since any society breaks down into a mass of individuals with different needs according to their social position. In later career, in works such *The Inhuman* ([1988c] 1991a), he is to be found defending difference against the massed forces of techno-science and development, which are pictured as wanting a homogenised world characterised by ultra-efficient systems focused on maximising performance, and even willing to dispense with humanity altogether if that is necessary for the achievement of this goal.

Little narratives exemplify difference, since they represent their own range of interests rather than those set down as the norm by the prevailing metanarrative, and develop independently of the central power base to their culture. Those interests may even clash with the metanarrative, and little narratives can find themselves in direct opposition to those in power – as happened, for example, in the *événements* of 1968 in Paris, with a loose grouping of students and trade unionists taking on the national government led by President Charles de Gaulle in protest at its policies. Lyotard conceived of little narratives as temporary projects, counselling against letting themselves grow into equivalents of the metanarratives they were opposing. If a little narrative did continue on indefinitely, becoming a political party perhaps, then it would become a power base in its turn, with longer-term interests to pursue which could only too easily harden into dogma. And dogmatism is what a sceptically inclined movement like poststructuralism is specifically designed to challenge.

The appearance of differends signals how difference can become a socio-political battleground. When incommensurable genres of discourse clash and one imposes its rules on the other to its detriment, then difference is being suppressed in the name of power. A colonised people cannot air their grievances properly if the legal system is set up to protect the interests of the colonisers; in effect, the former have been written out of the process, 'divested of the means to argue' as Lyotard sees it, and 'for that reason a victim' (*D*, 9) of the stronger narrative. Erasing difference in this fashion is a characteristic trait of metanarratives, which do their best to enforce conformity throughout their domain. One particularly shocking example of this trait can be found in the treatment of the Jewish race over the course of European history, an issue which Lyotard returns to persistently throughout his writings. The extent of the Jews' difference to Christian European culture means that they are always perceived as the 'other', and not just the other but a dangerous other that poses a potential threat to the host society – in a very real sense, unassimilable. 'Europe', Lyotard's reading of history tells him, 'does not know what to do with them' (*Hj*, 3). Difference is to be feared, and in the case of the Nazi 'final solution' even eradicated from European history in a grotesque attempt to guarantee an assumed European racial purity. Although this is an extreme example, metanarratives do have a distinct tendency towards homogenisation, and immigrant groups more often than not discover themselves to be the target of racial prejudice. Various kinds of minority groups can be marginalised in this way by dominant metanarratives, forming a category that Lyotard collectively refers to as 'jews', meaning that their difference renders then unassimilable by the cultural mainstream too.

Lyotard can be considered one of the foremost spokespersons for a politics of difference, therefore, and that is a consistent thread running throughout his work. Opposition to difference is presented as an ideologically loaded position that should be met with resistance by little narratives collectively.

Passages

DIFFEREND

Gary Browning

A differend is a technical term that Lyotard invokes in *The Differend* ([1983] 1988a). In that book Lyotard focuses upon language, maintaining that what is fundamental in language are phrases. There are always phrases of one sort or another but how they are to be understood depends upon how they are linked together. For instance, silence constitutes a phrase but its meaning is only determined by what comes next. Silence at a Quaker meeting is different from an uneasy silence at a business meeting that is then followed by an explosion of anger, and it is different again from the relaxed silence shared by intimates. Phrases can be linked together in phrase regimens such as counting, ordering or describing. In turn, phrase regimens are connected via genres of discourse such as dialogues, lectures or narratives that combine a number of phrase regimens. A Platonic dialogue, for example, contains a variety of styles, such as humour, stories, myths and philosophical speculation. The ways in which phrases are linked by both phrase regimens and genres of discourse shape their meaning. Certain styles of linking phrases and their distinctive forms of meaning might be recognised by some people but not others. Some discursive styles, for instance, satire and irony, either will not be recognised or else misunderstood. A differend occurs when something that may be said so as to express a standpoint is not in fact phrased, because it is excluded by other phrases and connecting conventions.

A differend represents a serious wrong that is neither easy to rectify nor to compensate for. Lyotard maintains that many forms of conflict or dispute can be resolved reasonably easily. Where both parties are agreed that a misdemeanour occurred and are at one on the terms in which it is to be understood then in principle rectification can be organised. A differend is more serious. It constitutes a wrong that does not lend itself to arbitration. A wrong occurs where there is a conflict over what has occurred or how an event may be described. In *The Differend* Lyotard provides the example of a Holocaust survivor whose experience is not captured in conventional forms of communication and who is unable to phrase his or her experience in ways that others will understand The wrong is not recognised because what has happened cannot be phrased in a way that will be recognised by others. Lyotard's analysis of the differend is radical in that it opens up a way of understanding and depicting a fundamental dispute between individuals. The relations between capital and labour, for instance, in some ways are not susceptible to arbitration. A proletarian might describe her or his experience in terms of exploitation and aliena-tion, which is not recognised by a capitalist or manager, who, in contrast, conceives of the worker as a flexible resource receiving a market rate of pay. Arbitration and compromise are neither possible nor expressible where the participants in a practice conceive of its conditions in radically different ways. Compromise presupposes some common measure or limit to which adjustments can be made.

Lyotard's notion of a differend stretches the notion of the political, and highlights what can be so intractable in political disputes. Lyotard imag-ines politics to be present wherever there is a fundamental dispute over terms and one party's perspective is excluded. Hence politics is not to be seen as merely pertaining to states and overtly public and conventionally recognised political activity, such as campaigning on behalf of a political party. Rather politics is present when an interlocutor is excluded from a discussion, when the perspective of an immigrant is not considered or when a partner to a relationship succumbs to the dominance of the other. Lyotard takes politics to be the radical intractable disagreement over terms and he aims to register the injustice of suppressing certain standpoints. The radicalism of Lyotard's stance can be appreciated by comparing his point of view with those, like Jürgen Habermas, who urge a deliberative standpoint in politics, maintaining that individuals can come to agree-ment. Indeed, deliberative democrats take it to be the aim of politics to arrive at agreement and the telos of a political association is to establish agreement over its ends and purposes. For Lyotard, there is the prospect of radical disagreement, which cannot even be expressed in terms that all parties would recognise. His viewpoint is a powerful counter to the aspira-tions of those who advocate a politics of consensus. The most fundamental beliefs currently maintained in liberal democracies might all be subject to challenge. For instance, the rights of man have been extended to women and might be extended to other animals besides mankind but the language of existing human rights might not be able to accommodate the extension of rights to non-humans.

Lyotard's notion of a differend is challenging. It is audacious in part because it is paradoxical. For if the common nature of differends could be stated then they would not constitute differends. Differends presume that there is no common metalanguage in which their status can be articulated. If the dilemmas associated with differends could be communicated unproblematically in clear objective terms then there would be no fundamental problem. For Lyotard, differends can only be suggested by the very inability to express them. This paradox has been cited as a problem for Lyotard by some Lyotard scholars (see Williams 1998; Browning 2000) and yet Lyotard could reply that it is rather the problem of politics itself.

Passages

Discourse
Dissensus
Genre
Philosophical Politics
Phrase, Phrasing
Politics

DISCOURSE

Stuart Sim

Treating human activities as self-contained discourses has become a convention in poststructuralist-postmodernist theory, part of the general commitment its practitioners have to the notion of difference. We are expected to treat each discourse on its merits, according to its own particular procedures and objectives, and to acknowledge what makes it different from others. The work of Michel Foucault in particular has been highly influential in establishing this conception of discourse within the critical community, and a whole school of 'discourse theory' has developed out of this line of enquiry. Foucault's major point about discourses was that they were in the main based on power, although those in control of each discourse used that power as a way of imposing their values on the population at large such that they took these to be the natural order of things and accepted any restrictions these may have involved on their lifestyle. Thus he could argue in *The History of Sexuality* (Foucault 1976–84 [1981–8]) that a discourse of sexuality was developed in the West from Christian times onwards that privileged heterosexuality, to the extent of eventually classifying homosexuality as a deviant practice. Equally, public behaviour came to be standardised within certain norms and anything perceived to be outside those became subject to control by the ruling authorities: the

mentally ill were rounded up into asylums, the modern, heavily regulated
and monitored prison system was created, and so on. Discourses set up
and institutionalised hierarchies of power which could be very difficult to
challenge.

Lyotard's take on this notion is that our culture is made up of a collection of genres of discourse, each with its own specific rules and ends.
Genres of discourse consist in their turn of phrase regimens and approved
linkages between the phrases they contain, the proviso being that these
linkages have purchase only within their particular regimen. A genre of
discourse has a bit more flexibility than that: it 'inspires a mode of linking
phrases together, and these phrases can be from different regimens' (*D*,
128). In doing so, the genre subsumes the phrases into its programme, the
'end' it is trying to achieve: it 'imprints a unique finality onto a multiplicity of heterogeneous phrases by linkages that aim to procure the success
proper to the genre' (*D*, 129). That is where the problems begin, however,
in the extent to which a genre might decide to go in order to procure the
success it regards as being proper to it. Genres of discourse can and do
clash, which is how differends emerge. In keeping with the anti–absolutist
tenor of his thought, Lyotard is against the idea that there can be such a
thing as an ultimate genre: instead, we are to recognise that '[g]enres of
discourse are strategies – of no–one' (*D*, 137) – that is, they have no transcendental quality.

Not all genres of discourse have admirable ends, therefore, and Lyotard
can be very critical of some on occasion – particularly when they attempt
to close down debate in other discourses. Success proper to one genre may
turn out to be a disaster for another. An example of this can be found in the
controversy over the Holocaust, with Holocaust deniers employing a radically different genre of discourse than their opponents. In Lyotard's scathing assessment, they were '"playing" another genre of discourse, one in
which conviction, or, the obtainment of a consensus over a defined reality,
is not at stake' (*D*, 19): which is to say that the deniers were spinning a
fantasy, and that fantasy was being transferred by them onto the genre of
discourse where events like Auschwitz did have a defined reality as well as
the means to prove it (in Lyotard's terminology, Auschwitz had a referent
that could be consensually determined). What made sense within the one
genre did not, and never could, within the other – the linkages governing
their respective phrase regimens simply did not match. The discourse of
the deniers was designed to render it impossible to make any judgement
regarding the Holocaust, because the Holocaust was assumed from the
beginning to be a non–event. No meaningful debate could take place under
those circumstances.

Misuse of a genre of discourse along these lines incenses Lyotard. In fact much of his philosophy can be seen as a campaign against misuse of genres and the differends that come in its wake. This aligns him quite closely with Foucault's worldview, where discourses are so regularly the province of the powerful and deployed to keep them in power at the expense of those they are engaged in exploiting. In real terms, however, it is a fallacy to think that a discourse can ever be completely controlled, certainly not on an indefinite basis, as it always has the disruptive force of 'figure' working within it to prevent it from achieving any sense of unity; figure constituting 'a violation of discursive order' (*LRG*, 293), much in the manner of the event and desire. Discourses can always be breached by such forces, no matter what those in power may choose to believe.

Passages

Difference
Figure
Genre
Links, Linkage
Phrase, Phrasing
Power

DISPOSITIF

Stuart Sim

Dispositif means 'apparatus' or 'device', and for Lyotard this gives it an interesting range of connotations (in fact the fluidity of the term has made it attractive to many thinkers in the French poststructuralist community). He tends to use it in the sense of an organising principle (or 'set-up') that gives some kind of structure or order to actions and events, a disposition towards interpreting these according to a particular scheme of thought – or at the very least a space, or framework, in which actions and events can be played out. *Dispositifs* are ways of channelling desire and libidinal energy for Lyotard therefore, although the extent of their success in doing so is always open to dispute: when they are worked up into metanarratives they generally overestimate their power in this respect, as Lyotard is at pains to point out in *Libidinal Economy* ([1974] 1993a). There is always an excess in desire and libidinal energy that *dispositifs* will fail to capture.

It is inevitable that we will make use of *dispositifs* (we are born into a world of these after all) and that they will play a significant role in shaping our view of experience, but the issue that always rises with them is whether they gravitate towards metanarrative status and lose sight of their essential contingency. It is when *dispositifs* claim precedence over others in this way that problems start (Michel Foucault sees this as a standard progression in modern culture, the end result being the exercise of social and political power by some dominant group). Lyotard's insistence that at the heart of all such explanatory theories there lies a 'Great zero' is designed to puncture the pretensions of all *dispositifs* and metanarratives. His argument is that ultimately they explain nothing, that they constitute instead a feedback loop: 'they bear within them knowledge and its "answers"' (*LE*, 6). One could just as easily put the word 'knowledge' in quotation marks too at this point; this has no claim to absolute truth either (rather in the nature of Friedrich Nietzsche's 'perspectivism'). Nevertheless, we do have a distinct tendency to assume that such a truth-value is invested in *dispositifs*, and to treat them as being more than mere perspectives on existence. Foucault certainly emphasises this repressive aspect of the phenomenon, and Lyotard is very aware of it too, hence his concern to draw our attention to the limitations that all *dispositifs* share. *Libidinal Economy* is an exasperated response to how we have allowed certain *dispositifs* to control our thought, with Lyotard repeatedly making the point that libidinal energy makes a mockery of all such pretensions to regulation. Given that any power the *dispositif* has is illusory, we have far more freedom within it than we tend to believe; freedom to construct oppositional little narratives, for example.

Perhaps we could even regard postmodernism as a *dispositif*, in that it has its own particular attitude towards desire and libidinal energy, and opposes the stratagems of metanarratives. It offers an alternative apparatus, or framework, to metanarratives, and constitutes a disposition towards viewing the world from a very different, resolutely anti-authoritarian and anti-systems perspective. That might go some way towards explaining Lyotard's often ambivalent attitude towards postmodernism, however, as he is by nature a restless thinker who never wants to get stuck in a particular mode of thought, someone temperamentally suspicious of explanatory schemes and how they can so readily be abused in the name of exerting power and control over others (by intellectuals as much as anyone). Postmodernism can become a programme, as it has to a notable extent in the arts and architecture (with practices such as double-coding coming to define aesthetic value), and Lyotard tends to shy away from it when that happens. Postmodernism is at its most useful for him when it is subversive and inducing scepticism of authority in a general sense.

Lyotard's commitment to svelteness means that *dispositifs* are to be treated lightly, indeed with a high degree of scepticism as to what they tell us about the world, since what they tell us is predetermined by the structure of the *dispositif* itself: a Marxist reading of history will always find class struggle, a religious one evidence of a divine master plan being worked out. *Dispositifs* must never be regarded as offering a definitive method of interpretation: one can, and should, move in and out of them as circumstances dictate, always recognising their contingent nature. As with Gilles Deleuze and Felix Guattari there is a nomadic quality to Lyotard's thought that resists being tied down to any set of methods or ideas; that for him is the best way of bearing witness to the intrinsic singularity of events.

Passages

Event
Great zero
Intellectuals
Libidinal Economy
Poststructuralism
Svelteness

DISSENSUS

Gary Browning

Lyotard valorises dissensus over consensus. He denies that there is an overriding unity to things and events. He refutes the possibility of essentialism. In *The Postmodern Condition* ([1979] 1984b), drawing upon Ludwig Wittgenstein, he argues for the absolute diversity of language games and the impossibility of an essential way of reading what they have in common. Difference is to be recognised and celebrated. He values dissensus because it recognises the differences that he takes to be fundamental to postmodernity. Dissensus for Lyotard harmonises with an incommensurability that is fundamental to the constitution of social practice. In *The Postmodern Condition* Lyotard presents the social world as constituting so many discrete practices or language games, which cannot be assimilated to one another. Dissensus is not contingent. It follows from the radical difference between ways of conceiving and acting. Constative statements are different from performative ones and aesthetics cannot be assimilated to scientific description. In *The Differend* ([1983] 1988a), Lyotard takes meaning to be constituted by distinctive ways of phrasing that do not allow for a consensual overview.

Perspectives are discrete and there is no common way of expressing them. Indeed the urge to accept or work for consensus is not only problematic but also politically unjust because it denies a voice to those whose standpoint is denied a phrasing. Dissensus is the appropriate way of responding to a political world in which there are radical differences between perspectives.

Lyotard's appreciation of dissensus and his suspicion of consensus is evident in his *Just Gaming* ([1979] 1985), co-written with Jean-Louis Thébaud, where he praises the sophists, whose paganism challenges the possibility of moral universalism. In *Lessons on the Analytic of the Sublime* ([1991b] 1994) Lyotard's support for an aesthetics of the sublime, in which the sheer inability to express a perspective is taken to capture its incommunicable aesthetic force, underlies his appreciation of distinct perspectives that resist straightforward articulation in a common consensual language.

Dissensus for Lyotard is a political perspective as well as a philosophical reading of the world. For if differences are radical and cannot be bridged by allegedly common forms of language it becomes politically significant to support causes that are marginal to or resist dominant forms of expression.

Dissensus is to be valued precisely because it resists the conformism engendered by the tendency for society to be increasingly dominated by an instrumental logic. Indeed, in *The Postmodern Explained to Children* ([1986] 1993c) Lyotard likens the developing cultural logic of instrumentalism to the kind of repressive social atmosphere captured in George Orwell's *1984* (1949). In the context of a one-dimensional repressive society dissensus is of signal importance and allows for the subversive creativity that is canvassed in Lyotard's late work, *The Inhuman* ([1988c] 1991a). Lyotard's lifelong concern for aesthetics and its inexplicable creativity resists consensus in its deeply singular character. From *Discourse, Figure* ([1971] 2010) through to *Signed Malraux* ([1996] 1999) Lyotard's preoccupation with aesthetics is linked to his association of it with an intractable creativity and an inherent fit with what resists consensus.

Passages

Aesthetics
Difference
Justice
Phrase, Phrasing
Sublime

DREAM-WORK

Roy Sellars

Sigmund Freud, dreamer and father of psychoanalysis, is a key figure for Lyotard. This much is clear; but why is it that he gives such importance to Freud's work? Lyotard was not a psychoanalyst himself and he does not seek to apply psychoanalysis considered as theory or doctrine; he insists even that he is 'not a theorist' (Olson 1995). In order to see what is at stake in Lyotard's long engagement with Freud, there is no better place to start than an essay first published in the fateful year 1968 and then, three years later, as a section of his *Discourse, Figure*: namely, 'The dream-work does not think' (*PW*, 19–55). The implications of this essay are still unfolding, and the complete translation of Lyotard's enormous and complex book, in 2010, will inaugurate a new phase of his reception in the English-speaking world.

If Lyotard is not a theorist, he is certainly a reader, and his essay on the dream-work constitutes a detailed and patient reading of the final chapters (6–7) of Freud's *The Interpretation of Dreams*. For Freud, the dream-work 'alone is the essence of dreaming' (Freud 1953–74: vol. 5, 506–7 n. 2). The dream-work is 'completely different' from waking thought and, supplying Lyotard with the title for his essay, Freud adds that it 'does not think' (Freud 1953–74: vol, 5, 507). We are to see the dream-work, instead, as a transformation of the dream-thought, and the question this raises is: 'How must a *text* be *worked over* for its stated meaning to be modified?' (*PW*, 21). The answer for Lyotard lies in the disruptive forces active within language, desire and the figure: 'Force occupies the very scenario of the dream as Van Gogh's brush-stroke remains recorded in his suns' (*PW*, 24).

In his introduction to a new translation of *The Interpretation of Dreams*, Ritchie Robertson writes: 'The extremely verbal character of Freud's mind leads him to underestimate visual imagery in dreams' (Freud 1999: xix). Robertson claims that Freud 'revelled in linguistic play, but, despite his appreciation of painting and especially sculpture, he did not know what to make of visual imagery in dreams'. This nexus of the linguistic and the visual, and of play and bafflement, is, however, exactly what interests Lyotard, who could never be accused of underestimating visual imagery. According to Robertson, furthermore, in 'assigning dreams to the primary process . . . Freud seems to distrust the imaginative activity by which dreams are shaped' (Freud 1999: xx; a more apposite guide to Freud on dreams may be found in Samuel Weber 2000: 101–20). For Lyotard, on the contrary, the imaginative activity by which dreams are shaped is

exactly what Freud trusts, even though it leads him into profound entan-
glements – including the entanglement of the supposedly secondary in the
supposedly primary.

As Samuel Weber emphasises in his Afterword to *Just Gaming* ([1979]
1985), Freudian dream interpretation is agonistic (*JG*, 110–13). In this
case, Lyotard is attempting to resist the conceptualism and the hypertro-
phy of language which he finds in Jacques Lacan's approach to psychoanalysis, which was influential to the point of being hegemonic when Lyotard
was writing: 'the imperial preference granted by the Lacanian system to the
concept' (*P*, 11) being a particular problem for him, as he described it in his
reflections on that part of his intellectual development in later career (on
Lyotard's Lacan, see Bennington 1988: 80–91). Hence the enduring appeal
of the dream-work to Lyotard: what it gives us is other than knowledge, it is
not language, and it forges links which cannot be reduced to the expression
of any given law: rather, 'it is the effect on language of the force exerted by
the figural (as image or as form)' (*PW*, 51). If Lyotard is a dreamer here,
then he is not the only one.

Passages

Agonistics
Art
Desire
Figure
Psychoanalysis
Thought

DRIFT, DRIFTING

Stuart Sim

Deliberate and systematic drifting between discourses is a recognisable
characteristic of Lyotard's methodology in later career, the intention being
to steer clear of fixed positions that would have the effect of curbing his
flexibility as a thinker. He drifts from Marx to Freud; from Marx to Kant;
from proto-Marxist political commitment in the Socialisme ou Barbarie
and Pouvoir Ouvrier groups to an anti-grand narrative, pro-little narrative
outlook in the aftermath of the 1968 *événements*; from politics to art (and
consistently back again in this latter case, although there is always a political dimension to be noted to Lyotard's thought whatever the topic might
happen to be).

Lyotard studiously avoids being pinned down in his thinking and strives to achieve a condition of mental svelteness, where he can approach each situation on its own particular merits, responding open-mindedly and creatively to developments as they occur, unencumbered by a pre-existing set of beliefs of the kind that constrains Marxists (the notion of having to follow a 'party line' is anathema to someone of his sceptical disposition). Practised properly that is what philosophy ought to be in Lyotard's view, rather than, as he argues it so often turns out instead, the defence of doctrines upholding various grand narrative schemes. To drift is to reject altogether the temptations of schematic thought, which serves only to subordinate the individual to the objectives of the grand narrative in question.

One might regard it as more of a shift than a drift from Marx to Freud and Marx to Kant, but in each case there is an abiding concern to keep engaging with the previous discourse, to acknowledge the extent of its sphere of influence. Marxism continues to obsess Lyotard as one of the most prominent examples in our time of a grand narrative (and one of the most insidious politically in its totalising prescriptions), and what he is searching for in the work of both Freud and Kant is ways by which to undermine its authority. From Freud he appropriates the concept of desire and uses that to challenge Marxism's claim to be able to control both historical events and human behaviour: libidinal desire is seen to escape this process entirely, constituting an unpredictable, and frequently highly disruptive, factor in human affairs. When Lyotard turns to Kantian dialectics instead of Marxist – 'Kant after Marx' as that move came to be known in the period, when Marxism rapidly was falling out of favour among the French intellectual class (see, for example, 'Judiciousness in dispute, or Kant after Marx' ([1985b] 1987)) – it is to contrast the paradoxes generated by the Kantian version against the certainties of outcome assumed by the Marxist. And paradoxes are much more to Lyotard's taste, vigorous proponent as he is of difference and incommensurability. The Kantian sublime becomes yet another way of calling into question the assumptions of the grand narrative system of thought, given the sublime's defining quality of unknowability – not to mention its implacable resistance to any kind of human management. Like desire, the sublime has its own trajectory and we cannot affect this.

Lyotard conceives of discourse in general as something we drift around in among various genres, each with its own sense of discreteness demanding that we shed any preconceptions that we might bring to it from our experience of other genres. We are to think of these genres overall as being like an archipelago, where we can drift from island to island, adapting ourselves to the local customs and conventions as we go; in other words, exhibiting svelteness. There is no universal genre of discourse by which we can explain the workings of all the others: we must engage with each and every one we encounter on its own specific terms. Thought itself involves drifting, since '[t]houghts are clouds' (*P*, 5) Lyotard contends. 'Accordingly' they 'are not our own. We try to enter into them and belong to them' (*P*, 6), subsequently finding ourselves carried along by their flow.

The ability to drift therefore becomes a philosophical ideal, an index of one's svelteness and freedom from ideological commitment; proof that we have developed the 'metamorphic capacity' (*PW*, 28) that Lyotard so admires as a character trait. Philosophy is closer to artistic practice than many of its adherents might like to believe in this regard – art being a subject in which Lyotard maintains a lifelong interest, as his extensive contributions to art exhibition catalogues alone would attest. At their best, art and philosophy stand opposed to the impulse to schematism and encourage a drifting mentality – and such a mentality, identified by its 'lightness' (*P*, 5), is a necessary prerequisite to the construction of little narratives.

Passages

Genre
Marxism
Paralogy
Philosophy
Svelteness
Thought

DUCHAMP, MARCEL (1887–1968) – see 'aesthetics', 'art', 'literature', 'modernism' and 'postmodernism'

EDUCATION

Bella Adams

In his 1979 report on the condition of knowledge in the most highly developed societies, Lyotard poses questions about knowledge and its transmission, or education. With a forty-year career in education at schools and universities in Europe and North America, and with a body of work that directly engages educational theory and practice, Lyotard is well placed to write *The Postmodern Condition: A Report on Knowledge* ([1979] 1984b). Importantly, however, he does so as neither an intellectual nor an expert, but only as a philosopher. Unlike these performance-driven scholars, a philosopher questions taken-for-granted assumptions and the subordination of knowledge to the demands of the social system. In *The Postmodern Explained to Children* ([1986b] 1993c), Lyotard asserts that 'you cannot be a philosopher (not even a teacher of philosophy) if your mind is made up on a question before you arrive' and that philosophising is 'an exercise in patience' (*PEC*, 101, 102).

Lyotard differentiates types of scholars, knowledge and education in terms of their various relationships to a social system that altered in the post-industrial or postmodern age at the end of the 1950s, most noticeably in the area of information technology. While traditional forms of knowledge appeal to truth, justice and beauty, even if such appeals are regarded with a postmodern incredulity and the knowledge they (de)legitimate merely one language game or micronarrative among others, technological knowledge eschews these metaphysical appeals for 'the performativity principle' (*PC*, 50) and its efficiency criterion: 'a technical "move" is "good" when it does better and/or expends less energy than another' (*PC*, 44).

If understood as a 'subsystem of the social system', education, particularly higher education, is legitimated through performativity and funded on its research and teaching efficiently disseminating the information needed to maintain the status quo (*PC*, 48). Thus commodified, education is not guided by truth and use-value, only 'prospection, development, targeting, performance, speed, contracts, execution, fulfilment' (*PEC*, 102). Although powerful, the performativity principle is not perfectly commensurate with social and educational systems since they comprise incommensurable language games or micronarratives. With the decline of the metanarrative and its legitimating apparatus, partly instigated by technological knowledge, these incommensurabilities require a knowledge responsive to 'dissensus' and legitimated by 'paralogy', rather than performativity, not least because the latter involves terror: 'be operational (that is, commensurable) or disappear' (*PC*, xxiv).

With experts and intellectuals meeting these respective fates, it is left to the philosopher and like-minded scholars to 'quest for paralogy' (*PC*, 66) through invention and experimentation. For Lyotard, postmodern knowledge produces 'not the known, but the unknown' (*PC*, 60), thus requiring a degree of patience at odds with technological and commercial demands to optimise performance. In terms of education, postmodern knowledge

cannot be transmitted and acquired in a way fully commensurate with the
performativity principle, and so offers no pedagogical method as such, but
this move from efficiency and, ultimately, terrorism towards experimentation is precisely why postmodern knowledge and Lyotard's understanding
of it are so important to educational theory and practice. 'Postmodern
knowledge is not simply a tool of the authorities; it refines our sensitivity
to differences and reinforces our ability to tolerate the incommensurable'
(*PC*, xxv): fine goals, indeed, for education, if not social justice.

Passages

Dissensus
Incommensurability, Incompatibility
Knowledge
Paralogy
Performativity
Terror

ENLIGHTENMENT

Lloyd Spencer and Stuart Sim

Like 'the Renaissance' and 'the Reformation', 'the Enlightenment' can
be used more or less unambiguously to refer to a historical period. It
is even fairly easy to assign convenient dates to the Enlightenment.
Britain's 'Glorious Revolution' of 1688 was a bloodless coup authorised
by Parliament. It not only put an end to the reign of the Catholic James II
but also meant that in England at least the perceived threat of Catholicism
began to recede into the historical past. Not so on the Continent. In
France, the power of the Catholic Church continued on through the
eighteenth century until it became one of the main targets of the French
Revolution.

The Glorious Revolution of 1688 provided one kind of touchstone
for the faith in Reason (a word often capitalised in the eighteenth
century), in parliamentary representation and in progress. The bloody
conflicts involved in the American War of Independence and the French
Revolution thus mark an end to the Enlightenment as a historical period
but not, of course, the Enlightenment as an ideal or intellectual project,
which we now see as underlying the phenomenon of modernity with its
belief in social and political progress (democracy, rising living standards,
etc.).

The Enlightenment was an era which – through its leading intellectuals – gave itself a programme: the enlightenment and improvement of the human race. To their own time certain eighteenth-century intellectuals gave the self-congratulatory label the 'Age of Enlightenment'. The label has stuck, and with some justification. The Enlightenment aimed at the overcoming of superstition and ignorance. Discussion, debate, and criticism came to be seen as an essential part of the process of developing independence in one's learning and thinking. The development of science and the expansion of knowledge are real accomplishments that result from this assertion of freedom of thought. In an age of continuing and resurgent fundamentalisms such as our own, this sense of Enlightenment as involving the removal of all shackles to free enquiry and debate seems as radical and necessary as ever. What Lyotard challenges is the claim that this should be in the cause of greater understanding, or even of consensus.

When Lyotard refers to the Enlightenment or to the Enlightenment project (which is often a term of abuse among the poststructuralist-postmodernist community, it should be noted) he is looking back over more than two centuries of the *legacy* of the Enlightenment rather than to the struggles and debates that characterised the century or so *before* the French Revolution. Thinking beyond narrow factional interests was a great achievement of the thinkers – the *philosophes* – of the eighteenth century. Some of the grander schemes and visions seem less relevant than the doubts and difficulties experienced in the struggles against political and religious misrule. What someone like Lyotard sees now, however, is an unrealistic belief in the powers of reason that can sanction repressive social and political policies in our own time. Theodor W. Adorno had been the first to make a link between the Enlightenment ethos and the Holocaust, and this line of thought had a profound effect on poststructuralists and postmodernists. Lyotard's own view of the Holocaust, as expressed in a range of works such as *The Differend* ([1983] 1988a) and *Heidegger and "the jews"* ([1988b] 1990b), is very similar: it represents for him what happens when humanity pursues a grand narrative at the expense of difference and diversity, when reason becomes ruthless in the headlong pursuit of its aims.

Another aspect of Lyotard's thought which cuts against the Enlightenment's championship of reason is his commitment to the notion of the sublime. The sublime was certainly around as a concept in the eighteenth century, with Immanuel Kant and Edmund Burke both writing important works on the topic; but it was the work of the latter that had the greatest influence on intellectuals and artists of the period, such as the Romantic movement in England. Burke's concept of the sublime emphasised the sense of terror it could cause in the individual when confronted by a power that far transcended one's own (which the novelists

and poets of the time often characterised in the form of the supernatural).
The Burkean sublime is mysterious and utterly unknowable, which tends
to be the way that Lyotard interprets it too: as a power that goes well
beyond human understanding and raises some very awkward questions
about the reach of reason. The failure to recognise this, indeed the deliberate refusal to countenance it, is a trait of grand narratives, which like
to picture themselves as exercising control over their world and able to
overcome pretty well any obstacles that might face humanity.

It would have to be said that the poststructuralist-postmodernist attitude towards the Enlightenment is not actually all that fair, since it is
made to carry most of the blame for what they do not like in contemporary
culture, as if there was a direct, unequivocal link between it and events
such as the Holocaust and politically exploitative policies such as Western
imperialism and globalisation. The very real advances in the human condition that the Enlightenment encouraged tend to be downplayed, not to
mention the positive role that reason, as opposed to superstition and the
arbitrary exercise of power, has played in human affairs. Reason too readily
can be scapegoated, creating a rather uneasy correspondence between
postmodernism and a contemporary religious fundamentalism which
downgrades reason in favour of unquestioning faith. Unquestioning faith
is not what postmodernists are promoting, but one can see why doubts
might arise about the wisdom of being quite so sceptical about the motiva-
tions of the Enlightenment thinkers and failing to acknowledge properly
the complexities of their cultural context. Lyotard is guilty of this when
he complains of 'the Enlightenment narrative' that 'if a metanarrative
implying a philosophy of history is used to legitimate knowledge, questions are raised concerning the validity of the institutions governing the
social bond' (*PC*, xxiv). Thinkers like Jürgen Habermas strongly disagree
with this view, and for him the Enlightenment and modernity are projects
it is in humanity's manifest interest to extend (see Habermas 1981). But
the point as always with Lyotard is to make us think through our political
actions and not to allow them to be worked up into universal maxims that
only serve to cloud our judgement.

Passages

Jews, Judaism
Legitimation
Modern, Modernity
Poststructuralism
Reason, Rationality
Sublime

ENTHUSIASM

Georges Van Den Abbeele

The concept of 'enthusiasm' emerges relatively late in Lyotard's work and as part of his turn toward Immanuel Kant in the early 1980s. In particular, the concept first appears in a paper he read in May 1981 at the Centre de Recherches Philosophiques sur le Politique. This paper, 'Introduction à une étude du politique selon Kant', would serve as the basis for his short book, *Enthousiasme: la critique kantienne de l'histoire* ([1986a] 2009).

Although brief and written as a philosophically technical reading of Kant, *Enthusiasm* also marks the full transition from Lyotard's earlier Freudian–Marxist preoccupation with libidinal politics and cultural revolution to his later work on more discursive models of social justice and ethics, as evidenced in *The Differend* ([1983] 1988a) and ensuing texts. In a sense, such a Kantian critique of history, pieced together from a set of late Kant texts that make up a kind of Fourth Critique, extends the work of the *Critique of Judgement* (Kant [1790] 2000), or so-called *Third Critique*, not only in terms of the latter's analytic of teleological judgement (or purposiveness) but also more crucially that of the analytic of aesthetic judgement, and even more specifically that of the analytic of the sublime. If, as Kant argues, the judgement of beauty occurs because of a harmonious interaction between faculties, the sublime proposes precisely a gap, a disharmony between faculties, an irreconcilability that cannot be translated, that is 'incommensurable'. It is the incommensurability between faculties (or phrases) that intrigues Lyotard and where he finds the ground zero of history and politics. For Lyotard, the feeling of the sublime is therefore as political as it is aesthetic, and it comes to the fore especially in those historical moments that do not follow the scripting of what Lyotard elsewhere calls grand narratives. Such unsuspected and unpredictable 'events' open up or deliver (*Begebenheit*) the potential for vastly different political/ historical outcomes by starkly revealing the incommensurability between phrases, whence a 'strong' sense of the sublime.

Enthusiasm would be such a strong sense of the sublime, for which Kant gives the example of the popular response to the French Revolution, that is, a widespread or 'common' expression of hopefulness toward a political reality better than the autocratic rule of feudal kings and princes. Such enthusiasm for the French Revolution was, of course, itself a risky expression in other countries, yet it is precisely that danger and its overcoming that qualify the sublimity of that feeling as enthusiasm and not merely the 'tumultuousness of exaltation' (*Schwärmerei*). What Lyotard finds especially intriguing in this Kantian notion of enthusiasm is that it involves not the great actors or participants in the historical events of the Revolution but rather the response (or judgement) of the *spectators* of those events, however far away, as a form of political engagement through their recognition of the *Begebenheit* as a 'sign of history'.

The contemporary enthusiasm of people around the world for the French Revolution is not a mere historical curiosity for Lyotard, but the very crux of a political thinking that highlights events such as those of May 1968 in France, Hungary in 1956, Czechoslovakia in 1968, or Gdansk in 1970 and 1980. Lyotard could not, of course, have cited the later popular uprisings that would sweep through Eastern Europe in 1989, some eight years after he wrote *Enthusiasm*, and yet this work uncannily foresees and theorises such unexpected and unscripted events – even the risks incurred in the manifestation of such enthusiasm, if we recall how the popular expression in China of 'enthusiasm' for the events in Eastern Europe was countered by the massacre at Tiananmen Square.

As such, this concept of enthusiasm remains for Lyotard a powerful way to think through such sudden historical/political change not just as nostalgia for past revolutionary action but as the spontaneous work of popular expression, the sublime as a *sensus communis*, with necessarily unpredictable results. This 'spontaneist' view of revolutionary action and concomitant distrust of political parties that claim a vanguard role (such as in the Marxist-Leninist tradition) hearkens back to the radical left of Rosa Luxemburg and Atonie Pannekoek. It also surfaces in the anti-bureaucratism of *Socialisme ou Barbarie,* for which Lyotard contributed a string of articles on the critical importance of spontaneous urban uprisings during the Algerian war. The analysis still obtains in our post-Cold War, neoliberal world order with its media-saturated environment and an increasingly interactive technology (such as the internet) that allows for ever-more unforeseeable and unscriptable moments of enthusiasm.

Passages

Aesthetics
Event
Incommensurability, Incompatibility
Libidinal Economy
Sublime

ETHICS

Anthony Gritten

Lyotard has an abiding concern with questions of ethics and justice. Like many other continental philosophers, Lyotard's ethics (more of a pragmatics) is non-foundational, and is not geared towards the kind of rationalisation that is habitually called 'an ethics'. His main concern is to preserve the potentially fluid and literally avant-garde phrasing of the event, rather than to formalise the activity of phrasing into knowledge, strategy, and goals to guide judgement. Nevertheless, there are consistencies in his thought that can be grouped together under the rubric of an ethics.

In 'The General Line' (*Postmodern Fables* [1993a] 1997), written for Gilles Deleuze, Lyotard tells a short story about what an ethics could be. He teases apart a distinction between, on the one hand, an ethics of the public sphere (communicative action), in which human rights are cited at every turn and ethics is a tool used predominantly as a defensive manoeuvre (defending the self under the politically correct guise of a concern for the other), and, on the other hand, an ethics of 'the second existence', a private abode somewhere on the other side of the general line, occupied by the intractable, that which makes the subject what he or she is and could be, but which withdraws from all contact, communication, conception, and consensus. Lyotard's point is that, since the territory across the general line is frequently targeted for assimilation into discourse, society and the world (a residual Cartesian project of mastery and possession), it must be protected. However, this is not a question of inventing rules and laws that state when, where, what and how this line and its space is to be safeguarded; it is not simply a matter of implementing 'an ethics'. The demand for protection is neither silenced nor passed, the biggest threat to ethical thought being that its tendency to claim sufficiency with regard to its subject and adequation between its subject and object. Indeed, protecting this second existence, this inhuman region across the general line 'requires', as Lyotard says, 'our time and our space in secret, without giving us anything in exchange, not even the cognisance of what it is, or what we are. We have no rights over it, no recourse against it, and no security' (*PF*, 121). Protection is never enough, and anything claiming to be an ethics suffers the indignity of never being able to institute a perpetual peace.

Needing to acknowledge and maintain the general line, or at least its possibility, but lacking the rights to control it (though still with a Kantian interest in it), creates anxiety. It might be argued that this is 'Because death is jealous of birth. Or if you will: the law is jealous of the body. Or again: ethics is jealous of aesthetics' (*TP*, 184), the point being that ethics is jealous because it came second, the body having had 'its time' prior to the law of ethics – its *anima minima*. Either way, it is clear that being ethical is troubling and troublesome, for, while it is a matter of action, linking and sharing, it is also a matter of patience, and Lyotard's point is that a quick solution is no solution to the continual question of how to protect and phrase the general line ethically. Indeed, Lyotard phrases judgement quite specifically, denying that it is simply a matter of the will in full possession of its desires and intentions (in fact, it is indeterminate), denying that possession is the name of the game when it comes to ethical judgement (actually, it lacks criteria), and even denying that phrasing the event ethically is a matter of passing over the general line in order to witness what is there (in fact, it lacks content).

Thus, for Lyotard, ethics involves a willingness to wait and abide, a mixture of patience, humility and resistance. Insofar as it can be phrased as a system or method, acting ethically involves a persistent feeling of resisting Ideas on behalf of the event, of resisting the system's desire to rationalise what lies across the general line. Resistance, however, is not the same as rejection, and Lyotard is careful to note that becoming aware of the limits of Ideas happens only in the very movement in which they are embraced. The task of living ethically, then, is not how to discover or resurrect an essential core of 'the ethical', still less 'an ethics', but rather to do justice to the incommensurability of all language games, including those of discovery and ethics, and to apprehend in the process how a pragmatics of feeling and judging might emerge out of an acknowledgement of precisely this incommensurability.

Passages

Antifoundationalism
Judgement
Language Games
Probity
Resistance
Subject

EVENT

Anthony Gritten

Numerous theories of the event were offered in the twentieth century in both continental and analytic traditions, including those of Martin

Heidegger, Jacques Derrida, Gilles Deleuze and Alain Badiou, and many others wrote on cognate subjects, including Jean Baudrillard and Guy Debord. A particular intensity in writing about the event occurred in the wake of *les événements* of May 1968. Although Lyotard did not pen an explicit theory of the event as such, his frequent writings on and around the concept made a profound contribution to the subject, and include texts on the sublime, contemporary art, techno-science and complexification, psychoanalysis, language, politics and much more. The theory that can (slightly against the grain) be extrapolated and synthesised from his writings has at least three phases or versions corresponding to a rough periodisation of Lyotard's writings into libidinal, differend and sublime phases.

In general, an event is an occurrence beyond the powers of representation, something that the subject experiences but which he or she is unable to comprehend or think through adequately, let alone phrase coherently. In fact, the event has a deeper effect on the subject: it disarms his or her desire to be spontaneous, causal and originating, to be master and commander of him- or herself (Lyotard criticises Hannah Arendt for conceiving the event as anthropomorphic action). It is the brute fact that something happens, disrupting pre-existing theories, frameworks, models and experience through which it might otherwise be understood: it is 'the occurrence "before" the signification (the content) of the occurrence' (*D*, 79), and its arrival is thus, paradoxically, always belated. What is important about an event is that it is otherwise than a matter of language or Being; it is an occurrence. A matter of 'it happens' rather than 'what happens', *quod* rather than *quid*, what marks the event out is its radical and questioning singularity. Lyotard often phrases the matter interrogatively: is it happening? The event thus can be forgotten even before it has had the chance to be phrased and understood (though Lyotard does not go as far as Baudrillard in this direction), though it always presents itself as a demand for linkage onto further events.

While the essence of the event is that 'that there is' comes before 'what there is', its sheer irruption draws attention to its essential connection to nothingness (and all that comes with it: absence, failure, withdrawal, death, etc.). At his most direct, Lyotard calls the event the face to face with nothingness, but elsewhere he frequently invokes the event in terms of the feeling that something will happen rather than nothing, that a minimal occurrence – *anima minima* – will be awoken and the soul forced into existence, that survival might continue. This minimal occurrence is far removed from the Debordian spectacle, the Baudrillardian media event, and the generally capitalist thrill of exchange and profit following managed innovation.

The event's imbrication of presence and absence, something and nothing, is a function of its energetic constitution. This is something that Lyotard discusses explicitly in later essays, where he tells fables about the potential survival of the human species against the background of the broader relationship between entropy and complexification (of which human techno-science is merely one embodiment). The concept of energy recurs throughout Lyotard's writings on events, inflected in various ways, along with its cognates and relatives, such as force (*puissance* and *pouvoir*), intensity and tension. The event is subject to entropy and its energy cannot be mastered, since it 'does not have an ear for unity, for the concert of the organism' (*PC*, 91) – it is intractable, like lightning (a metaphor Lyotard uses in *The Differend* ([1983] 1988a) and *Lessons on the Analytic of the Sublime* ([1991b] 1994)).

Nevertheless, events demand responses, linkages, phrasing. Responding to an event is not a matter of competence or even of performance per se. It is not that there are various types of events, but that there are many different ways of phrasing them, and what matters is, not what the event means, but what it does and incites. A common way of phrasing an event is to impose a narrative structure upon it. Stories, after all, seem to protect themselves against the unknown threat of the event, and to provide a technology that helps people to categorise and manage information. Lyotard finds this type of response to the event insufficient, for while increasing the ability to structure and predetermine information is not in itself bad, it is less useful – less just – than inventing ways to increase our passibility to the event; in any case, the event is not a story or a sign. Therefore, responding justly to an event is a matter of 'a working through attached to a thought of what is constitutively hidden from us in the event and the meaning of the event' (*I*, 26), rather than of prediction, of anticipating what the event will be or incite or mean, or of retreating from the contingency of each event into custom. Indeed, while to be able to paraphrase 'what happens' is to draw the event into consciousness and slot it into a genre of discourse, what the 'it happens' really needs is a receptivity to the event in which the response is not determined by prior guidelines and in which genres of discourse are themselves open to change in response to the event. For responsible phrasing of the event is not found in an abstract subject carrying out his or her abstract duty but in this particular person linking onto the singular event confronting him or her in its specific non-predetermined and unrepeatable context. This is reflective judgement in a broadly Kantian sense, in which judging the event is in the grip of the case, and the case is judged on the basis of feeling, though it is worth noting, first, that Lyotard rethinks Kant's project in terms of sensibility and the sensible, and second, that his anti-Platonic inflection of Kant is such that justice comes literally after the event.

Passages

Is It Happening?
Links, Linkage
May '68, *Événements*
Narrative
Phrase, Phrasing
Subject

EXISTENTIALISM

Stuart Sim

The poststructuralist generation of philosophers in France very self-consciously distanced themselves from the existentialist movement, as typified by Jean-Paul Sartre and his circle, that had held sway in France in the postwar years, attracting considerable popular attention. Both groups drew extensively on phenomenology, as in the work of the German philosophers Edmund Husserl and Martin Heidegger, but constructed apparently very different world pictures from their source material. In the case of the poststructuralists that world picture had an anarchic character, with a concentration on the gaps and contradictions in human knowledge, whereas the existentialists were more inclined to emphasise the anxiety attendant upon recognition of the absurdity and lack of meaning to human existence.

However, when one looks back at both movements from a twenty-first century perspective there seems to be significant correspondences between them that hint at more common ground than the poststructuralists usually care to admit. This can be seen in the work of Lyotard, with many of his concepts having a distinct family resemblance to those found in the existentialist canon – especially when it comes to such topics as the nature of the future, human freedom of action and the necessity for political commitment. In *Being and Nothingness* (Sartre [1943] 1958) great stress is laid on the factor of choice in human affairs, and that means the future can unfold in various ways depending on the nature of our choices – it is manifestly open in this respect. Thinkers like Lyotard may have less belief in our ability to exert control over events (which for him are unpredictable phenomena anyway), but he is just as emphatic that we have the ability to respond to them and that the choices we proceed to make really do matter. Neither theory views us as mere pawns in a game (unless we choose to allow that to happen), although Lyotard's conception of the sublime does ask us to recognise that there are powers that lie utterly beyond our capacity to affect – or even to understand.

Lyotard's concept of the little narrative has an existentialist resonance that invites exploration. Little narratives deliberately choose to resist the power of the oppressive metanarratives in their society, on the assumption that such actions will count in how their culture develops. They constitute a refusal to surrender to force and arbitrary authority, and there is a definite suggestion of Sartrean-style commitment about such a stance – as there is also in Lyotard's notion of a 'philosophical politics', where philosophers help marginalised social groups create a discourse to articulate their complaints. There are various metanarratives which Lyotard wants us to subvert: Marxism, capitalism, techno-science and development, for example, all of which set out to channel human behaviour into a pattern they have established for their own ideological ends – in existentialist terms, they constrain personal choice. Metanarratives are essentially inimical to individualism (which always holds out the possibility of the emergence of dissent), and that is something both poststructuralists and existentialists are keen to protect: unless we leave space for the individual then we shall find that difference and diversity are being eroded. Both groups oppose the efforts made by metanarratives to ensure cultural conformity as a way of maintaining their power.

Lyotard's conception of the sublime also recalls Sartre's nothingness, an all-pervasive force lying constantly in wait to envelop us that Sartre insists we should strive constantly to hold at bay. Although nothingness will claim us all in the end, the act of defiance against this ultimately unbeatable force is one of the defining features of being human and expressing our selfhood. To give in to nothingness by, for example, committing suicide, is an unacceptable act for Sartre because it negates both our selfhood and the power it grants us to make meaningful choices. Similarly, Lyotard asks us to acknowledge that there is a realm of the unknowable to be contended with in our existence, but does not regard that as a basis for fatalism on our part. We still have scope for freely chosen actions against human forces bent on enslaving us, no matter how large they may loom in our culture: events are not predetermined, and we must not fall into the trap of thinking they obey the dictates, or prove the predictions, of any particular theory. He invites us to respond with an attitude of svelteness, much in the manner of the free existential subject as pictured by Sartre. It is not unreasonable, therefore, to identify echoes of existentialism within poststructuralism: they should not be thought of as incompatible projects.

Passages

Event
Little Narrative
Phenomenology
Philosophical Politics
Poststructuralism
Sublime

FARÍAS, VICTOR (1940–) – see 'Heidegger, Martin' and 'Jews, Judaism'

FEMINISM

Pamela Sue Anderson

The critical role of feminism in both the contexts of twentieth-century epistemology and the debates of moral and political theory has significant parallels with the role of Lyotard in the postmodern critiques of Immanuel Kant and various other prominent theorists in the modern period from the Enlightenment onwards. This remains true, even though decisive divergences ultimately develop between Lyotard's philosophy and feminist epistemology, ethics and politics. Lyotard's *The Postmodern Condition* ([1979] 1984b) has been used as the archetypal postmodern manifesto by feminist philosophers and political theorists who explore the conflictual relations of 'feminism and/or postmodernism' (see Nicholson 1990: 1–16; cf. Benhabib 1992: 203–11; Kimberly Hutchings 1996: 173).

Lyotard's epoch-making, postmodern argument targets not only Kant but also G. W. F. Hegel and Karl Marx – each of whom assume a metanarrative that promises truth and justice at the end of all philosophical pursuits. Insofar as the metanarrative of philosophy has been oppressive to women and non-privileged men, notably in assuming an exclusive God's-eye point of view, Lyotard argues against it, while arguing for a multiplicity of heterogeneous and incommensurable language games. This multiplicity would also open up new possibilities for at least some feminist discourses. According to Lyotard's argument against any modern form of a unifying or totalising narrative, thinkers and practitioners who reject the incommensurability of epistemological narratives must be working from a rigidly doctrinaire and exclusively privileged standpoint.

Feminist standpoint theorists, for example, find at least partial support for their epistemological projects from the political critiques of Lyotard. In particular, his critiques help to expose the sexual, racial and other salient biases in the supposedly neutral and impartial God-standpoint (see Hartsock 1998: 205–6; Battersby 2007: 16–17). However, feminist philosophers have been cautious in taking Lyotard's views of disorientation and the loss of both subjectivity and objectivity too far. Just when women are gaining their own voices, feminists will not advance their causes either by embracing disorientation, if it only confuses their words, or by giving up any shared sense of subjectivity, truth and justice.

Another way in which feminists have drawn on Lyotard's postmodern manifesto is by appropriating his critique of the universalising perspective in twentieth-century epistemology. Basically, knowledge for Lyotard is the same as any other narrative: it is a 'language game' (*PC*, 63) with only provisional agreement on its conventions by players at any one time. Following Lyotard, postmodern epistemologists have maintained that knowledge is fragmentary; and so they reject any ontology of a unitary human nature. Similarly feminist postmodernists assert the contradictory, partial and strategic nature of our identities (see Haraway 1990). Yet again, feminist epistemologists might still be worried: how can women as subjects take a stand against injustice or for truth, if they are contradictory? Equally worrying for women in epistemology is Lyotard's contention that knowledge cannot be distinguished from power by the 'truth' of a knowledge-claim (Assiter 2003: 7 and 129). For Lyotard, knowledge as a narrative like any other could be true, but equally could be a fiction.

Taking a similar line to that of Lyotard, some contemporary feminist philosophers recognise that the Kantian sublime leaves gaps: 'the unrepresentable' creates a space for women to breathe, freeing their emotion, desire and imagination. However, this Kantian opening to the sublime can also become a trap for women, if it is reduced to a 'feminine principle' generating the gaps in reason (Battersby 2007: 16–18). The attraction of the postmodern sublime is mobilising difference in the motion of incommensurable discourses (*The Postmodern Condition*). The fear of the postmodern is dissolving human differences into the inhuman (*The Inhuman* ([1988a] 1991a)).

Passages

Incommensurability, Incompatibility
Justice

FIGURE   77

Knowledge
Language Games
Subject
Sublime

FIGURE

Roy Sellars

Lyotard challenges us, as Americans would say, to 'go figure'. 'Figure' is undoubtedly a key term in his work – but what is a figure? (see Auerbach [1959] 1984, on the early history of *figura*, which came to mean 'form' or 'imprint', in the typological sense, in the Roman world). Wallace Stevens, in his poem 'Man Carrying Thing' (Stevens 1997: 306), could be describing the effect of the figural when he asserts that poetry should work against our reason, actively 'resisting it'. So the figural is shady. The figural in Lyotard is to be seen as different from figurative language or indeed from tropes. It is that which prevents discourse from ever presenting as a unity, as structuralists believe it to be, and in this respect its effect is comparable to desire, with which it has close links (indeed, Lyotard speaks of there being 'a connivance' (*LRG*, 293) between them). Lyotard identifies three main components: 'image-figure' ('traces' of images, as found in hallucinations or dreams), 'form-figure' (the underlying 'schema', to, say, an artwork) and 'matrix-figure', with the last consisting in 'a violation of discursive order' (*LRG*, 293). In that sense of 'violation' the figure is to be considered as an event, with all the potential for disruption that involves – figure is, above all, a force.

The title of Lyotard's early book *Discourse, Figure* ([1971] 2010) already implies a tale of a comma. (The full translation of *Discourse, Figure* by Mary Lydon, which had been contracted to Cambridge University Press, was still unfinished at the time of her death in 2001; fortunately Antony Hudek's completion is now available from Minnesota University Press (2010).) The English-language reception of Lyotard's early work has until now therefore been somewhat skewed. Discourse and figure are not opposed to one another; rather, they are heterogeneous, anachronous states that are nonetheless found in juxtaposition. As Geoffrey Bennington explains, the figural is a third space at work between signification, which is systemic-structural in orientation, and designation or reference, which is subjective-phenomenological, and it can be seen to 'disrupt visual or perceptual space' (Bennington 1988: 70) no less than discursive. What the figural does, as both Bennington and Bill Readings point out (see Readings

1991: 28–52), is akin to deconstruction, working in terms of difference rather than opposition.

Before part one of the book ('signification et désignation') comes the manifesto-like 'Le parti pris du figural', which emphasises that the given is not a text, that it has a thickness or rather a difference, constitutive, which is to be seen rather than read – and that this difference keeps getting lost in signifying. Lyotard presents his book as a defence of the eye, going after shade and penumbra, displacing the system of discourse; but it is not a question of abandoning discourse; the figure is itself lodged *in* language. Turning the unconscious into a discourse, as Jacques Lacan does, is for Lyotard to omit energetics – thus effectively killing off both art and the dream. Discourse already is traversed by force and calls for the work of the eye. For Freud, truth is utopic, not happening where you expect it.

Part one begins by distinguishing the negativity of the visual from that of the readable. Lyotard argues persuasively against the confusion of signification and designation; but there is no signified except by virtue of a necessary mirage. Language is fascinated by what it is not, trying to *have* it, in the phantasm of science, or to *be* it, in the phantasm of art. A figure creates a linguistic event because it is a discharge coming from elsewhere. In part two ('L'autre espace'), Lyotard analyses the line in Paul Klee ('La ligne et la lettre'). Desire stages figure, and Klee gives us the atelier of the primary process.

The academic context in which *Discourse, Figure* was conceived was one in which structuralism was the intellectual paradigm, and Lyotard is to talk later of '[t]he anger I felt against Lacan's reading of Freud' (*P*, 10), heavily biased towards structuralism as it was. As he remarked in an interview with Gary Olson, he deliberately set out to challenge this state of affairs:

I remember in the sixties when structuralist ideology was dominant in France and elsewhere I resisted this way of thinking. It was with a sort of pride (or arrogance) on my part to observe that finally a book like *Discours, figure* – which was completely ignored at the time because it was explicitly against structuralism, not only in terms of linguistic structuralism but even Lacanian structuralism because at that time the Lacanian reading of Freud was similar to Althusser on Marxism – has gained acceptance. I was against this way of thinking, and I am pleased that now readers have discovered this book. I was waiting thirty years – no problem. The point is that I'm not a theorist. ('Resisting a Discourse of Mastery' 1995)

At the time of this interview was Lyotard being rather optimistic about the acceptance or discovery of his book? No matter how many years pass, it remains indeterminable whether readers in the English-speaking world will finally be ready for it. At the same time, the academic theory industry becomes ever more voracious in its search for raw materials, and the appearance of the full translation of *Discourse, Figure*, after forty years, comes with the risk that it may merely inaugurate a new phase in the assimilation of Lyotard and the transformation of the figure into so many commodities. It is all the more important, then, to remember that the figure, for him, is what survives such transformation, in the shadows and as the shadows. This is the revolutionary force of the figure, to which Lyotard calls us to bear witness.

Passages

Deconstruction
Desire
Difference
Discourse
Event
Structuralism

FORGETTING

Stuart Sim

Lyotard lays great emphasis on the need to bear witness to the events of our world and to take care to remain aware of what we have witnessed. Since he does not believe we have any absolute criteria by which to make value judgements (about good and evil, for example), that makes it all the more important to retain events in our memory so that we can work toward some method of assessing them ('case-by-case', with no precon-ceived notions, being one such outlined in *Just Gaming* ([1979] 1985)). The cardinal sin would be to forget what has happened, especially when it involves some momentous historical event like the Holocaust, as Lyotard argued was the case with the German nation in general, and such high-profile figures within it as the philosopher Martin Heidegger.

    The Holocaust had been an example for Lyotard of 'a "politics" of absolute forgetting' (*Hj*, 25), with the Nazi state apparatus striving to eradicate all evidence of the event, as if to make it seem that the Jewish population of Germany, and then those of the countries it invaded in the Second World War, had never actually existed. Without written documentation the Holocaust had to be reconstructed from the physical evidence that was left at the end of the war, in camps such as Auschwitz.

Given such a policy of effacement it became easier for the German nation to forget the fate of the Jews, who systematically were removed from the national picture. Lyotard finds this unforgiveable and emphasises the wilful aspect of the exercise: one can only 'forget', in this sense of the term, what one knows somewhere in one's mind has been suppressed. For such a committed supporter of oppressed and marginalised groups throughout history ('the jews' in his catch-all phrase) it is politics at its most cynical: a case of making problems disappear rather than engaging openly with them such that public dialogue could ensue. That was not possible with a policy of genocide, since '[t]he "politics" of extermination cannot be represented on the political scene' (*Hj*, 29), even if anti-Semitism was rife in Western society during the Nazis' time in power. So there is only one 'solution' if one is determined to go ahead: 'It must be forgotten' (*Hj*, 29).

It is in order to prevent such practices from being successful that Lyotard devises his notion of a 'philosophical politics', where oppressed and marginalised groups are aided in finding ways to state their case in the public arena. The objective is to counter the 'politics of forgetting' that play a part in all grand narratives, which inevitably involve the suppression of at least some groups within society – with the Jewish race as the most visible instance of this in recent European history. Forgetting is to be seen, therefore, as a deliberate policy deployed by grand narratives as a means of reinforcing their power. The trend is always towards cultural homogenisation, and when this cannot be achieved then the demand that the unassimilable groups in question 'must be forgotten' all too easily arises.

Passages

Anamnesis
Ethics
Heidegger, Martin
Jews, Judaism
Judgement
Philosophical Politics

FOUCAULT, MICHEL (1926–84) – see 'discourse', 'Jews, Judaism', 'little narrative', 'philosophy', 'pluralism', 'politics', 'posthumanism' and 'poststructuralism'

FRACTALS

Stuart Sim

Fractals present an intriguing concept to Lyotard because they seem to provide evidence for his belief that we can never aspire to a condition of complete knowledge of our world. As thinkers like René Mandelbrot had demonstrated, we could keep going down to more microscopic levels of any object being studied and continue to find self-similar structures, the implication being that this exercise could be carried on to infinity and that we could never have a full grasp of the nature of phenomena. For Lyotard, this constituted a characteristic feature of postmodern science, that it was revealing how partial our picture of the physical world was – and would have to remain: we could never exhaust a fractal search.

Lyotard seizes on things like fractals in *The Postmodern Condition* ([1979] 1984b) because they suggest a world that is more elusive than modern science had conceived it; a world full of mysteries and paradoxes that our theories of physics were finding it increasingly difficult to explain. Fractals are indicative of a world which is characterised by 'incomplete information' (*PC*, 60), and where the incidence of catastrophe and chaos are challenging long-held scientific beliefs about how nature operates. There is far more discontinuity to be accounted for than previous theories had thought, and Lyotard draws various metaphysical and political conclusions from this observation. The ultimate effect of the researches which yield entities like fractals is to alter our entire conception of knowledge, which is now to be considered as not just partial but also very provisional – no matter how sophisticated it goes on to become. The more that science identifies paradoxes in the course of its enquiries then the more provisional we have to accept that our scientific knowledge actually is, and the less predictable our control over the environment is likely to be: 'It is not true that uncertainty (lack of control) decreases as accuracy goes up: it goes up as well' (*PC*, 56). Science for Lyotard, therefore, becomes a method of generating ideas rather than a source of hard and fast truths about the world: more like game theory than our traditional view of the enterprise.

Mandelbrot's work identifies various areas where the limitations of scientific method become very evident. We cannot make precise measurement of non-linear systems such as clouds, for example, because their behaviour is too chaotic for us to plot. Lyotard homes in on such theories and concepts because they reinforce his worldview, which emphasises the unpredictability of the future and the lack of a determining pattern to existence. This does leave him rather exposed to any changes that subsequently take place in scientific theory however (and these tend to occur with rather bewildering frequency these days), since we have no way of knowing the long-term status of the material Lyotard appropriates for his own purposes. Fractals, for instance, may look like a rather quaint concept at some not too distant point, and that is always a danger when hooking up any cultural theory or philosophy to hard science.

Passages

Catastrophe Theory and Chaos Theory
Clouds
Game Theory, Gaming
Knowledge
Postmodern Science

FRENCH REVOLUTION (1789) – see 'Enlightenment', 'enthusiasm', 'modern, modernity', 'postcolonialism', 'postmodernism' and 'sublime'

FREUD, SIGMUND (1856–1939) – see 'anamnesis', 'desire', 'dreamwork', 'drift, drifting', 'enthusiasm', 'figure', 'great Zero', 'legitimation', 'libidinal economy', 'Marxism', 'May '68, *événements*', 'post-Marxism', 'psychoanalysis', 'sexuality', 'Socialisme ou Barbarie' and 'tensor'

FUNDAMENTALISM – see 'Enlightenment', 'incredulity', 'knowledge', 'pluralism' and 'politics'

GAME THEORY, GAMING

Stuart Sim

In *The Postmodern Condition* ([1979] 1984b), Lyotard approvingly quotes the game theorist Anatol Rapoport's claim that game theory is to be prized primarily for its ability to generate ideas, as well as the scientist Peter

Medawar's that generating ideas is science's greatest achievement. In each case, players are creating narratives; what differentiates the scientist from the game theorist is that the former 'is duty bound to verify them' (*PC*, 60). One senses, however, that Lyotard is less interested in the verification than the constant stream of new ideas that scientific research can produce. Scientists are continually pushing into the unknown, and cannot tell beforehand where their explorations will take them or what they will yield. For Lyotard that is a very healthy state of affairs in preventing consensus from forming, since it is his view that consensus deadens enquiry; dissensus is to be preferred. From this perspective science is a game, and while it may have rules these do not determine what is going to be found: the unpredictable can always occur, which means that our knowledge is in a state of flux without the fixed points of reference we tend to assume there are. As someone opposed to universal theories this is what Lyotard appreciates most about the scientific enterprise: 'that someone always comes along to disturb the order of "reason"' (*PC*, 61).

Originally devised by the mathematician John von Neumann and economist Oskar Morgenstern (*Theory of Games and Economic Behaviour* (1944)), game theory describes situations where each player's actions have an effect on the welfare of all the other players, the assumption being that each player acts in such a way as to maximise the benefits to themselves within the overall parameters of the game. All those in the game have to weigh up the consequences of their actions in terms of their effect on others and the actions they might take in response, so there is a strong strategic element involved.

Lyotard applies game theory more generally to human activity and regards it as a model of how societies should operate. Games need no metanarrative, just a set of rules which govern what kind of moves can be made – although these rules can always be altered in the light of developments. Justice is no different from science in this respect, and for Lyotard it is a large-scale game the goal of which is to come up with satisfactory judgements without recourse to universally applicable criteria. *Just Gaming* ([1979] 1985) explores this topic in detail, with Lyotard defending his 'case-by-case' method against the criticisms of his interviewer Jean-Loup Thébaud, who clearly would be happier with more precise concepts of good and evil than Lyotard is willing to countenance. Conceiving of justice as a game whose outcome cannot be determined in advance ('It is a game without an author' (*JG*, 72) as Lyotard understands it) goes against the grain of traditional views of the phenomenon, which do favour universally applicable criteria that require little in the way of interpretation. Lyotard's conception is very much geared towards interpretation, however, and allows far greater flexibility than traditionalists think is safe.

Language is also a series of games to Lyotard, who follows on from Ludwig Wittgenstein in the first instance, although eventually he adopts a more radical version of the concept of language games with phrase regimens, where the element of human control still there in Wittgenstein is largely missing. The point about such games is that they are self-contained, their rules only applying internally, and problems only arise when this injunction is broken and one language game infiltrates another. Genres of discourse can draw on various phrase regimens to construct and pursue their ends, but the same restriction applies to them that those ends should not be foisted on other genres of discourse, otherwise differends will appear.

Ultimately, what Lyotard gets from game theory is a sense of an open-ended process where there is always something at stake (although crucially, never truth). He is a great advocate of the local dimension to human affairs, and that means that every move we make in whatever game we are playing has significance. There is no need to refer to an overall controlling agency, the game is in a perpetual state of development and there is no ultimate destination to dictate how we should proceed at any one moment (such as the dictatorship of the proletariat, or heaven in any of its various religious formulations). That could well sum up Lyotard's political creed: that there is always something to play for, that the end has not been decided in advance, nor could it ever be. Unfortunately, that is not the way politics is usually conducted, hence Lyotard's lifelong campaign against those who claim to be in possession of the definitive narrative by which to run society.

Passages

Differend
Discourse
Justice
Language Games
Narrative
Postmodern Science

GENRE

Karen Langhelle

To Lyotard, the term 'genre' denotes various modes for linking together heterogeneous phrases or phrase regimens. This linkage follows a set of rules which attempt to secure the attainment of certain goals or ends. As such, rules for linking phrases vary according to what is at stake in each particular genre, that is, whether its goal is 'to know, to teach, to be just, to seduce, to justify, to evaluate' (*D*, xii) and so forth. A linkage is considered a success when the stakes tied to a specific genre of discourse are attained. Taking the economic genre as an example, we may say that its rules are those of an exchange between two interchangeable parties. Thus, in an initial phrase, the addressor x cedes the referent a to an addressee y, and this phrase is then linked onto by a second phrase, where the addressor y cedes the referent b to the addressee x. What is at stake here is the freeing up of both parties: the linking is successful if the cessation of b annuls the cessation of a and the sum of the exchange is therefore null. If by chance the sum of the exchange is not null, the balance, whether positive or negative, falls to either x or y, and the linking of the two phrases resumes.

Lyotard sees genre in terms not only of success but also of victory and conflict. A phrase 'happens', and, since 'to link is necessary' but 'how to link is contingent' (*D*, 29), there will always be any number of possible ways in which to link onto a phrase. Yet since only one linkage can take place at a time, one phrase necessarily 'wins' whereas all other possible linkages are ignored. Thus any linkage is also a potential for conflict. Lyotard stresses that this is never a question of conflict between human beings. Rather, conflict is the result of tensions between opposing phrases. We may think the stakes of a certain genre are the product of our will, but it can never be our intention to, for example, persuade or seduce. If there is persuasion or seduction, it is because a genre of discourse – in this case, the rhetorical or the erotic – 'imposes its mode of linking onto "our" phrase and onto "us"' (*D*, 136). As Lyotard puts it: 'Genres of discourse are strategies – of no one' (*D*, 137).

Whereas there are rules *within* a genre that guide linking, we have no rules for linking *between* genres of discourse. The fact that there is no universal genre able to regulate the conflicts or differends that arise when 'the success . . . proper to one genre is not the one proper to others' (*D*, 136) has not prevented various genres from trying to achieve generic hegemony. In Ancient Greece, the hegemonic genre was that of dialectics or rhetoric, whereas during the Industrial Revolution it was the technical genre and its emphasis on performance. Today, in the age of capital, the hegemonic genre is arguably the economic genre of exchange, whose criterion of success is extended to areas not previously under its rule, such as communication theory, where phrases become countable units that can be exchanged as commodities. The economic genre seeks to repress the inevitable heterogeneity of genres of discourse: as its rules dictate, one cessation must cancel out another.

Yet there are ways in which to respect the heterogeneity of genres of discourse. Borrowing from Immanuel Kant, Lyotard compares this heterogeneous multiplicity to an archipelago, where genres are akin to islands separated from each other by the sea, which simultaneously marks the abyss between genres as well as the potential for passages between them. Unlike Kant, however, Lyotard does not find in this idea grounds for a synthesising substrata uniting all genres. To Lyotard, all 'passages promised by the great doctrinal syntheses end in bloody impasses' (*D*, 179–80), the bloodiest of all being Auschwitz, which put an end to the hegemony of speculative genre and its claim that everything that is real must also be rational. The best way to effectuate a passage between genres is through political deliberation, which is 'par excellence the question of linkage' (*D*, 138). A multiplicity of genres rather than *a* genre, politics 'lets the abysses be perceived that separate the genres of discourse from each other' (*D*, 150) and thus renders visible the differends between them.

Passages

Archipelago
Auschwitz
Discourse
Links, Linkage
Phrase, Phrasing
Politics

GRAND NARRATIVE, METANARRATIVE

Angélique du Toit

One of the fundamental attacks postmodernism subjects modernism to is on the latter's belief in a 'grand narrative'. It is a rejection of the idea that the ultimate truth associated with a grand narrative is possible and that the world as experienced is as a result of hidden structures. A grand narrative or metanarrative can also be understood as an ideology or paradigm; a system of thought and belief. Such a belief exerts a strong influence on what is considered true and just. Furthermore, such a truth is seen to have an existence independent to that of the individual or society and also to act as a measurement against which other truths are to be judged. Grand narratives or metanarratives, as they are also referred to, are defined as large-scale theories and philosophies of the world which, according to Lyotard, should be viewed with deep scepticism. Instead, postmodernism, as depicted in Lyotard's work, argues for multiplicity and endless variety. He strongly suggests that society is not held together by such a perceived truth represented by a particular structure, but by a multiciplicity of beliefs and discursive practices.

Lyotard argues that as a society we have ceased to believe that grand narratives as described are adequate to represent and contain us all. Instead, we have become conscious of difference or the differend, as defined by Lyotard, and diversity which characterises postmodernism by an abundance of little narratives. Lyotard argues that the domination of the ideology of a metanarrative leads to the suppression of other ideologies. He contends that the very nature of a metanarrative leads to the annihilation of what is different and in opposition to the metanarrative. Lyotard's aversion to grand narrative can be found in *The Postmodern Condition* ([1979] 1984b), in which he argues that grand narrative should be replaced by little narratives, rejecting the dependency on a guarantor of truth. Furthermore, the metanarrative or grand narrative is accompanied by an assumption of prediction and control which is shown by recent science to be a futile waste of energy. Instead, Lyotard suggests that a postmodern society functions on a high level of abstraction and uncertainty and is marked by a search for instabilities which in turn reflects the complexity and heterogeneity of society.

Lyotard argues forcefully that the grand narrative has lost its credibility 'regardless of whether it is a speculative narrative or a narrative of emancipation' (*PC*, 37). Instead, little narratives are seen to come into being through the interaction of a group or groups for a specific reason and at a particular moment in time. By their nature little narratives accept difference and the transient nature of knowing which is in opposition to the modernist structure of binary opposites. Postmodernist knowledge then becomes a reflection of everyday life inviting a multitude of alternative voices.

What is important is not whether the little narratives are true or false, but whether they serve a purpose at a given time. According to Lyotard grand narratives repress individual creativity. Instead he argues that the postmodern environment is characterised by diversity and conflict. Society is complex and filled with uncertainties. Grand narrative is seen as the oppressive force of authoritarianism. The death of an overarching metanarrative reveals knowledge not as universal, but grounded in local knowledge instead. The perspective of a grand narrative has, by its nature, to reject difference. While the metanarrative imposes choice of one over the other, postmodernism resists closure and explores the interconnection of opposites. Truth is fluid and ever changing and the most that can be hoped for is a snapshot at a particular moment in time.

In addressing the debate on the Enlightenment, Lyotard argues that all aspects of societies are reliant on grand narratives or meta-theories, which seek to explain dominant modes of thought such as religion and philosophical schools of thought. For Lyotard the Enlightenment represents yet a further attempt at authoritative explanation with its associated ideologies. He therefore bases his definition of postmodernism on the notion that postmodernist thought sets out to challenge and deconstruct metanarratives. Instead of grand narratives which seek to explain all, Lyotard puts forward the notion of mini- or little narratives that are, as Peter Barry sums it up, 'provisional, contingent, temporary, and relative' (Barry 2002: 87).

Lyotard's arguments for the little narrative in *The Differend* ([1983] 1988a) provide a powerful antidote to the totalitarianism of the grand narrative which seeks to reduce everything to a single genre in order to stifle the differend in the process. Stifling the differend also means the suppression of new and different ways of thinking and acting. Instead Lyotard argues that the postmodern age is recognised by an 'incredulity toward metanarratives' (*PC*, xxiv). He goes on to propose that these grand narratives are attempts at putting forward large-scale theories and philosophies of the world in which he suggests we have ceased to believe. Instead, we are much more open to difference, diversity and the incompatibility of our aspirations, resulting in the little narratives which display his postmodernist ideas. Instead of the grand narrative, Lyotard argues for a multiplicity of little narratives which resist and challenge the dominant narratives, the fragmented quality of the former protecting them from being incorporated into any of the latter. The little narrative is the antithesis of the grand narrative, representing flexibility and constantly reinventing itself, free from the weight of tradition and the restrictions of preconceived ideologies.

According to Lyotard the universal theories which underpin Western culture are nothing less than mechanisms with which to suppress the individual. Instead, the little narrative emerges to meet the needs of a particular situation without any reference to a larger and dominant philosophy. Furthermore, little narratives serve to underwrite and legitimise other ideological beliefs. It could be argued that metanarratives have given rise to various forms of fundamentalism and that little narratives will serve as a challenge to extreme forms of ideology.

Passages

Difference
Incredulity
Little Narrative

GREAT EPHEMERAL SKIN

Stuart Sim

Libidinal Economy ([1974] 1993a) contains some of Lyotard's densest philosophical writing, as in the chapter on the 'Great Ephemeral Skin' where that concept itself proves very difficult to pin down with any great precision. (As one commentator has justifiably enough remarked, the book itself often sounds 'more like an avant-garde novel than a philosophical text' (Ashley Woodward 2005).) The subject here is libido, desire, and how this lies beyond our control, and even our understanding except in the sense of being aware of its effects as it works through ourselves and others. Desire is expressed physically through our bodies, but it eludes explanation as to its motives or ultimate objective: indeed, like most post-structuralist thinkers Lyotard does not believe that it *has* any ultimate objective. It is yet one more aspect of existence that lies beyond human power, particularly the power of reason, and thus, even more importantly for this anti-authoritarian thinker, the power or reach of any metanarrative also. The libido traverses our body in an unorganised and compulsive fashion: 'it is infinite . . . intensities run in it without meeting a terminus, without ever crashing into the wall of an absence, into a limit which would be the mark of a lack' (*LE*, 4). Libido is, too, an insistent part of our experience, something which, as Lyotard acknowledges, does not 'lack regions to invest' (*LE*, 4). Much of the socialisation process through which we all go is concerned with trying to organise and contain libido, but this can only work up to a point: whatever our efforts, libido's internal dynamic remorselessly drives it on.

The chapter begins with a virtuoso description of a dissection of the human body, but this does not reveal the secret behind the operations of the libido, which requires us instead 'to spread out the immense membrane of the libidinal "body" which is quite different to the frame' (*LE*, 2). All that the physical dissection can show us is the site on which the intensities of libido go to work, but a full understanding of the 'libidinal body' and its economy will always escape us, not least because Lyotard contends that 'thought itself is libidinal' and 'what counts is its force (its intensity)' (*LE*, 31). We are in fact subjected to a 'tumult of intensities' that undermine our pretensions to rationality, Lyotard dismissing those

pretensions on the grounds that 'the criterion of true and false is irrelevant
. . . when the latter is an intensely spun top' (*LE*, 31). Libido is a primal
process that cannot be reduced to the strictures of reason: it no more offers
an organised structure for analysis than any other form of natural energy
does. Trying to pin it down or rationalise it is a bit like trying to do the
same thing with lightning.

Lyotard emphasises the role of the ephemeral in our lives, arguing that
'there is nothing permanent from one encounter to another' (*LE*, 38) – as
in our love lives, for example. Again, the claim is that we cannot dictate
the course of events and that we are instead stuck inside a labyrinth,
making our way through it as best we can, always responding to libido
rather than directing it. Being within the labyrinth is like being within a
skin ('ephemeral like the eye of a tornado' (*LE*, 41), in Lyotard's striking
phrase, conjuring up the notion of an existence surrounded by uncontrollable intensities). The critical point is that, unlike our physical body with
a skin that could be slit to reveal its structure, '[n]o-one has the power to
draw up the map of this great film' ('film' being another sense of the word
'skin'), 'whose constituent parts would change according to unforeseeable
modulations, would appear and disappear with the same terrifying ease as
virtual images on a screen' (*LE*, 36).

Although there is a certain tragic dimension to this picture of the libidinal body, bringing us as it does sharply up against the limitations of human
reason, for Lyotard it is a case of daring to come to terms with the actual
nature of existence – a nature over which no metanarrative can really exercise dominion: 'Imagine the universe in expansion: does it flee from terror
or explode with joy? Undecidable. So it is for emotions, those polyvalent
labyrinths to which, only after the event, the semiologists and psycholo-
gists will try to attribute some sense' (*LE*, 42). The point about metanarratives, of course, is that they claim to be able to attribute sense *before* the
event, so for Lyotard the libido and the great ephemeral skin become part
of his armoury in the campaign to demolish such pretensions.

Passages

Body
Desire
Great Zero
Libidinal Economy
Poststructuralism

GREAT ZERO

Stuart Sim

The great Zero shares at least some of the opaqueness and density of meaning of the Great Ephemeral Skin in the chapter of that same name in *Libidinal Economy* ([1974] 1993a), which remains one of Lyotard's most challenging pieces of writing, where concepts are used in a very fluid manner. The chapter can be considered as a series of meditations on desire and the libido, where their intensity and power are emphasised, the critical point being that they lie beyond human control and can be understood only in terms of their effects on us. Human history features many attempts to come up with a universal theory which can explain all aspects of human behaviour, including desire and the libido, and these generally posit some kind of directing force behind them – such as a God with a master plan. Dialectical materialism or Freudian theory or the Platonic theory of forms would be other examples of such theories, all of which Lyotard lumps under the heading of the great Zero.

Lyotard challenges the claims of the great Zero to be able to contain desire and libido within any master plan: 'Far from taking the great Zero as the ontological motif, imposed on desire, forever deferring, re-presenting and stimulating everything in an endless postponement, we, libidinal economists, affirm that this zero is itself a figure, part of a powerful *dispositif*, wise like the god of the Jews and pale like the void of Lao-tzu' (*LE*, 5). In other words, the great Zero does not really offer a satisfactory explanation for the workings of desire (such as that it is motivated by a sense of 'lack'), and in that sense is empty: as Lyotard puts it at another point, 'this Nothing, it is their desire that produces it, it is not it that produces their desire' (*LE*, 13). Lyotard is once again rejecting the viability of metanarratives, and encouraging us to be similarly suspicious of their claims to universal knowledge. To acknowledge that emptiness is for him a positive step: 'we want all that affirms that this zero not only does not engender itself, and no more is it engendered by another force . . . but most of all that questions of engenderment are trapped, they bear within them knowledge and its "answers" ' (*LE*, 5, 6). The great Zero assumes a master signifier which endows everything with meaning, thus providing a basis for explanation and interpretation; but of course it cannot explain itself; it has to be accepted as a given whose value is transcendent. When it comes to a religion like Christianity, for example, that means that theologians are repeatedly forced to refer to the mysteriousness of God's ways since their meaning can never be known to us.

This all amounts to saying that universal theories impose a scheme on human existence that is not really there, as in the example Lyotard gives of Karl Marx's belief that 'the force of labour' – and the theory of class struggle lying behind that – will eventually dictate the course of human history. Thinkers like Marx reveal themselves to be 'in the grip of an obsession with the great Zero, when, at any cost, one wants to produce a discourse of so-called knowledge, when therefore one never ceases . . . to proclaim that now, this is it, one holds the true *dispositif* of the logic of propositions, of the theory of numbers, of whatever' (*LE*, 12–13). The dismissive 'whatever' sums up Lyotard's enduring scepticism towards metanarrative projects, with their master signifier pretensions, as does the deliberately provocative use of 'Zero' to describe any and all universal theories or systems of knowledge.

Passages

Desire
Dispositif
Great Ephemeral Skin
Libidinal Economy
Marxism

HABERMAS, JÜRGEN (1929–) – see 'aesthetics', 'differend', 'legitimation', 'little narrative', 'modern, modernity' and 'reason, rationality'

HARAWAY, DONNA (1944–) – see 'body', 'feminism' and 'inhuman'

HEGEL, GEORG WILHELM FRIEDRICH (1770–1831) – see 'aesthetics', 'dialectics', 'feminism', 'links, linkage', 'modern, modernity', 'phenomenology', 'postmodern, postmodernity', 'postmodernism', 'speculative narrative' and 'sublime'

HEIDEGGER AFFAIR – see 'forgetting', 'Heidegger, Martin', 'Jews, Judaism' and 'philosophy'

HEIDEGGER, MARTIN

Keith Crome

Martin Heidegger (1889–1976) is one of the most important philosophers of the twentieth century. His thought, 'equal to the "greatest"' (*Hj*, 52) as Lyotard puts it, has been widely influential, particularly in France where it had a significant impact on the development of existentialism, phenomenology and deconstruction.

Heidegger's major work is *Being and Time* ([1927] 1962), the aim of which is to enquire into the meaning of Being. Heidegger argues that such an enquiry animated Greek philosophy, through which it determined the meaning of Being as presence. This determination continues to exert a powerful, fateful hold over us, conditioning the ways in which we relate to beings, ourselves included. The task for Heidegger, then, is to return to and readdress the question of the meaning of Being. This is initiated in *Being and Time* by the argument that the Being of the human being – or Dasein – cannot be properly understood as a mere being-present. Rather, Dasein actively exists, and is always beyond itself in the sense that it is a being-able-to-be that defines itself in terms of its projects. While this specific claim concerning Dasein was taken up directly by the French existentialists, it is Heidegger's broader attempt to think Being otherwise than as being-present, and in particular to think it as the event of presencing that itself withdraws in favour of what it grants, that decisively influenced later French philosophy, Lyotard's included.

However, if Lyotard's work is influenced by Heidegger's, it is neither exclusively nor uncritically indebted to it. Lyotard's most sustained and complex engagement with Heidegger's thought is in *Heidegger and "the jews"* ([1988b] 1990b), which is a response to the debate occasioned by Victor Farías's *Heidegger and Nazism* ([1987] 1991). In 1933 Heidegger was appointed Rector of Freiburg University by the Nazi regime and joined the Nazi Party. Although he resigned from the rectorship in 1934, and withdrew from political activity, he did not renounce his membership of the NSDAP until the end of the war, and thereafter remained reticent about the atrocities perpetrated by the Nazi regime. While Heidegger called his involvement with the Nazi Party his greatest stupidity, Farías's book purports to show, with 'evidence' from Heidegger's personal and public life, that his allegiance to Nazism was deep-rooted, that it continued until the end of his life, and that it was intrinsic to his thinking.

Against Farías, Lyotard argues that Heidegger's involvement with the

Nazi Party was not a necessary consequence of his philosophy, and that his activity as Rector of Freiburg 'was divergent from . . . the party line' (*PW*, 144). However, he goes on to point out that Heidegger's political speeches from the period of the rectorship are pervaded by the terms and tone of the existential-ontological analysis of *Being and Time*, and if Heidegger's master work is not intrinsically Nazi, it did not exclude the possibility of an engagement with Nazism.

As serious as it is, the question of the significance of Heidegger's involvement with the NSDAP is not, for Lyotard, the most crucial issue. Of greater significance is his almost total silence concerning the *Shoah*. This silence, Lyotard argues, is neither a matter of personal discretion nor avoidance on Heidegger's part, but is inextricably related to the import of his thinking, revealing its complicity with the philosophical tradition that it delimits and deconstructs. While that deconstruction shows how with the advent of philosophy the truth of Being becomes forgotten through its submission to a thinking that determines it only from and in relation to beings, it itself forgets – and thus repeats – another forgetting by means of which Western thought, conditioned by philosophy, has submitted beings to the virile mastery of its will to know. That 'Forgotten' is the immemorial liability of the soul, its sense of being affected by an obligation which it can never adequately represent and of which it cannot acquit itself. Within Western history, it is the Jews, Lyotard suggests, who bear witness to this pathos of the soul, hostages to 'the Covenant that the (unnameable) Lord has imposed on [them]' and which they 'are not ready to submit to and respect' (*PW*, 143). Consequently, the Jews cannot be incorporated within the political and social practices of the West (practices installed by its will to truth), and are thus subject to conversion, expulsion and extermination. Thus for Lyotard, Heidegger's silence concerning the *Shoah* is a mark of his philosophically conditioned insensitivity to this radical pathos of the soul, so alien to the imperatives of the Western will that he otherwise seeks to delimit.

Passages

Anamnesis
Deconstruction
Existentialism
Forgetting
Jews, Judaism
Phenomenology

HISTORY, HISTORIANS

Stuart Sim

Lyotard has an ambivalent attitude to historians and the project of history in general, regarding them as all too often concerned to advance the cause of a grand narrative. Historical narrative can make the past seem far neater and tidier than it was in reality, and that imposition of form on events is something of which Lyotard is always going to be suspicious. From such a perspective Marxist history would be a particularly dubious project, forcing history to conform to a predetermined scheme of class struggle and the desirability of the dictatorship of the proletariat, as if that was the only possible interpretation to be made.

Lyotard identifies two main methodologies at work in the field, 'memorial history' and 'history-as-science', and even though he thinks the latter is the more defensible, he still finds it based on many questionable assumptions. Memorial history is very much in the service of a grand narrative, and its value in helping to build up a sense of socio-political unity is acknowledged, Lyotard noting, 'how indispensable this memorial is to the constitution and the perpetuation of a community governed by this entirely new and unprecedented law of political equality'. Such a form of history replaces myth as the foundational narrative of the state, but that means it is necessarily very selective indeed: 'it requires the forgetting of that which may question the community and its legitimacy'. Memorial history compresses everything that happened into a 'single representation' (*Hj*, 7) that by its very nature excludes the validity of any alternative explanation.

History-as-science takes issue with this older form, and does its best to bring what the former had hidden to the surface. Such historians, 'choose, simply because of this claim to "realism," to confront the community with what menaces it, that is, with the forgotten of the memorials, with discord, rather than serve the political projects of legitimation and perpetuation' (*Hj*, 9). Historians of this persuasion are critically minded, striving to amass as much evidence as they can from archives and documents to put together a picture of what '*really* happened' (*Hj*, 9), rather than what the grand narrative would like to have happened.

But even this, laudable enough in its way, attempt to uncover the truth behind the forgetting is fatally flawed. Here, too, the assumption is that everything can be brought under a thesis, can be fixed and pinned down, and this is to fail to recognise the sheer complexity, and even mystery and incomprehensibility, of what has happened. As usual with Lyotard, the problem lies in starting from preconceived notions – such as that one can ever reach the full truth of what happened. Thus his reminder that 'one forgets as soon as one believes, draws conclusions, and holds for certain' (*Hj*, 10). The historian is to be contrasted with the philosopher in this respect, the latter, in Lyotard's idealised image of the profession anyway, avoiding preconceived notions and refusing to claim certainty for any judgements he or she might reach in the course of their analyses.

Passages

Event
Forgetting
Intellectuals
Marxism
Philosophy

HOLOCAUST – see 'Auschwitz', 'bearing witness', 'differend', 'discourse', 'Enlightenment', 'forgetting', 'intellectuals', 'Jews, Judaism', 'justice', 'philosophy', 'politics', 'posthumanism', 'referent' and 'scepticism'

HUMANISM – see 'inhuman' and 'posthumanism'

HUSSERL, EDMUND (1859–1938) – see 'Christianity', 'existentialism', 'phenomenology' and 'post-Marxism'

I DON'T KNOW WHAT

Stuart Sim

It is a consistent refrain of Lyotard's writing that we never are, or can be, in complete control of our world, and that circumstances can always deflect us from even the most carefully worked-out plan we might have constructed. We should consider the future not just as open, but also as fundamentally unpredictable – and this goes for the development of our own careers as well, as he makes clear in his most personal book, *Peregrinations* (1988b [1990]). There, he claims that we should be 'guided only by feelings' in choosing the direction we take, since there are no 'unequivocal criteria' (*P*, 12) we can deploy that will tell us what is the right thing to do.

Intriguingly enough, Lyotard does suggest there will be something that draws us and that we need to be attentive to, even if we do not understand it entirely: 'I think that every writer or thinker carries in him or herself as a particular temptation the weakness or the possibility of ignoring that he or she is committed to a "I don't know what"' (*P*, 12). There is a definite echo here of the 'strange attractor', one of the key concepts of chaos theory, which as part of the changing world of physics has a noticeable influence on Lyotard's thought and worldview. A strange attractor lies behind all systems and systems duly respond to it, but we cannot determine any pattern to its workings, which remain a mystery we are unable to solve – it seems to involve a counter-intuitive combination of chance and determined elements that we can only regard as profoundly paradoxical.

Lyotard cites a personal experience of being guided by his feelings in the writing of *Libidinal Economy* ([1974] 1993a), 'my evil book, the book of evilness that everyone writing and thinking is tempted to do' (*P*, 13), as he rather ruefully perceives it in retrospect. *Libidinal Economy* was a vicious attack on Marxism which brought to a head the problems Lyotard had been undergoing with the theory for at least a couple of decades. One interpretation is that his 'I don't know what' had been leading him away from Marxism for some time (anyone reading his Algerian writings will recognise the early symptoms), and that he was finally opening himself up to what this meant: 'My only law . . . was to try to be as receptive as possible to emerging impulses, be they of anger, hate, love, loathing, or envy' (*P*, 13). Receptivity to the 'I don't know what' is seen to be a necessary part of one's development, and for all his criticism of the book in *Peregrinations*, one suspects that Lyotard does not really regret having followed his gut instincts in *Libidinal Economy*. The book marked a watershed in his career, and his outsider status on the left became progressively more pronounced afterwards, as he opted for the insecurity that goes along with the 'I don't know what' instead of the apparent certainties of theory. From a Marxist standpoint, that is tantamount to opting out of politics altogether.

Passages

IDIOM

Karen Langhelle

Of all of the terms integral to Lyotard's philosophy of the phrase in *The Differend* ([1983] 1988a), 'idiom' is the one that receives the least elaboration, this despite the fact that it is crucial to Lyotard's discussion of the differend, that 'instant of language wherein something which must be able to be put into phrases cannot yet be' (*D*, 13). Since this 'something' cannot be phrased in a common idiom, such as that of the tribunal, a victim suffers a wrong because his or her case is settled in an idiom that is not the victim's own. There being no words with which to phrase what is happening, the differend thus gives rise to a silence. Yet this silence signals a feeling of both pain and pleasure: pain because we cannot find the words with which to phrase what is happening, but also pleasure in realising that not everything has been said and that for this reason we are called upon by language, indeed conscripted into it, to begin to search for idioms that do not yet exist in order to bear witness to the differend.

Beyond the above, however, Lyotard appears almost reluctant to provide further detail as to how we are to understand his use of the term. What differentiates one idiom from another? What would a search for new idioms actually entail? Lyotard does intimate that idioms are largely equivalent to 'language' or even 'culture' (*PF*, 132), to the extent that all three can accommodate various different genres, each of which comes with its own set of rules and stakes. Thus Lyotard can speak of a Jewish idiom, which, with its emphasis on the genres of discourse of questioning and interpretation is an idiom that is open to the unrepresentable instant, to the *Is it happening?* of the event. As such, this idiom is at the furthest possible remove from that of Nazism, which seeks to eliminate any idiom that is foreign to the stakes of its genre, a mythic narrative of exception that through endless repetition of the same must constantly legitimate the permanence of a closed *we* and reaffirm its superiority. Their idioms are so opposed that between them 'there is not even a differend' (*D*, 106) since not even the tribunal can provide a common idiom with which at the very least to begin to formulate damages.

More than merely being a question of language in the purely linguistic sense, Lyotard also ties idioms to the body and to affects, and, as such, he also proposes the term 'existence' as a suitable synonym. To Lyotard, therefore, idioms are 'every expression loaded with affect' (*LR*, 258) that form 'an absolutely singular, untranslatable way of deciphering what is happening' (*PEC*, 92) that in language is signalled through the use of deictics. Though idioms may be untranslatable and singular – the points where the sensible reaches you through touch, hearing, sight and so forth can never be mine, nor mine yours – this does not mean this 'singularity of existence' that is the idiom is not present in the plural: indeed, idioms 'constantly come into contact with one another through these fragile antennae of sensibility' (*PEC*, 92).

We find this difference between linguistic language and affective 'idiomatic' language in Lyotard's contrasting of Orwellian Newspeak with what he calls writing. The former is bureaucratic language at its most static and inflexible; the latter involves phrasing with and against language so that through violence and seduction one introduces new idioms into it in order to make it say what it ought to but cannot yet say. The aim of writing is 'to save the instant from what is customary or understood', whereas 'Newspeak has to tarnish the wonder that (something) is happening' (*PEC*, 91).

We begin to see why Lyotard should give the impression that a certain element of vagueness must necessarily surround the idiom. Indeed, we cannot know in advance what form an idiom will take and what new rules, addressors and addressees it will generate, for to anticipate it means to reduce this 'wonder' to pre-established categories, which is to wrong it and even prohibit it. What is called for is a complete openness to the singularity of the event. Though it is the task of literature, philosophy and politics to look for new idioms with which to bear witness to the differend, it is perhaps the idiom of avant-garde art with its expressed rejection of representation and resolution that is best suited to presenting 'the unpresentable' (*PC*, 78).

Passages

Bearing Witness
Deictics
Event
Is It Happening?
Phrase, Phrasing
Writing

LES IMMATÉRIAUX – see 'postmodernism'

INCOMMENSURABILITY, INCOMPATIBILITY

Lloyd Spencer and Stuart Sim

Incommensurability has become an issue of some note in contemporary philosophy, particularly in regard to debates over truth and meaning. Anyone espousing a relativist position, as poststructuralists and postmodernists generally do, will want to claim that incommensurability is an intrinsic feature of discourse, and Lyotard is certainly disposed that way as regards communication in a general sense. The concept itself is derived from mathematical theory, where it denotes two qualities or magnitudes having no common measure. That notion has been carried over into debates about the nature of language: two languages are deemed to be incommensurable if exact translation between them proves to be difficult or even impossible.

The idea that our thought is shaped, even determined, by our language has been around for quite some time, as in the Sapir-Whorf hypothesis, formulated from work done on native American languages by the anthropological linguists Edward Sapir and Benjamin Whorf in the earlier twentieth century. Willard van Orman Quine has made a very influential contribution to this debate with his concept of the 'indeterminacy of translation', which contended that every language maps the world and its contents in its own unique way (see Quine 1964), and that this process extends from the objects of common sense to those of the physical sciences. It is not just a case, therefore, of there being shades of meaning which get lost in translation, more that this is a pointless concept when it comes to moving from one language into another. One can see how this notion of indeterminacy could be used to reinforce relativism, although Richard Rorty for one argues that we should not be alarmed by the relativist implications of incommensurability, on the grounds that '[i]ncommensurability entails irreducibility but not incompatibility' (Rorty 1980: 388). We have no reason to believe that there is massive difference in kind between what is being said in one language and another, at the very least comparison is possible. Nevertheless, postmodern theorists have shown themselves very inclined to assume that incommensurability equals incompatibility.

Not surprisingly, given their commitment to difference, postmodernists have been quite taken by the Sapir-Whorf hypothesis, although they generally interpret it in stronger terms than the original, to the point of implying that speakers of different languages in effect inhabit different worlds. This is an idea which is consistent with Lyotard's views about the way discourses and phrase regimens work: 'For each of these regimens there corresponds a mode of presenting a universe, and one mode is not translatable into another' (D, 128). The implication is that, *pace* Rorty, even phrase regimens *within* a language are incompatible with each other.

Postmodernists are equally prone to take a very strong version of incommensurability from their reading of Thomas Kuhn. Kuhn had postulated the existence of scientific 'paradigms' which regulated how scientists perceived the physical world, meaning that they interpreted the data from their experiments through particular theories, and continued to do so even when anomalies arose that their theories could not explain. The tendency instead was to try to shore up the existing theory. Scientists were unable, in other words, to think outside their theoretical discourse, the scientific language with which they had grown up. If another theory was subsequently developed by the next generation to explain those anomalies then it posited a new paradigm with a totally new theoretical perspective, as when Copernican astronomy challenged Ptolemaic. As in that example, the two paradigms were incommensurable: you had to believe in one or the other; they were constructed on mutually exclusive worldviews. From the debates opened up by such theories, Lyotard is moved to put forward his notion of 'postmodern science', where experimental research keeps yielding the unknown and scientific practice is effectively dominated by anomalies: 'undecidables', 'incomplete information', 'catastrophes', 'pragmatic paradoxes' (PC, 60). Another way of putting that would be to say that for Lyotard science nowadays keeps producing evidence of incommensurability.

The political implications of incommensurability come forcefully into play in Lyotard's concept of the differend, where opposed interests confront each other without a common discourse or phrase regimen in which to articulate their respective positions. What Lyotard refers to as 'the heterogeneity of phrase regimens and . . . the impossibility of subjecting them to a single law (except by neutralizing them)' (D, 128) prevents any resolution being achieved. In a very real sense neither side is talking the same language, and no meaningful communication is taking, or can take, place. Thus colonisers and colonised confront each other over an unbridgeable divide, since there can be no common ground between them: the phrase regimen of colonisation and that of being in control of one's own national territory can never correspond. We know what generally happens in such cases historically, however: the colonisers impose their will on the native population and simply refuse to acknowledge that they have any grievance at all to voice. Force wins out as a grand narrative quashes dissent in time-honoured fashion (as it also did memorably in the case of Nazism and the Jews). Lyotard wants us instead to bear witness to this incommensurability, and for narratives to respect each other's autonomy. Unfortunately, as he recognises, this is rarely what happens in the real world, where grand narratives consistently feel the need to erase any semblance of incommensurability in order to cement their power. The politics of the little narrative is specifically designed to be a corrective to this state of affairs.

Such a political perspective offers a more straightforward way into the issues raised by the notion of incommensurability than some of the more arcane linguistic and epistemological debates. Lyotard's interest in questions of justice and injustice leads him to a sense of what is at stake in the relation between languages, and enjoins us to be vigilant against attempts by one discourse to exert dominance over another, as repeatedly happens in the political domain. The notion of the differend suggests that we pay attention to what cannot be translated, what may effectively be silenced when we attempt to reach general agreement – generally to the benefit of the stronger party. Similarly, the concept of the sublime asks us to be aware of what cannot be represented, since it lies beyond even the possibility of translation.

Passages

Difference
Differend
Little Narrative
Phrase, Phrasing
Postmodern Science
Sublime

INCREDULITY

Stuart Sim

Incredulity is what marks out the postmodern condition for Lyotard, the general lapse in belief that he argues has occurred in the later twentieth century with regard to political and institutional authority: 'I define *postmodern* as incredulity towards metanarratives. This incredulity is undoubtedly a product of progress in the sciences: but that progress in turn presupposes it' (*PC*, xxiv). Whereas previously grand narratives had been able to count on fairly extensive popular support, that had eroded as their weaknesses and contradictions had increasingly come to light, and we were in consequence no longer disposed to follow their dictates. Marxism, to take an obvious case, had signally failed to overturn capitalism or to create a completely new world order. By the time that Lyotard was writing *The Postmodern Condition* ([1979] 1984b) in the late 1970s, the communist world was beginning to show definite signs of disarray, and as we now know was indeed on the verge of collapse, with the Soviet bloc crumbling within just a few years.

The world that was developing was to be one in which universalising theories would cease to exert the appeal they had done, and in which a far more sceptical temper would prevail. It would be a world where little narratives came to prominence, and these would involve no commitment to grandiose theories, being concerned instead to challenge the abuse of power by grand narratives. Once success had been gained on that front, they would be expected to dissolve such that they did not become substitutes for the grand narratives they had undermined – incredulity was to remain the default position for all attempts to impose an authoritarian system on human affairs.

A decline in belief in authority has been a notable factor of life in the West of late. Politics in general, for example, is viewed with a great deal of scepticism by the public and respect for politicians has plummeted. The aesthetic theory of modernism has also lost its hold on practitioners, and there has been a general turn away from its doctrines, particularly the insistence on originality as the primary criterion of aesthetic value. Postmodern artists have simply stopped believing that, and have made a point of reviving older styles and entering into a dialogue with the past where possible.

Lyotard saw incredulity as a widespread phenomenon, but in retrospect it is clear he overstated the case on this and that grand narrative was in fact beginning a significant comeback in the form of various kinds of fundamentalist belief. Religious fundamentalism is the most obvious of these, and there is no denying that it has become an increasingly powerful force globally in recent decades. Market fundamentalism and globalisation are further proof of this trend: the grand narrative of capitalism has been extending its reach very considerably in recent times, and the project of modernity is far from being exhausted in the way that thinkers like Lyotard had been hoping. Incredulity has turned out to be in much shorter supply than he had assumed.

Passages

Little Narrative
Marxism
Modern, Modernity

Modernism
Politics

INHUMAN

Stuart Sim

Lyotard's collection of essays, *The Inhuman: Reflections on Time* ([1988c] 1991a), raises the issue of the extent to which the forces of techno-science are seeking to marginalise humanity and the notion of the human in favour of a machine-led, computer-controlled culture. Techno-science stands accused of introducing the factor of the inhuman into our world through the process of development (the relentless spread of advanced capitalism), in support of which its computer systems are continually being improved to increase operational efficiency. Lyotard puts the problem in a fairly stark form: 'what if human beings were in the process of, constrained into, becoming inhuman . . . ? And . . . what if what is "proper" to humankind were to be inhabited by the inhuman?' (*I*, 2). His claim is that development is forcing us to become progressively more machine-like and, even more worryingly, that we are under threat of computers replacing us altogether, turning collectively into a self-enclosed system with no need of any human input. Such a scheme is said to be attractive to techno-science as a means of surviving past the death of the sun, when it finally burns out in around 4.5 billion years. In a rather portentous phrase, Lyotard insists that this 'is the sole serious question to face humanity today' (*I*, 9), and clearly he is very exercised by it.

In an admittedly far-fetched, but nevertheless still striking, piece of argument, Lyotard suggests that techno-science is actively preparing for the sun's extinction, writing off the human race in the process. As far as techno-science is concerned the human is simply too unpredictable, whereas computers are programmable into the indefinite future, offering a guarantee of operational efficiency largely foreign to humanity. In other words, what techno-science wants to eliminate is difference, including the difference encoded in gender. Computers also mean the end of the unexpected (symbolised by the 'event' for Lyotard, without which he can hardly conceive of human history), since their programming predetermines how the future will turn out. In Lyotard's view, that is one of the most effective ways of exercising control over one's culture, almost as if time itself is being overcome.

Computers may seem to offer the intriguing prospect of 'thought without a body', therefore to be ideal candidates to outlive the sun; but

Lyotard is unwilling to grant them the status of thinkers. Instead, he argues there is a necessary element of suffering, in fact pain, in thinking that can only occur in a body. Computers cannot experience this, and are incapable of questioning or resisting the commands of their programming system. Dissent is not possible under a computer regime, and without dissent we are indeed constrained into the inhuman, where nothing matters except the performance of the system (a concern Lyotard had already raised in *The Postmodern Condition* ([1979] 1984b)). One of the most insidious side-effects of a move towards computerisation would be the eclipse of free will, and without that we do not have the human as traditionally we have understood it.

Lyotard advocates resistance against the overweening power of techno-science in an effort to preserve the human against what is for him the fundamental 'inhumanity of the system' (*I*, 2). Techno-science plus development (which could be read as the multinationals plus globalisation) now constitutes the major global metanarrative, and it is a consistent aspect of Lyotard's thought that metanarratives are there to be challenged, with little narratives striving to destabilise their power base and the authority that emanates from this. Once again, we see that Lyotard is promoting the cause of difference, and it is certainly true that the multinationals and the globalisation system they work through have sought to create a more homogenised world where difference is minimised as much as possible – difference being considered a barrier to operational efficiency.

Behind Lyotard's argument lies a fear of the development of Artificial Intelligence and Artificial Life, areas which of late have attracted a great deal of research funding on the part of techno-science. The goal in both cases is to produce self-sustaining, and even perhaps self-replicating, systems, and although proponents are generally sceptical about the likelihood of these escaping human control entirely and competing with humanity for resources, it is by no means an impossible scenario to imagine. Artificial Intelligence and Artificial Life are already claimed as new life-forms by their more enthusiastic advocates, and that surely carries the risk of them becoming rivals of humanity at some point in the future. At the current stage of development such a risk may seem very small, but it depends how much we trust techno-science to act in humanity's best interests – and Lyotard for one is deeply suspicious of the objectives of the techno-scientific establishment. For all its science-fictional elements, *The Inhuman* is a heartfelt defence of our human nature that resonates more strongly with each passing year and new technological development that emerges. At the very least, Lyotard is calling for significantly increased monitoring of techno-scientific activities, and for constant pressure to be exerted on governments to ensure that these are not allowed to take an inhuman turn.

For all Lyotard's sceptical attitude towards the humanist tradition in Western culture (in common with most postmodernist thinkers he can be very critical of what the Enlightenment has meant or has been used to justify), he is espousing what looks substantially like a humanist position in *The Inhuman*. Anti-humanist though he is generally described to be (sometimes posthumanist), few humanists would disagree with the line he takes in the book. He is certainly on the other side of the divide from enthusiastic champions of a machine-led culture such as Donna Haraway, for whom a conflation of the human and the inhuman, in the form of the cyborg, is a highly desirable development: '[t]he machine is us' (Haraway 1991: 180), as she provocatively proclaims. From a Lyotardian perspective, to go down the road of cyborgisation, to cultivate such an affinity, is to surrender to the inhuman, and he is calling on little narratives to do their utmost to prevent this from ever happening.

Passages

Development
Event
Posthumanism
Resistance
Techno-Science
Thought Without a Body

INTELLECTUALS

Georges Van Den Abbeele

An abiding concern with the role and status of intellectuals in contemporary societies runs through the work of Lyotard from his early essay, written in 1948 for Jean-Paul Sartre's *Les temps modernes*, on the intellectual generation 'Born in 1925', through his 1996 biography of André Malraux, a figure whose variegated career from colonial art thief to novelist to resistance fighter to cultural minister under Charles de Gaulle incarnates the longstanding tradition or myth of the French intellectual as a powerful social voice.

While Lyotard addresses many issues and situations that have implications for intellectuals (the Algerian war, the student uprisings of May '68, Soviet bureaucracy, Holocaust history), he most directly engages the topic in a short essay, 'Tombeau de l'intellectuel [The Intellectual's Tomb]' (English translation, *PW*, 3–7), written in 1983 and published in

Le Monde. The article appears in the context of dozens of responses to a provocative editorial penned by Max Gallo, spokesman for the new social- ist government headed by François Mitterand. Gallo launched an appeal to France's intellectuals to become more involved in helping the govern- ment plan the social and economic modernisation of France. While many respondents bristled at the suggestion that intellectual labour should be placed in so servile and utilitarian a role, Lyotard broached a more general discussion of the relation between civic engagement and the work of those individuals loosely referred to as 'intellectuals'.

For Lyotard, an intellectual in the traditional sense is a thinker, a writer or an artist whose 'intellectual' reputation is such as to empower that indi- vidual to speak authoritatively to the larger society on behalf of a univer- sally valued subject (for example, the people, the nation, the working class, humanity). In this regard, the intellectual has not only the authority but also the responsibility to speak up on the subject's behalf. Within a French context, this progressive or 'Enlightenment' view of the intellectual as a specifically empowered spokesperson conjures up the names of Voltaire, Émile Zola and Sartre, among others.

Is this role of the intellectual still possible, asks Lyotard, in a post- modern world, where highly skilled labour that requires the use of 'intel- ligence' is rampant but increasingly specialised and determined solely by the object of realising the performance metrics specific to the job at hand? These metrics are overt in areas such as civil or social administration, in scientific research or in policy development. But they are also dominant in the world of cultural institutions, where success is measured by increased participation, patronage and funds raised. As for the arts and philosophy, where resistance to the value of increased performance is the greatest, the stakes of one's work, says Lyotard, are in being faithful to the question of what art or thought or writing is. The task of 'creation' in these fields is not one that can be legitimately placed in a servile relation to social, eco- nomic or political *ends* (which is not to deny that creative work may have *outcomes* in such areas).

Given this particular confluence, can there still be a social engagement that recalls that of the classic intellectual (such as Sartre's concept of 'com- mitment' or Antonio Gramsci's organic intellectual)? More directly, to what extent can one's reputation or competence in any given field (whether administrative or scientific or artistic) *legitimately* transfer into another? The temptation to authorise such transfers remains greater than ever while the erosion and disappearance of universalist values undermine the cred- ibility of such efforts. Even when one wishes to speak in one's capacity as a citizen of a community, 'nothing proves that optimal performance defines the best mode of coexistence or even contributes to it' (*PW*, 5).

At the same time, the decline of universalist values does not mean an inevitable collapse into the solipsism of professional specialisation, where administrators only administer, painters only paint, or philosophers only philosophise. Beyond any mourning over the tomb of a now-defunct vision of the intellectual, Lyotard proposes that,

the multiplicity of responsibilities, and their independence (their incompatibility), oblige and will oblige those who take on these responsibilities, small or great, to be flexible, tolerant, and svelte. These qualities will cease to be the contrary of rigor, honesty and force; they will be their signs. (*PW*, 7)

It is in such flexible negotiation of the manifold differends between one's various responsibilities (for example, to one's profession, to one's art, to one's place of citizenship) that a renewed sense of intellectual engagement is to be found.

Passages

Algeria
Differend
Legitimation
May '68, *Événements*
Performativity
Philosophy

IRIGARAY, LUCE (1932–) – see 'difference' and 'poststructuralism'

IS IT HAPPENING? about Burkes terror awe before the sublime

Daniel Whistler

The question *Is it happening?* (*Arrive-t-il?*) dominates Lyotard's late work on aesthetics. It originates, however, in the ethical and political discussions of *The Differend* ([1983] 1988a), and even has a 'cosmic' dimension. *Is it happening?* is opposed to *What is happening?*; the difference corresponding to that between the Scholastic categories *quod* and *quid*. The latter question assumes that 'something will happen', and what is at issue is merely its content, the information it transmits. The former *questions this very assumption*; it is 'the feeling that nothing might happen' (*I*, 92). In fact, for Lyotard, the initial moment in the feeling of the sublime is the) terror pertaining to the question, *Is it happening?*: 'What is terrifying is that the *It happens that* does not happen, that it stops happening' (*I*, 99). The paintings of Barnett Baruch Newman are paradigmatic of this. Newman's paintings refuse to communicate information, leaving merely the sheer presence of the painting: 'It happens here and now. What (*quid*) happens comes later' (*I*, 82). *Is it happening?* is therefore the fundamental question to which Newman's sublime artworks give rise. Lyotard writes of Newman's painting *Who's Afraid of Red, Yellow and Blue?*, 'The question mark of the title is that in *Is it happening?*, and the *afraid* must, I think, be taken as an allusion to Burke's terror, to the terror that surrounds the event' (*I*, 88).

As with all Lyotard's categories, *Is it happening?* is not confined merely to the aesthetic realm, but has crucial ethical and political connotations. Grand narratives try to neutralise the *Is it happening?* by focusing on the question *What is happening?*. For them, 'there is no *Is it happening?* It happened' (*AEP*, 106). The appropriate attitude of resistance therefore is one that opens up to the possibility of nothing happening, and so asks *Is it happening?*. Again, it is art and philosophy which best exemplify this procedure by exhibiting 'the misery that the painter faces with a plastic surface, of the musician with the acoustic surface, the misery the thinker faces with a desert of thought, and so on' (*I*, 91).

In consequence, the political role for the question *Is it happening?* is immense. It is the only way of thinking that can resist capitalism and other versatile grand narratives which are premised on one assumption alone: *that something happens. Is it happening?* is not concerned with 'the new' (what innovative information is going to be communicated next), but with 'the now' (the very possibility of anything being communicated at all). It thus discovers 'hidden in the cynicism of innovation . . . the despair that nothing further will happen' (*I*, 106–7). *Is it happening?* is the very question that disrupts the efficiency of capitalist and technological thinking by remaining faithful to the terror of nihilism.

The ethical implications of *Is it happening?* are most evident when Lyotard first develops this question in *The Differend* ([1983] 1988a). In section 160 (*D*, 104–6), he introduces the question in terms of the differend generated between the discourse of SS officers and that of the imprisoned Jews. While Nazism culminated (as well as parodied) the modern grand narratives by imposing 'what will happen', the Jewish prisoners opened themselves up to the terror of the question, *Is it happening?*: 'In eliminating the Jews, Nazism eliminated a phrase regimen where the mark is on the addressee . . . [The Nazi grand narrative] is placed under the regimen of the already there, the Jewish idiom is placed under that of the *Is it happening?* Nazism assails the occurrence, the *Ereignis*' (*D*, 106).

How did this particular Rabbit Solar Extinction jump out of Lyotards Magic HAT here??

110   JEWS, JUDAISM

In the subsequent paragraphs of *The Differend* Lyotard works out an ethical obligation to open oneself up to the *Is it happening?* in dialogue with Emmanuel Levinas. 'The unpresentable calls out' (*D*, 116), and, as such, imposes an obligation on the subject to do justice to what is silenced and fails to reach presentation. *Is it happening?* testifies to 'the nothingness that suspends and threatens the linkage from one phrase to the next' (*D*, 179). *Is it happening?* even has a cosmic significance for Lyotard. The sun's extinction – 'the sole serious question to face humanity today' . . . 'is the *quod* itself . . . Pure event' (*I*, 9, 11). 'something happens' is put into question most absolutely by this cosmic catastrophe. When one asks *Is it happening?* of an artwork or an ethical differend, one is transforming this situation into a precursor of the solar catastrophe. Cosmic extinction is prefigured every time one asks *Is it happening?*.

This is pretty wierd and not very intelligble

Thus is a wild leap into the DARK Unknown

Passages

Aesthetics
Ethics
Jews, Judaism
Politics
Sublime

J

JEWS, JUDAISM

Stuart Sim

Jewishness plays an important role in Lyotard's thought as a symbol of difference. The Jewish race is pictured as keeping the fact of difference very much alive in European culture throughout the centuries, being an element that always stands outside it and can never be properly absorbed into the mainstream: for Europeans, the Jews are to remain irredeemably other. They are, as Lyotard puts it, 'within the "spirit" of the Occident that is so preoccupied with foundational thinking, what resists this spirit' (*Hj*, 22) – a permanent threat to its value system based on Christianity, as a case in point. On those grounds Lyotard strongly identifies with the Jews, and makes a strong case in *Heidegger and "the jews"* ([1988b] 1990b) for the term itself to become shorthand for all those groups that our culture tries to repress because of their perceived difference (in Lyotard's terminology, the distinction between 'jews' and 'Jews'). Almost any oppressed group could be labelled as 'jews' because of society's intolerant attitude towards them, an intolerance that is all too pervasive a phenomenon in our cultural history (a point also made insistently in the writings of Michel Foucault). In his Introduction to *Heidegger and "the jews"* David Carroll suggests that it would seem to be one of Lyotard's intentions 'to make "jews" of all of us' (*Hj*, xii); that is, to invite us to reflect on our own sense of difference and how any of us could find ourselves marginalised by an overbearing cultural metanarrative.

Lyotard emphasises the otherness of the Jews, regarding this as a critical part of their heritage: '"The jews," never at home wherever they are, cannot be integrated, converted, or expelled. They are also always away from home when they are at home, in their so-called own tradition, because it includes exodus as its beginning' (*Hj*, 22). It is because of this ineradicable otherness and difference that the Jews come to be seen as a problem in European society, which 'does not know what to do with them' (*Hj*, 3), leading eventually to such horrific events as the Holocaust. The modern European nation-state has, at least until recently, had a distinct tendency towards cultural homogenisation, emphasising national identity first, although this could be subsumed to some extent under European or racial identity if an outside threat presented itself. Jewishness does not really fit in with any of these, and even when the attempt is made by individual Jews to integrate themselves into host cultures the fact of difference remains, with non-Jews always aware of this. Whereas difference is something to be respected and encouraged as far as postmodernist and poststructuralist thinkers are concerned, all too often it can appear problematical to the general public (as well as many in the political class), and a trigger for prejudice. Cultural diversity may be promoted as an ideal in current culture, but it is striking just how superficial the support for multiculturalism can be, and how easily intolerance of the other can reassert itself – even in the face of official disapproval (as in campaigns against immigration, which have arisen in most Western European countries in recent years). The Jews have been at the receiving end of this fear of the other throughout most of their history.

Europe's failure to cope with the Jewishness in its midst culminates in the 'solution' of the Holocaust, a systematic attempt to erase cultural difference altogether. In that respect it is to be considered an extreme version of a trait latent in all European society. The denial of this event by various historians, a debate which has rumbled on for some years now, is for Lyotard yet another attempt to deny difference, and it prompts his response to what he describes as 'a "politics" of absolute forgetting' (*Hj*,

25). Difference was to be excised so that no trace of it remained, an unforgiveable decision for Lyotard.

Martin Heidegger, too, becomes a highly symbolic figure in terms of the fate of the Jews in modern times, one of those who contrived to 'forget' their fate under the Nazi regime, refusing to comment on this in the postwar years (a 'leaden silence' (*Hj*, 52) in Lyotard's assessment). Heidegger was an enormous influence on postwar French philosophy, informing the work of several generations of thinkers, from Jean-Paul Sartre through to the poststructuralists (including figures such as Jacques Derrida and Lyotard himself). The so-called 'Heidegger Affair' of the late 1980s – generated by an attack on Heidegger's politics in Victor Farias's book *Heidegger and the Nazis* ([1987] 1991) – divided opinion very sharply in French philosophical circles. Derrida, for example, could argue of Heidegger's work that it could be read from either a left-wing or right-wing perspective regardless of what the author's politics were (see *The Ear of the Other* (1988)), whereas others like Lyotard took a far more critical line and saw the work itself as tainted by Heidegger's overall worldview. While he cautioned against the idea that Heidegger's politics could be read off from any of his major works, Lyotard nevertheless identifies a commitment to totality in works like *Being and Time* ([1927] 1962) that could then find expression in Nazism and its belief in the destiny of the German *Volk*. The Jews could never be incorporated into such a project as this, failing to qualify on ethnic grounds, and that came to be an unacceptable situation to the Nazis, hence their development of the 'final solution' with its disgraceful objective 'to "terminate" the interminable' (*Hj*, 25).

The fate of the Jews under Nazism demonstrates the extent to which metanarratives will go to remove difference from the cultural equation, and Lyotard feels it holds a critical lesson for all of us. Ultimately, we are all potentially at risk from the politics of forgetting, which could be visited upon any group deemed to be resisting the general will ('jews' of whatever description), and difference needs to be vigorously defended against it if we are to have anything like a just society. The symbolic import of the Jews needs to be stressed to remind us of this.

Passages

Difference
Forgetting
Heidegger, Martin
Modern, Modernity
Poststructuralism

JUDGEMENT

Neal Curtis

Lyotard's writings on judgement are guided in the main by two philosophers: Immanuel Kant and Aristotle. From at least the time of his dialogue with Jean-Loup Thébaud in *Just Gaming* ([1979] 1985), the problem with which Lyotard wrestled is the need to think the possibility of judgement in the absence of any criteria that might determine what makes a judgement just. The lack of criteria arises from two distinct but related problems. First, the inability to think justice in terms of a theoretical model and, second, the irreducible singularity of events. In relation to the former, Kant is perhaps the most important philosopher, while Aristotle provides the theoretical tools for one approach to thinking the latter.

In talking of the withdrawal of the moral law Lyotard resisted the problem where justice is seen as compliance with a pre-established definition, or conformity to the signification of some philosopher's or politician's discourse. The lack of fit between the prescriptive phrase 'Be Just' and, for example, the descriptive phrase 'justice is democracy' comes about because each sets in play a phrase universe with its own set of rules for its formation. To find a possible solution to the problem of this heterogeneity Lyotard turned to Kant. First of all it should be noted that for Kant thinking and judging are the same, because all thinking involves the unification of a sensible object with a concept of the understanding. Put another way, judgement is the union of phenomena that produces a cognition proper. In the introduction to *Critique of Judgement* Kant writes that 'the business of the judgment in the use of the concept for cognition consists in *presentation* (*exhibitio*), i.e. in setting a corresponding intuition beside the concept' (Kant [1790] 1951: 29). Presentation is 'an adjoining, a conjoining, a setting side by side, a comparison, between an established or an unknown rule and an intuition' (*D*, 64). Where the rule is established judgement is determinate, where the rule is lacking and needs to be found judgement is said to be reflective. Determinate judgement, for Kant, pertained to cognitions of objects of experience, objects in the world that could be tested and verified. This was the proper field of theoretical reason, or science, and dealt with concepts of the understanding.

There are, however, other concepts that do not correspond to testable, verifiable objects: these Kant referred to as concepts of reason, or Ideas. These were concepts like justice, freedom, totality, first cause, etc. Because there is no object called justice in the world it cannot be tested, measured or quantified, meaning that rules cannot be established to determine if something we experience actually is just. In these instances the rule for producing the cognition has to be created via the imagination. This means that the mode of presentation cannot be 'direct' but must be indirect, or by *analogy*, as either *symbol* or *type*. This analogical reasoning is the key to Lyotard's thinking around the question of justice because such presentations aid conception without reducing Ideas of reason to cognition. Reason, in effect, borrows from the world of experience intuitions which, through reflection, share similar rules of causality and effectivity although there is no identity. Such symbolic presentations are evident in the representation of justice as a pair of scales, connoting the 'weighing up' of both sides, or as blindfolded, connoting resistance to prejudice. In this way it is now clear how communication regarding the Idea of justice itself is also possible in the absence of determinate criteria.

Lyotard's other approach to judgement was via Aristotle. Although this is not as central to Lyotard's philosophy as Kant's approach to judgement, Aristotle's discussion of practical wisdom, or *phronesis*, remains important for the sensitivity of case-by-case judgement that Lyotard advocated. *Phronesis* is the ability to respond in the right way to practical problems without the right way being determined. For Lyotard, in keeping with Ronald Beiner's analysis of *phronesis*, it is a response to 'the ultimate particulars that constitute a practical situation' (Beiner 1983: 75). The necessity of judging according to the particularity or singularity of a case is most evident in Aristotle's doctrine of the mean found in *The Nicomachean Ethics* (Aristotle 2009). This doctrine talks of excellence, happiness, justice, etc. as a balance between the two poles of excess and deficiency. This balance might be understood in terms of the object, where a universal rule is assumed, or it can be understood relatively, that is, with reference to the particular subject, requiring, for example, happiness. According to the objective mean the intermediate may be assumed to be a gauge for all action, but this fails to recognise that relative to a particular situation that mean might either be excessive or deficient. Aristotle uses an example of a trainer prescribing the diet of an athlete where, if ten pounds is too much to eat and two pounds is too little, it is not necessarily the case that six pounds is the correct amount of food to eat, because in relation to the athlete and the particular requirements demanded of his exercise this may still be excessive or deficient.

What is especially significant for Lyotard is that in spite of the desire for rulings to apply universally, as in the objective mean, Aristotle is only too aware of specificity and the need to respond to particular cases. This inability of rulings to account for all instances is called 'equity', a process of supplementation where the law is amended in the light of a problematical case. Although Aristotle suggests that the judge should be restricted to as few judgements as possible the judge's role is primary for it is he who must judge whether this particular case can be subsumed under the universal rule. This also shows that *phronesis* has a strong connection to *praxis*. For Lyotard, this is especially important, because judgement for him is always connected to action understood as the politics of phrasing. In Lyotard's idiom, judgement is inseparable from the necessary practice of phrasing or linking without a rule.

Passages

Descriptives and Prescriptives
Justice
Links, Linkage
Phrase, Phrasing
Reason, Rationality
Rules

JUSTICE

Stuart Sim

Justice is a particularly problematical issue for Lyotard given his steadfast refusal to countenance the use of prescriptive criteria in the act of judgement. His provocative remark in *Just Gaming* ([1979] 1985) that 'I have a criterion (the absence of criteria) to classify various sorts of discourse here and there' (*JG*, 18) brings to the fore the difficulty anyone following Lyotard's line on judgement faces when it comes to trying to build a just society: it has to be an ad hoc, pragmatic process which gives no guide to future practice. Everything is thrown back on the particular judge in question in each instance of seeking to establish justice; or, as some commentators have complained, the judge's feelings, raising the spectre of emotionally biased judgements – exactly what most justice systems are generally striving to avoid. Most justice theorists want justice to be dispassionate and predictable, operating according to agreed principles which in the main are to be applied unilaterally (some limited scope can sometimes be allowed for negotiation on the ground of extenuating circumstances). Human rights, and the laws that protect them, for example, are held to obtain at all times and all places rather than to be a matter for debate every time around. The ideal in the standard legal system we have become used to in the West is for everyone to be treated the same before the law, subject to the same rules and procedures. That is what cannot happen under a Lyotardian dispensation, which is at once more flexible and less reliable:

we could never know in advance what would constitute justice, as Lyotard rejects the notion of there being any universal laws.

Justice proves to be an abiding concern of Lyotard's, however, and much of his writings is devoted to outlining his opposition to manifold injustices that have taken place in human history. Events like the Holocaust worry him a great deal, and it is a theme he returns to throughout his work (lying at the heart of *The Differend* ([1983] 1988a) and *Heidegger and "the jews"* ([1988b] 1990b), most notably). As far back as the Algerian writings of the 1950s he is noting how metanarratives – French colonialism and revolutionary Marxism equally, in his reading of the situation – can lead to injustice being visited upon the mass of a country's population by means of what he later comes to term a differend. The concept of the differend is based on a recognition of the deplorable ubiquity of injustice in human affairs, the repeated incidence of one discourse suppressing another, with those in control deploying it to render opposition all but invisible, thus entrenching themselves all the more firmly in power. The injustice in such cases lies in the stronger party preventing the weaker from even being able to complain of their oppressed state, with the former's discourse offering no way for dissenting views to be framed. Lyotard clearly feels very strongly about the existence of such injustices (a residual left-wing outlook keeps him on the side of the underdog), but does not believe they can be corrected through the standard legal systems we have developed in advanced societies. He argues that

Ordinarily, when the problem of justice is raised, it is from a problematic of the Platonic type. It will be said that the distribution of all that circulates in a given society is just if it conforms to something defined in Plato as justice itself, that is, as the essence, or the idea, of justice. (*JG*, 19)

But for Lyotard, 'the question of justice for a society cannot be resolved in terms of models' (*JG*, 25), and we should be adopting what he calls 'paganism' instead.

In a pagan society judgements have to be made on a case-by-case basis, meaning that that there is no overall conception of justice in operation. That would be closer to a just society in Lyotard's opinion, since it was treating each case on its own merits rather than according to a pre-established prescription. Prescriptives are frowned upon in Lyotard's scheme of things and for him militate against justice, which then becomes a mere mechanical exercise of checking whether judgement and prescription coincide. The argument back, of course, is that justice should be independent of individual circumstances and that such a state can only be achieved when there are universally accepted criteria in place by which to make decisions, which can then be compared in terms of their fidelity to the system's principles.

Lyotard has a keen awareness of injustice, particularly against scapegoated minorities (that left-wing bias in operation, for all his turn against traditional leftist politics in later career), and a lifelong interest in making philosophy responsive to it. Commendable though that is, his proposals for ending injustice are more problematic and rely heavily on a change of consciousness taking place in wider society. If we all bore witness to differends and the injustice they enshrine, as he recommends, then the world would no doubt be a better place; but how we are to bring about that desirable state remains more than a bit vague in Lyotard's writings. Philosophical politics would play its part in helping to overturn differends but, again, precisely how it would do so stays rather obscure – as would whether this would be enough to effect the wholesale change of social consciousness that is being looked for. In his defence, it can be said that Lyotard is hampered by not having a specific political theory to fall back on (as most of the left generally do, giving them ready-made answers to whatever issues may arise). That can be regarded as a mark of his intellectual honesty, however, in that it would run counter to his overall philosophy if ever he became a spokesperson for any metanarrative. The upshot is that, as we would expect from such a committed relativist and pragmatist for whom prescriptives are all too frequently an excuse to wield power over others, Lyotard will always be stronger in pointing up injustice than in providing us with a programmatic method by which to prevent it occurring.

Passages

Descriptives and Prescriptives
Differend
Jews, Judaism
Judgement
Paganism, Pagus
Philosophical Politics

KANT, IMMANUEL (1724–1804) – see 'aesthetics', 'archipelago', 'dialectics', 'drift, drifting', 'Enlightenment', 'enthusiasm', 'ethics', 'event',

'feminism', 'genre', 'judgement', 'legitimation', 'links, linkage', 'obligation', 'paralogy', 'phenomenology', 'philosophy', 'probity', 'sublime',
'unknown' and 'unpresentable'

KNOWLEDGE *Interesting*

Stuart Sim

The Postmodern Condition ([1979] 1984b) starts by announcing that its
concern is with 'the condition of knowledge in the most highly developed
societies' (*PC*, xxiii), and that condition is for Lyotard one that raises questions of legitimation above all. Who decides what is knowledge, and how do
they justify their decisions? Knowledge, he argues, has been for the modern
world an issue of matching data or statements against some 'metadiscourse
. . . making an explicit appeal to some grand narrative' (*PC*, xxiii), which is
assumed to hold the power of legitimation. The modern world has several
examples of such high-powered legitimating grand narratives: Marxism,
for example, or the various theories of emancipation that have emerged out
of the Enlightenment movement (based on principles such as democracy
and universal human rights). Postmodernism will be what Lyotard memorably dubs an attitude of 'incredulity towards metanarratives' (*PC*, xxiv)
of this kind, which dramatically changes the way we view and conceive of
knowledge. He goes on to claim that the more advanced forms of scientific
enquiry ('postmodern' in his reading) now offer the best example of the
changed status of knowledge in our society; their concern being to produce
not the known, but the unknown, to keep calling into question our theories
of the world by generating data that those theories cannot satisfactorily
explain. The argument is that there is no longer any credible legitimating
discourse that holds over time enabling us to decide unequivocally what
is true or false, and that what counts as knowledge is in a constant state of
flux. That, essentially, is the 'postmodern condition', and for Lyotard it is
an exciting and socio–politically radicalising state to be in, where authority
is always being challenged and institutional power undermined.

   The problem is, however, that those who control most of the systems
by which we live are now fixated on performance, and use that as a legitimating criterion. This is not good news for the majority of us since, '[t]he
application of this criterion to all of our games [by which Lyotard means
language games] necessarily entails a certain level of terror, whether soft
or hard: be operational (that is, commensurable) or disappear' (*PC*, xxiv).
We are reduced to subservience by the systems, which cynically impose
their will on us. This is a line of argument that Lyotard also pursues in

The Inhuman ([1988c] 1991a), which takes an even more pessimistic view of just how comprehensively the operational imperative has embedded itself in our daily lives and is worried that it may eventually lead to the marginalisation of the human race in the name of ever-greater efficiency. Machines, after all, can offer a degree of reliability in following programs that human beings simply cannot.

Rather than knowledge in its generally understood sense of true in accordance to a universally applicable legitimating principle, Lyotard champions the cause of narrative knowledge instead – and that in a fairly traditional form. The virtue of traditional narrative (as used in tribal contexts, for example) is that it requires no legitimating principle at all: 'it certifies itself in the pragmatics of its own transmission without having recourse to argumentation and proof' (*PC*, 27). Such narratives are merely handed down from generation to generation and the question of legitimacy never really arises for users. Lyotard regards this as a model from which we could still learn today, since the transmission from generation to generation does not involve any issue of power.

The upshot of the move that we have made into a postindustrial age is that we need to reassess what we mean by knowledge, particularly how we go about verifying it. Clearly, the modern method of doing so has fallen into disrepute, Lyotard speaking of its 'obsolescence' (*PC*, xxiv), and we must now think of knowledge as something much more fluid and changing, something to be processed through a range of language games without necessarily being transferable from one to another. We cannot fall back on the notion of some master narrative unproblematically conferring legitimacy on statements, and will have to settle for a relativist notion of truth instead where we just have to live with the fact of paradox and ambiguity in our discourses. The ideal for Lyotard from now on is the development of the little narrative ethos, which he contends drives 'postmodern' scientific enquiry. Under this dispensation knowledge is at best provisional, which at least in theory ought to work against the powerful interests that are at work in our society, the 'decision makers' as Lyotard pointedly refers to them (*PC*, xxiv), whose primary goal is to keep us in subjection to the demands of their systems. The more we emphasise the difference and incommensurability of the language games we play then the less power those decision makers will be able to exercise over us, and that for Lyotard is a healthy state for us to be in – even though it has to be said that grand narratives (for example, religious fundamentalism and neoliberal economics) have in fact reasserted themselves with something of a vengeance in the years since Lyotard submitted his 'report on knowledge', suggesting that he was overoptimistic about their apparent decline.

Perhaps the most critical point about knowledge in the current socio–political order for Lyotard is that it is only considered useful if it can be translated into information that can be incorporated into computer programs. Knowledge then simply becomes a product to be bought and sold on the market, and whoever controls this process wields enormous power. Lyotard's response is to call for the world's data banks to be thrown open to the general public: only in this way, he claims, could we have 'a politics that would respect both the desire for justice and the desire for the unknown' (*PC*, 67). Knowledge is for Lyotard a political battleground therefore and, as recent science has shown itself to be particularly effective at 'producing . . . the unknown' (*PC*, 60), we should follow its lead rather than allow ourselves to be taken in by the pretensions of grand narrative.

Passages

Language Games
Legitimation
Little Narrative
Performativity
Postmodern Science
Relativism

L

LACAN, JACQUES (1901–81) – see 'desire', 'dream-work', 'figure', 'May '68, *événements*', 'post-Marxism', 'poststructuralism', 'psychoanalysis' and 'tensor'

LACLAU, ERNESTO (1935–) AND **MOUFFE, CHANTAL** (1943–) – see 'Marxism' and 'pluralism'

LANGUAGE GAMES

Stuart Sim

Lyotard's view of human discourse draws heavily on the notion of language games formulated by Ludwig Wittgenstein in his *Philosophical*

Investigations ([1953] 1976). For the later Wittgenstein, language was a matter of learning how words are used and then deploying them in the approved fashion (as he saw it, a case of asking not for the meaning but the use). We come to regard this as a fixed system of communication, the natural order of things, but in fact it is only one 'game' among many other possibilities that could be instituted. The rules and procedures of any game were to be considered as conventional only, and could be changed to encompass different worldviews. Language games go on to play a central role in the argument of *The Postmodern Condition* ([1979] 1984b), where Lyotard makes three key observations about the activity: (1) 'their rules do not carry within themselves their own legitimation, but are the object of a contract, explicit or not, between players', (2) 'if there are no rules, there is no game', (3) 'every utterance should be thought of as a "move" in a game' (*PC*, 10). The conventional aspect is made particularly explicit.

Lyotard situates language games 'within the domain of a general agonistics' (*PC*, 10), meaning that they can be highly competitive, with players continually testing themselves against the particular game and its conventions in such a way as to induce countermoves from their peers. The more imaginative these countermoves prove to be then the better, with Lyotard arguing that displacement and disorientation are to be prized for their ability to generate the unexpected and keep altering the trajectory of the game. Predictable countermoves that offer no challenge to the other players are frowned upon. The whole point of discourse for Lyotard is to widen our knowledge, which ideally means confronting us with the unfamiliar on a regular basis. Social relations are held to thrive on this agonistic bias and the range of thought-provoking utterance it is capable of producing; indeed, for Lyotard, 'language games are the minimum relation required for society to exist' (*PC*, 15).

When we turn to *The Differend* ([1983] 1988a), however, Lyotard proceeds to move away from Wittgenstein's original conception, on the grounds that there is too much of the traditional sense of the 'subject' still left in it. As Lyotard put it in an interview: 'it seemed to me that "language games" implied players that made use of language like a toolbox, thus repeating the constant arrogance of Western anthropocentrism' (Van Den Abbeele 2004: 249). From now on he prefers to speak of phrase regimens, and despite a surface similarity to language games (internally applicable rules, no universal concepts), there are significant differences in the way that the former operate. In a typically poststructuralist gesture, Lyotard insisted it was language that set the conditions for discourse: '"Phrases" came to say that the so-called players were . . . situated by phrases in the universes those phrases represent, "before" any intention' (Van Den Abbeele 2004: 249). We were under an obligation to make links with phrases (and for Lyotard even silence counted as a link; in effect, we could not *not* link), but we could only be part of a chain that went on unfolding past our own individual contribution, meaning that we were never really in control of the process. In fact, we had no way of knowing where the chain would go after us or what links would be added to it. Discourse was a process in a constant state of becoming, not something determinate or determinable, conditions that meant no toolbox could ever exist.

This indeterminacy could be seen most strikingly in the sciences, where, Lyotard claimed, what was being produced most of the time these days by researchers was the unknown, thus raising severe doubts about the possibility of there ever being a Grand Unified Theory to explain the entire workings of the universe. As far as Lyotard is concerned, there will always be an unknowable, never a total picture. His own philosophical writing is no more complete than any other kind of phrasing: what happens to his books after they leave him is something he can neither control nor predict – 'you cast bottles to the waves' (*JG*, 9), as he conceived of the process. Although there are obvious echoes of Roland Barthes's 'death of the author' notion here, it would have to be noted that the Lyotardian reader would have no more control over the destination of the phrasing than the author did: all of us are engaged in casting bottles into the waves.

Passages

Agonistics
Incommensurability, Incompatibility
Links, Linkage
Obligation
Phrase, Phrasing
Unknown

LAW

Neal Curtis

Traditional, that is to say liberal democratic, approaches to the law are founded on the idea of autonomy. The laws made by liberal democratic governments are understood to be representative of the people's collective will, which is in turn made up of the rational deliberation of reasonable, autonomous individuals. The legal institutions and practices of the judicial system are also founded on this idea of autonomy in that 'due process' ought to satisfy a certain number of inalienable human and civil rights, and prevent the exercise of arbitrary power. For Lyotard, in contrast, the law takes the form of a radical heteronomy that directly challenges the basis of liberal democratic conceptions of law. He argues that the law is nothing more than the practical condition whereby we are first and foremost addressed. Having been born without wanting to be, and having been given our place by language, the subject is continually immersed in, and affected by, events to which he or she cannot but respond. The law, then, is both this condition of being held, and the necessity of a response. But because the law is empty of content, it does not signify what is to be done. It remains completely indeterminate in this regard.

In the first lecture of his *Peregrinations* (1988b [1990]) Lyotard explains that '[t]he desire to explore [thoughts, forms, phrases] is the duty we are committed to by the law' (*P*, 12). But he reminds us that 'very many ways are available to fulfill this duty. Moreover such a diversity would be more respectful of the constitutive withdrawal of the law than the exclusive privilege arrogated by theory' (*P*, 12). There is, then, a summons to respond and explore, but we do not know what this law commands for 'the law is only prescription as such' (*P*, 10), that is, *the prescript of being held in a prescriptive position.*

The law calls for a doing without determining what is to be done. It is the necessity of linking onto phrases without ever mastering them. This space of hesitation before the law, 'which forbids and prevents us from identifying with it and profiting from it' (*P*, 10), means two things for Lyotard. First, this ban on identifying with the law displaces theory, for no discourse, account or model is adequate to the law. In an essay in his *Political Writings* (1993) entitled 'The Grip' Lyotard shows how Jewish thought is exemplary of this condition. It does not *provide for itself*, but belongs to the Other. It is in the condition of *mancipium*, the gesture of taking hold. It is bound and obligated, rather than self-possessing and emancipated. Jewish thought, for Lyotard, is defined by a covenant made in an immemorial past to be fulfilled in an undisclosed future. The realisation of the promise is not in the hands of the Jews; there is simply a ceaseless waiting; and the waiting itself is uncertain. A key feature of anti-Semitism, for Lyotard, is the disbelief that the Jews will not absolve themselves of this incessance by adopting the sacrifice, reconciling themselves and guaranteeing their own destiny. But Lyotard argues there is no grace in sacrifice. Irrespective of the number or content of redemptive symbols we internalise in order to rid ourselves of this condition – be they Christian, techno-scientific, National Socialist, Communist, capitalist, liberal, etc. – the eschatology is deluded for we always remain held, in *mancipium*.

Second, as a consequence of this lack of a model, experimentation is required in the fulfilment of our duty to it. But returning to the argument in *Peregrinations* Lyotard warns us that every thinker 'carries . . . as a particular temptation the weakness or the possibility of ignoring that he or she is committed to a "I don't know what"' (*P*, 12). This is not to say that thinkers act as if there is no law to which they are beholden, rather, they seek to overcome the ban and our abandonment to this 'I don't know what'. They argue that the law is deducible. In this way the law is made our own; we are commensurate with it. No longer the anxiety of a radical questioning, it is now something determinate against which we might measure our judgements and actions as correct. Resistant to such model building, Lyotard's own writings constantly move in search of ways to answer the appeal. If anything, it might be characterised as a philosophy of the remainder, with the law itself being emblematic of that which remains or resists.

Passages

I Don't Know What
Jews, Judaism
Judgement
Justice
Links, Linkage
Power

LEGITIMATION

Derek M. Robbins

Some initial consideration of the work of Max Weber and Jürgen Habermas is necessary to contextualise Lyotard's contribution to the debate on legitimation. In a speech delivered at the University of Munich in 1918 – 'Politik als Beruf' ('Politics as a vocation') – published in 1919, and subsequently republished posthumously in his *Gesammelte Politische Schriften* (*Collected Political Works*) in 1921, Weber argued that 'If the state is to exist, the dominated must obey the authority claimed by the powers that be' (Max Weber 1948: 78). He proceeded to ask: 'why do men obey?'. He distinguished between the 'inner justifications' leading men to obey and the 'external means' adopted to enforce domination. The former can be regarded as types of *legitimacy* and the latter as mechanisms of *legitimation*. Weber famously suggested three types of legitimacy, which he called 'traditional', 'charismatic' and 'legal'. Whatever type of legitimacy might justify domination in any society at any time, Weber argued that continuous domination has to be maintained by administrations whose loyalties are enforced. Although Weber sought to articulate an explanatory model which might be universally applicable, his specific concern was with the analysis of developments in Germany. Whereas his model assumed that legitimated leaders used administrations to maintain their domination, he considered that, in the rational-legal state of his day, the leaders had undermined the autonomy of their administrators such that legitimation per se had marginalised the originally social grounds of legitimacy.

For Weber, modern political organisation is based on legal authority. Discussing the same formal circumstances in relation to religious organisation, Weber argued that, in our modern situation, a leader or official never exercises his power 'in his own right; he holds it as a trustee of the impersonal and "compulsory institution"' (Max Weber 1948: 295). Weber's definition of the modern situation corresponded with what Habermas was to describe as that of the modern bourgeois state. Habermas's *Strukturwandel der Offentlichkeit* (*The Structural Transformation of the Public Sphere. An Inquiry into a Category of Bourgeois Society*) was first published in 1962. It was a socio-historical account of the way in which, in the eighteenth century and, particularly in Britain, the traditional authority of the monarch, which was the legacy of feudal society, was controlled by the institution of a parliament representing the new bourgeoisie. His *Legitimationsprobleme im Spätkapitalismus* of 1973 (published in English translation in 1976 as *Legitimation Crisis* and in French in 1978 as *Raison et légitimité*) extended historically the earlier discussion so as to consider social organisation in 'capitalist' and 'post-capitalist' societies, with a view to speculating whether the examination of crisis tendencies 'in late- and post-capitalist class societies' might disclose 'possibilities of a "postmodern" society' (Habermas 1976: 17). Jürgen Habermas suggested that 'advanced capitalism' is of a different kind from the 'competitive capitalism' or 'liberal capitalism' which operated within and between political states. Systemically, 'advanced capitalism' operates independently of state regulation except when malfunctions occur causing states to 'intervene in the market' (Habermas 1976: 33). Habermas argued that 're-coupling the economic system to the political' in times of crisis 'creates an increased need for legitimation' (Habermas 1976: 36) and he devoted the third part of his book ('On the logic of legitimation problems') to consideration of the consequences of alternative views of the 'relation of legitimation to truth' – whether, in effect, *force majeure*, legitimacy and legitimation coincide or whether 'every effective belief in legitimacy is assumed to have an immanent relation to truth' (Habermas 1976: 97).

This is the immediate context for Lyotard's consideration of legitimation in *The Postmodern Condition* ([1979] 1984b). As its subtitle indicates,

Lyotard's book was concerned with the nature of knowledge within post-modern society. He did not dissent from Habermas's characterisation of the historical progress of Western social, political and economic organisation, but he differed from Habermas in refusing to accept that legitimation had to be either the consequence of a process of sociological/ social-psychological acceptance or of rationally grounded truth claims. As Lyotard says of legitimation, specifically contrasting himself with Habermas, 'I use the word in a broader sense than do contemporary German theorists in their discussions of the question of authority' (*PC*, 8). Lyotard's concern was more fundamentally epistemological and he argued that the kind of rationality invoked by Habermas to resolve legitimation problems was predicated on a view of 'science' that was no longer tenable. Habermas's recourse to rationality to resolve the legitimation crisis of 'postmodern' society involved the mobilisation of precisely the form of thinking which that society is in the process of superseding. It involved reference to a redundant 'grand narrative' and wrongly sought to secure communicative consensus. Lyotard's contention was, rather, that we have to determine 'whether it is possible to have a form of legitimation based solely on paralogy' (*PC*, 61) or scientific and linguistic pragmatics, and he concluded that, as a result of viewing legitimation pragmatically, we are now 'in a position to understand how the computerization of society affects this problematic' (*PC*, 67).

Lyotard explicitly stated that *The Postmodern Condition* was the report of a 'philosopher'. As a philosopher, he was already wrestling specifically with the problem of the kind of 'judgement' that would be compatible with the demands of postmodern legitimation. Following on from his attempt in *Discourse, Figure* ([1971] 2010) to liberate aesthetic experience from the tyranny of cognition, and his attempt in *Libidinal Economy* ([1974] 1993a) to characterise that liberated condition in a post-Freudian discourse, he attempted to find a way out of the alternative legitimacies proposed by Habermas, through detailed scrutiny of the work of Immanuel Kant. Whereas Kant's *Critique of Pure Reason* (1999 [1781]) and his *Critique of Practical Reason* (1997 [1788]) had seemed to emphasise forms of a priori regulation of thought and action, Lyotard sought to show (notably in *Just Gaming* ([1979] 1985), *The Differend*, 'Judicieux dans le différend' in Jacques Derrida et al., *La Faculté de juger* (1985) and in *Lessons on the Analytic of the Sublime* ([1991b] 1994)) that Kant's *Critique of Judgement* ([1790] 2000) represented a transition to a form of pragmatics, reconciling sensation and reason, which acceptably deployed aesthetic legitimation as a paradigm which could be deployed for all the kinds of legitimation needed in postmodern society.

Passages

Judgement
Knowledge
Law
Modern, Modernity
Postmodern Science
Reason, Rationality

LEVINAS, EMMANUEL (1906–95) – see 'Is it happening?', 'obligation', 'phenomenology' and 'poststructuralism'

LIBIDINAL ECONOMY $N\beta$

Ashley Woodward

Libidinal Economy ([1974] 1993a) is the title of one of Lyotard's most important books, and the name of an idea elaborated in that book and related essays. The 1974 book was in part a response to Gilles Deleuze and Felix Guattari's *Anti-Oedipus* ([1972] 1983), and a decisive point in Lyotard's break with his Marxist past. The book made little impact, and Lyotard quickly changed his theoretical frame of reference. He later execrated it as 'my evil book' (*P*, 13), and Lyotard scholars have generally either ignored it, preferring to focus on later works, or followed him in criticising it. More recently, however, some have begun to give the work renewed and more positive attention (Williams 2000; Woodward 2009).

The idea of libidinal economy originates with Sigmund Freud. For him, it indicates the system of energy (libido) circulating in the human body and psychic apparatus, investing regions and undergoing metamorphoses. Lyotard greatly extends the idea of libidinal economy into a global metaphysics and identifies it with political economy. In 'A Short Libidinal Economy' he asserts that libidinal economy is not limited to the organic body: 'It extends well beyond this supposed frontier because words, books, food, images, looks, parts of the body, tools and machines, animals, sounds and gestures are able to be invested, and thus function as charged regions and as channels of circulation' (*LRG*, 205). This extension then allows a libidinal economic model of society:

One can imagine any society as an ensemble of persons ruled by a system whose function would be to regulate the entry, the distribution, and the elimination of the *energy* that this ensemble spends in order to exist . . . The institution . . . would in general be any stable formation . . . transforming related energy into bound energy within a given field of the circulation of objects (the linguistic field, the matrimonial field, the economic field, etc.). (*LE*, 63)

Lyotard's libidinal economy is a description of social reality which allows him to map its stabilities and instabilities from the perspective of relatively kinetic or quiescent energies. Freud indicates two types of desire: wish-desire and libido-desire. Wish-desire is teleological and negative: it aims to possess something that is felt lacking. Libido-desire is a positive force of transformable energy. For Lyotard, Libido-desire is itself divided according to two regimes: Eros and the death drive. Eros contributes to the stable functioning and regulation of a system and operates according to Freud's principle of constancy (energy maintained at a low, stable level). The death drive deregulates the system and works against its unity and stable functioning: it produces intensities at very high or very low levels of energy, which Lyotard characterises as 'events'.

Lyotard explains the relation between libido-desire and wish-desire with the figures of the libidinal band and the theatrical volume. In itself, libido operates according to the primary psychical processes (the unconscious), which knows nothing of negation, space or time. This is envisaged as the libidinal band, a Möbius strip (without inside or outside), along which intensities run at infinite speed, such that their position cannot be localised in time or space. Wish-desire is described according to the slowing, folding over and hollowing out of the libidinal band to form a 'theatrical volume'. This describes wish-desire as a function of representation: that which is lacked is represented on the stage, while the real thing lies outside the theatre walls. The theatre also describes the secondary psychical processes: space, time, the concept and language, all of which depend on a basic distinction (this/not-this) absent from the libidinal band. The theatre dampens intensity, and Lyotard characterises it as a nihilistic depression.

The transformations of energy in the libidinal economy are described by what Lyotard calls *dispositifs* (set-ups or dispositions), arrangements that channel energy and which are themselves relative stabilisations of energy. *Dispositifs* include the organic body, social institutions, concepts, books, works of art, theories, systems of financial regulation and so on. They have two 'poles'. At one pole, energy is transformed into a well-regulated whole, stabilising the *dispositif*. At the other pole, intensities disrupt and deregulate the whole, causing it to change or be destroyed. *Dispositifs* thus distribute and transform energies according to the regimes of both Eros and the death drive, but the distributions of these regimes will differ markedly between different *dispositifs* (from the extremely ordered to the extremely disordered).

Reading Freud and Karl Marx together, Lyotard insists that every libidinal economy is a political economy (and vice versa). This identification is justified by an equation of Freud's libido and Marx's labour-power. Both are energetic plenitudes subject to similar systems of regulation: Freud's principle of constancy finds its parallel in Marx's law of value, both of which reduce the intensity of energy through a levelling equalisation. Lyotard sees capitalism as deeply duplicitous because, while the desires are dampened by the law of value (the 'concentratory zero'), this very law acts as an expedient to the circulation of desires in the system and the seeking out and production of new intensities (the 'zero of *conquest* . . . of profit or surplus-value' (*LE*, 211)).

In *Libidinal Economy* Lyotard rejects revolution and liberation in favour of a politics of conspiracy. Instead of the liberation of desire, he asserts the mutual *dissimulation* of desire and reason:

Let us be content to recognise in dissimulation all that we have been seeking, difference within identity, the chance event within the foresight of composition, passion within reason – between each, so absolutely foreign to each other, the strictest unity: dissimulation. (*LE*, 52)

Dissimulation means that there is no pure, free desire: desire is always channelled in *dispositifs*, but conversely all *dispositifs* contain an excess of desire they cannot fully regulate. In general, Lyotard tends to criticise theatricality, nihilism and excessively rigid *dispositifs*, and to privilege the transformative potential of libidinal intensities. The aim of the libidinal economist is to encourage a life-affirmative, creative flow of energy *within* systems, encouraging them to change and to produce new intensities. The highly experimental style in which *Libidinal Economy* is written is aimed at encouraging this flow.

Passages

Desire
Dispositif
Event
Great Ephemeral Skin
Great Zero
Tensor

Tom Waits Alice 2002 CD Release (music from a play by Wilson)
You haven't looked at me that way in years – but I'm still here
I love you till all time is gone, Turn the lights back on Come on.

LINKS, LINKAGE

Stuart Sim

One of the most pressing tasks in Lyotard's universe is establishing links between various genres of discourse, language games and narratives. Lyotard sees all of these as being like archipelagos, with each island in the group having its own internal system of organisation that distinguishes it from the others. Without such linkage we are left with the spectre of differends, which generally bring out the worst in human nature, with narratives, for example, attempting to gain control over their competitors, suppressing their identity in the process. Linkage, in contrast, does not, or should not, have such imperialist ambitions. Thoughts, too, require linkage, although Lyotard is at pains to remind us that our ability to do this should not be mistaken for meaning 'that we ever master them' (*P*, 12), thought as such being extraneous to us.

Lyotard explores linkage in some detail in *The Differend* ([1983] 1988a), highlighting its creative nature: 'to link is necessary; how to link is contingent' (*D*, 29). Problems arise, however, when those linking forget, or ignore, that latter point and assert an authority for their linkages. Immanuel Kant's philosophy is deeply concerned with finding such linkages between the various faculties, and he clearly wants these to be more than just contingent. Lyotard is not persuaded by his efforts, any more than he is by those post-Kantian philosophers 'who claim to assure passages over the abyss of heterogeneity or of the event' (*D*, 179). This applies to the philosophies of history put together by such as G. W. F. Hegel and Karl Marx, who from a Lyotardian perspective are linking together various genres of discourse with the intention of constructing a grand narrative that will invalidate other linkages. Lyotard's position is that it is only possible to make rules for the linkages inside a genre of discourse – where it is a case of specifying what phrases are permitted to be added to particular others, consistent with the genre's 'stakes' and 'ends' (*D*, 30). What we must never do is assume that those rules can be transferred to other genres, this being the mistake that Marx is guilty of when he moves from a philosophy of history to a narrative of emancipation.

Linkage involves an imaginative leap, although it is important to recognise that it leaves the identity of the linked entities intact, with each acknowledging the other's difference. Lyotard is adamant that 'contact is necessary', and that if we handle it with sensitivity then we can 'escape the differend' (*D*, 29). Human beings are held to be under an obligation to link (although Lyotard is careful to differentiate between obligation and necessity, the latter being a concept he is rarely willing to promote); in fact, we 'cannot do otherwise' (*D*, 80) than enter into the chain of communication constantly developing around us. Importantly, the act of linking, and thus extending the communication chain, keeps generating new states of affairs (that is, new events) for us to respond to creatively – precisely what Lyotard thinks we should be doing, rather than blindly following the grand narrative line.

Passages

Discourse
Genre
Language Games
Obligation
Pragmatics
Thought

LITERATURE

Stuart Sim

Lyotard tends to show a greater interest in painting than any of the other arts, and his writings on the subject run to several books, articles and exhibition catalogues; but the subject of literature also crops up at various points over the course of his oeuvre. This is often in the context of discussions about the difference between the modern and postmodern sensibility, as well as the impact of the concept of the sublime on both modernist and postmodernist aesthetics. Thus his remarks on James Joyce and Marcel Proust in 'Answering the Question: What is Postmodernism?', Lyotard conceives of the modern in the arts as that concerned 'to present the fact that the unpresentable exists. To make visible that there is something which cannot be conceived and which can neither be seen nor made visible' (*PC*, 78). In other words, to recognise that there is an unknowable and a sublime. For Lyotard, this comes through in the novels of Joyce and Proust, who 'both allude to something which does not allow itself to be made present' (*PC*, 80). As Lyotard sees it, that something is an excess that cannot be captured in their work – that of time in Proust's case, and of the book and literature in general in Joyce's (similar points are made about Joyce in the essay 'Return upon the Return' (published in *Toward the Postmodern* (1999), in which it is argued that *Ulysses* ([1922] 2008) demonstrates that language itself constitutes an excess the author can never exert control over).

The work of François Rabelais and Laurence Sterne are also seen to bear out Lyotard's contention that the modern and the postmodern interact continually with each other in recurring cycles, being taken as examples of postmodernists *avant la lettre*, 'in that they stress paradoxes, which always attest the incommensurability of which I am speaking' (*PW*, 28). (Sterne in particular has been claimed for the postmodern of late by many literary critics and theorists; see, for example, Pierce and de Voogd 1996.)

It is towards the end of his career, however, when Lyotard has his most sustained engagement with the literary world in two works on the French novelist, and then later Minister of Culture in President Charles de Gaulle's government, André Malraux: *Signed Malraux* ([1996b] 1999), and *Soundproof Room: Malraux's Anti-Aesthetics* ([1998a] 2001). Malraux is ostensibly a classic type of French public intellectual, but Lyotard sees him as a more complex version of this than the norm that he so ofen castigates elsewhere. Although Malraux's fiction clearly lacks the experimental quality that Lyotard seems most attracted to in creative activity (particularly apparent in his artist preferences, such as Barnett Baruch Newman and Marcel Duchamp), his overall approach to it is still very sympathetic. This comes across most vividly in *Soundproof Room*, where he praises his subject's lack of anti-Semitism (a rare enough trait in the 1920s and 1930s when Malraux is establishing his reputation, as Lyotard pointedly observes), as well as his general antipathy towards totalitarian political systems, whether fascist or communist. While there are 'some compositional shortcomings' to be noted on Malraux's part, such as 'a tendency toward the epic, a public speaker's eloquence', Lyotard nevertheless aligns him with figures like Georges Bataille and Albert Camus as writers who exhibit an 'ontological nausea' (*SR*, 10) about the state of their culture.

Malraux is someone who comes to recognise the transitory and unpredictable nature of existence, how it resists being directed by any ambitious grand narrative out to claim its superiority as a belief system over all others. He is, in Lyotard's terms of reference, an author sensitive to the event, and in that sense, '[h]is writing is not tragic but dramatic. No *fatum* commands from the outset the development or fulfillment of a singular life or guides it to its end' (*SR*, 58). While Malraux may be described as something of a formalist in his approach to writing (and Lyotard takes several sideswipes at the period's various aesthetic formalisms over the course of *Soundproof Room*), he manages to transcend this background: this is a writer who, as Lyotard approvingly notes, 'distrusts manifestoes and treatises' (*SR*, 66). Malraux's novels 'show rather than tell' (*SR*, 56), and that for Lyotard is one of his most commendable traits as a writer of fiction, and why his work still holds value for a postmodern age.

Passages

Event
Incommensurability, Incompatibility
Modernism
Sublime
Unknown
Writing

LITTLE NARRATIVE

Tony Purvis

'We can no longer have recourse to the grand narrative – we can resort neither to the dialectic of Spirit nor even to the emancipation of humanity' (*PC*, 60). Thus begins Lyotard's short prelude prior to his more detailed discussion of 'little narrative' under the subheading 'Legitimation by Paralogy' (*PC*, 60). We start this definition of little narrative with Lyotard's preamble, rather than his actual definition. This is because Lyotard is keen to provide a context for his deliberations as well as to establish one of the principal claims which runs throughout *The Postmodern Condition* ([1979] 1984b). Society, he argues, no longer has recourse to grand narratives in order to account for its government, its laws or its sciences.

Lyotard's own immediate context for these observations is the 1970s and the changing status of science and knowledge in an increasingly computerised, cybernetic society. He considers how the notion of 'emancipation' and 'progress', two of the key features of the knowledge secured by the grand narratives of science and history, take shape in modern culture. In postmodern cultures, grand narratives are met – and Lyotard urges that they should be met – with some measure of incredulity, so that their validation and validity are brought into doubt. The sense of scepticism here is in part due to the computerisation of knowledge as well as the shift from macro- to micro-political formations. This has led to a proliferation of little narratives. Knowledge legitimation in little narratives is not based on accepted or stultifying rules of argument but seeks out local and vernacular agreements. This is Lyotard's *paralogic* way of referring to the conversational, local and dispersed nature of knowledge production in post-industrial societies. The circulation of knowledge in contemporary cultures, he continues, is not centred on a single source or origin.

Little narratives highlight the quintessentially postmodern 'problem of the legitimation of knowledge today' (*PC*, 60). The 'petit récit' (*PC*, 60) or little narrative serves as an alternative and a challenge to the knowledge produced in the totalising account of the grand narrative. History, progress, science, law and morality, Lyotard proposes, have been conceived in terms of grand narratives which, in the recent past, served to structure society on the basis of an imagined consensus. Grand narratives are centripetal in their operation, tending to bring together that which is contradictory and dispersed. Little narratives function by casting doubt on common-sense claims, and are centrifugal, functioning on the basis of paralogy and indirection. If grand narratives promise a knowledge secured on the basis of consensus, little narratives show how knowledge is both decentralised and localised.

The notion of the little narrative initially arises out of Lyotard's analysis of late twentieth-century cultures and the spread of information technology. In contemporary society, competing narratives challenge a consensus which, in the past, validated and made credible the grand narrative's epistemological status. Little narratives, or local knowledges, are postmodern to the extent that they are accounts that signify an incredulity towards metanarratives, a crucial argument in all of Lyotard's work after *The Postmodern Condition*. Lyotard intends the phrase little narrative to evoke the mundane and often discontinuous ways in which (paralogic) knowledge circulates in postmodern cultures. He aims to show how a given system of thought is not axiomatically tied to scientific, rational or consensual modes of engagement but comes about in relation to contingency rather than historical inevitability. Although his work departs from archaeological and genealogical modes of inquiry, some of Lyotard's arguments in *The Postmodern Condition* are not dissimilar to those of Michel Foucault. Both critics suggest that the culture's *frameworks* for the production of knowledge ('epistemes' is how Foucault refers to these frameworks; and 'language games' is the phrase Lyotard borrows from Ludwig Wittgenstein) are not governed by the same rules as science, grammar and logic.

Language games are powerful in shaping knowledge. Although they might appear to operate beneath the immediate consciousness of the subject, they constitute, none the less, a nexus of conceptual possibilities and determine the boundaries of thought in a given domain and period. It is Wittgenstein's model of language games, but also speech–act theory and the associated notion of language performativity, that Lyotard openly appropriates in his own theory of the little narrative. In *The Postmodern Condition*, Lyotard states how language, no longer simply a (realist) means of representation or indeed communication, has become effective and culturally more significant than the period of the Enlightenment, on the basis of its performativity rather than the transmission of truth. Indeed, much of Lyotard's own writing has as its backdrop speech–act theory and the notion of language games. *Libidinal Economy* ([1974] 1993a), for instance, and his writings on art and aesthetics, are innovative in their combination of linguistic playfulness and social critique.

Postmodern cultures, typified as they are by a proliferation of little narratives competing with grand narratives, do not bemoan either the loss of the latter or of an imagined cultural coherence. Rather, the deconstruction of narrative means the locus of legitimation is no longer achieved on the basis of a (Habermasian) notion of consensus. However, because late capitalist cultures function in part on the basis of the endless advertising of the same product by means of new images and new languages, so paralogy is required by the culture itself in order for markets and products to seem always *more-than* new or *always* postmodern. Alternatively phrased, little narratives have always been central to a system that is in need of continual reinvention. Paradoxically, modernity's 'now-ness' and its paradigm of progress, are always threatened by a postmodern paralogy in which new rules of language entail changing the game of modernity.

Lyotard recounts in *The Postmodern Condition* how grand narratives are themselves objects of invention and experimentation which result in the production of new statements. This leads Lyotard to show how the model of knowledge as the inevitable or progressive outcome of consensus is obsolete. Little narratives, akin now to Lyotard's notions of both desire and paralogy, make way for the possibility of a new sense of ethics, as well as justice and knowledge, as subjects invent language games in order to talk anew about human complexity.

Passages

Dissensus
Enlightenment
Knowledge
Legitimation
Narrative of Emancipation
Paralogy

MALRAUX, ANDRÉ (1901–76) – see 'dissensus', 'intellectuals' and 'literature'

MANDELBROT, BENOIT (1924–) – see 'catastrophe theory and chaos theory', 'clouds', 'fractals', 'postmodern science' and 'thought'

MARX, KARL (1818–83) – see 'capitalism', 'desire', 'dialectics', 'drift, drifting', 'feminism', 'great Zero', 'libidinal economy', 'links, linkage', 'Marxism': 'modern, modernity', 'peregrination', 'post-Marxism', 'post-modernism' and 'sublime'

MARXISM

Stuart Sim

Marxism was an immensely influential force in French political and intellectual life in the years when Lyotard was growing up and he could hardly be unaffected by it. For the rest of his career he is in regular dialogue with it, even if this is to mean eventually that he considers himself to be in a state of 'profound *différend*' (*P*, 46) with it as a system of thought.

As a theory Marxism can be very seductive, offering a fully worked-out, philosophically sophisticated programme for resolving all humankind's social and political problems, and many French intellectuals found it to be very congenial on that basis: society was to become completely egalitarian, economic exploitation to be ended, and humanity liberated from the poverty and socio-political repression that had dogged it throughout so much of its history. The Soviet Union came to be regarded as the bright hope for humankind's future by such thinkers, and it would not be until after the Second World War that any really serious criticism came to be offered of its policies in their circles. Even then, Marxism's stock continued to be high among the French intellectual community, and the French Communist Party (PCF) remained an important voice in French political life. Significant reinterpretations of Marxist theory were still being put forward well into the 1960s by such as Louis Althusser and his followers, with their structural Marxism (see, for example, *Lire le Capitale* (1965), later translated into English in abridged form as *Reading Capital* (1968)). Lyotard was working in an intellectual and academic context in the 1950s and 1960s, therefore, in which Marxism was a highly respected tradition of thought and setting much of the agenda for debate.

The year 1968 and the aftermath of its tumultuous *événements* brought about a radical change in Marxism's fortunes in this milieu, however, prompting defection from the official Marxist cause among many of the French intelligentsia, alienated by the PCF's support for the Gaullist government against the alliance of students and workers that had emerged as an oppositional force. This sense of alienation helped to promote a shift, as thinkers like Lyotard conceived of it, away from Marx and towards theorists of desire like Freud (see Lyotard's *Dérive a partir de Marx et Freud* (1973a)). It marked a generalised reaction against universal theories that was to become one of the hallmarks of postmodern thought, as conspicuously present in the work of such as Gilles Deleuze and Felix Guattari, and Jacques Derrida, for example, as in that of Lyotard. In Lyotard's ringing words, '[t]he decline, perhaps the ruin of the universal idea can free thought and life from totalizing obsessions' (*PW*, 7).

Lyotard's *Libidinal Economy* ([1974] 1993a) is one of the landmarks of this growing anti-Marxist trend, and he becomes one of the most vociferous critics of Marxism as both philosophy and political theory – and, as such, a critical voice in the development of post-Marxism. Marxism ultimately represents everything that Lyotard dislikes about grand narrative and what he regards as the hijacking of philosophical discourse by politics. Marxists end up uncritically defending their own particular narrative, thus putting themselves in the service of their political masters – precisely what Lyotard believes philosophers should at all costs avoid doing. When philosophers operate according to a prearranged scheme, and Marxism is a very schematic doctrine indeed, then they cease to be proper philosophers as Lyotard understands the term and turn into mere intellectuals. And, as Lyotard never tires of pointing out to us, intellectuals have shown themselves only too willing over the years to be seduced by political establishments, succumbing to the temptation 'to turn themselves into the representatives of an authority' (*PW*, 95). Marxism has had more than its share of such individuals, prepared to turn a blind eye to the excesses that a totalising obsession could inspire (Jean Baudrillard's demolition of the Marxist obsession with production in *The Mirror of Production* ([1973] 1975) is another notable example of the sea-change taking place in French intellectual life of the period.)

Nor was *Libidinal Economy* Lyotard's first sally against Marxist orthodoxy. In his Algerian writings of the 1950s and 1960s for the *Socialisme ou Barbarie* journal, he had complained that the imposition of Marxist categories and revolutionary methods on that nation was not answering its real needs; that it was instead most likely leading to eventual dictatorship by the main revolutionary party, the FLN, 'a dictatorship that does not shrink from the use of terror' (*PW*, 208) as Lyotard is moved to report. Algeria was being made to conform to a theory designed for Western industrialised societies, and its difference from these as a largely peasant-based economy was simply not being acknowledged. The doubts about how grand narratives can distort people's lives are to crystallise later in the uncompromising attack on Marxism in *Libidinal Economy*, with the *événements* as a crucial intervening experience for Lyotard, whose faith in universalising political theories, never very strong in the first place, now completely evaporates.

Given his insistence on the importance of the event in human affairs – and the 1968 *événements* certainly qualified as an instance of this, an irruption into everyday life that no-one really foresaw – Lyotard could only have difficulty with the notion of a dialectic working its way through history and largely determining human behaviour. From such scepticism comes the 'profound *différend*' with both Marxism and his former colleagues in the Socialisme ou Barbarie and Pouvoir Ouvrier groups, particularly with the historian Pierre Souyri, with whom Lyotard had developed a close working relationship in their role as political activists. As Lyotard records in *Peregrinations* (1988b [1990]), Souyri himself felt this differend to be so profound 'that he considered it pointless to try to resolve' (*P*, 48), professing an unshaken belief in Marxism's value as philosophical theory and political method. Lyotard, however, was by this stage having severe doubts about 'Marxism's ability to express the changes of the contemporary world' (*P*, 49) (a line later to be elaborated on by Ernest Laclau and Chantal Mouffe in their post-Marxist writings such as *Hegemony and Socialist Strategy* (1985)), and particularly 'its claim to absolute universality' (*P*, 50). Marxism henceforth becomes for Lyotard merely one among a multitude of competing genres of discourse in the political sphere, and from his perspective no longer one of any great relevance.

Passages

Algeria
Differend
May '68, *Événements*
Libidinal Economy
Post-Marxism
Socialisme ou Barbarie

MAY '68, *ÉVÉNEMENTS*

David Bennett

As a philosophy lecturer at the University of Paris X-Nanterre in 1968, Lyotard was actively involved with the prime movers of the student-led, anti-government riots that began in Paris and briefly paralysed the French state in May of 1968. Inspiring a general strike of eleven million workers that brought France's economy to a standstill for a fortnight, the student protests against the French education system, technocratic rationalism and consumer capitalism – not to mention its cold-war alternative, Stalinist totalitarianism – prompted President Charles de Gaulle to take refuge over the German border in the French air base at Baden Baden and almost caused the collapse of his government.

Already disillusioned with theory-driven political movements, Lyotard had ended his twelve-year membership of the militant Marxist collective Socialisme ou Barbarie ('either socialism or barbarism') two years earlier (1966), and his jaundiced view of political organisations and their founding abstractions was confirmed by the French Communist Party's (PCF's) notorious failure to support the student revolt, its insistence on itself holding the reins of any revolutionary movement, and its siding with the de Gaulle government in the interests of containing the revolt. At the time of the initial riots, Lyotard promised to write a history, or rather an 'anti-history', of the Movement of March 22, the group of Nanterre student '*enragés*' (rowdies) who had ignited the uprising that would become known as 'May 68'. For good reason, he never got beyond drafting what he called 'an unpublished introduction to an unfinished book on the movement of March 22' (*PW*, 60–7). Preferring to interpret the '*événements*' or happenings of May '68 as an explosion of irreducibly singular energy-events, Lyotard had an investment in *not* making historical sense of them – not assimilating them to a 'grand narrative' such as governed the PCF's vision of its own historical role and destiny. The student radicals had caught Leninist doctrine unawares by showing that there *could* be a revolutionary movement without a revolutionary theory, and Lyotard thanked them for changing his political mood, which he said had been swinging between party-line dogmatism and impotent doubt, by staging the explosive energy-event of May '68 which proved that newness could enter the world.

For Lyotard, as for other influential poststructuralist thinkers of his generation, the key feature of May '68 was that it didn't fulfil anyone's master plan. Catching all established theories of politics off-guard, the *événements* were explosive evidence of 'what this society represses or denies, a figure of its unconscious desire' (*PW*, 63), a subversive force in what Lyotard would later call the 'libidinal economy' of contemporary capitalism and its politics. An 'event', in Lyotard's sense of the term, is a singular, unpredictable occurrence whose strangeness 'dismantles consciousness' (*I*, 7), challenging existing codes of interpretation and genres of representation, demanding that everything that had led up to it be rethought. Thus, an irreducibly singular political event is one that forces a rethinking of politics as such, of what political conditions, action, agency, strategy, goals and value might all be (and much the same goes for an artistic 'event' or a historical 'event'). Lyotard sometimes characterises the 'event' in terms of the Freudian notion of the 'return of the repressed', the traumatic eruption of unconscious material (or of what Jacques Lacan called 'the Real'), as when he writes of an artistic event: 'it is what consciousness cannot formulate, and even what consciousness forgets in order to constitute itself' (*I*, 90).

The Movement of March 22 may have had its precedents in the long anarchist, anti-organisational tradition in which independently formed councils of workers, soldiers or peasants seized the initiative from the existing parties, but the student 'rowdies' extended their critique to *all* forms of representation, perceiving them 'as immediate and lasting obstacles to the liberation of potential critical energy' (*PW*, 61). In Lyotard's vitalist ontology, 'representation' blocks or binds energy, much as Sigmund Freud's neurotic symptom, 'representing' repressed desire, is interpreted as a blockage of libidinal energy. Any society is composed of institutions, including those of representative politics, which are relatively stable formations that, as such, transform 'free energy' into 'bound energy'. Hence, Lyotard argues, 'One could call an event the impact, on the system, of floods of energy such that the system does not manage to bind and channel this energy; the event would be the traumatic encounter of energy with the regulating institution' (*PW*, 64). Capitalism is such a system, regulating the introduction, circulation and elimination of ever greater quantities of energy, with its 'labour theory of value' enabling any object to be exchanged for any other that 'contains the same number of units of energy'. The young rowdies of Nanterre are thus heirs to the likes of Dada, Paul Cézanne, John Cage and Werner Heisenberg, who mounted their critiques of representation in the spheres of literature, painting, music and physics. Lyotard suggests that the movement's 'destruction of representation in the socio-political sphere should be placed in parallel with the structural autocritiques carried out over the past century in mathematics, physical science, painting, music and literature in turn' – except that the anti-social or post-social *enragés*, 'by extending their critique of representation to society itself, marked not only the end of specific spheres, but also the end of specific *ends*' (*PW*, 61).

Given the impossibility of representing this critical end to representation – of writing a history of this end to historical ends or goals – it is unsuprising that Lyotard's antihistory of May '68 remained unwritten. As he put it in his unpublished introduction to his unwritten book: 'a history book always aims to produce a *historian's knowledge* . . . a discourse . . . in which the non-sense of the event will be rendered intelligible, fully signified, and thus in principle predictable' (*PW*, 66), whereas the Movement of March 22 had 'performed a work of unbinding, an antipolitical work, that brings about the collapse rather than the reinforcement of the system' (*PW*, 65–6).

However, in the event (as we say), the system survived. Following brutal police suppression of student protesters (many of whom had travelled to Paris from the provinces and abroad to join the heady cause for 'liberation' – the writer of this entry among them), the violence evaporated, the trade unions and PCF did shabby deals with Prime Minister Georges Pompidou, the workers returned to work, the students went on summer vacation, and the general election of 23 June returned the Gaullist party to power in even greater numbers. But the radical promise of the failed revolution continued to resonate in French intellectual life, especially among once-militant leftists whose disenchantment with party politics it confirmed. Their insistence that *mai 68* remain a proper-named 'event' that punctuates or punctures History, rather than being 'explained away' by assimilation to either a socialist or a capitalist 'master-narrative' of modern European political history, is arguably symptomatic of the ideological impasse and bankruptcy that the French Left was experiencing by June of 1968. Western Marxism since the 1930s had been trying to fuse itself with psychoanalytic theory in an effort to explain why the proletariats of industrially developed nations failed to translate their class consciousness into socialist revolution. Both the spontaneous explosion and the rapid defusion of the May '68 uprising confounded many of the basic assumptions of Western Marxists. Much of their radical vision would be displaced from the discourse of politics into that of aesthetics. Lyotard was not the only disappointed '*soixante-huitard*' (sixty-eighter) and philosopher of his generation who subsequently looked to modernist art for those epistemologically confounding 'events' that he had once hoped for from politics.

Passages

Event
History, Historians
Marxism
Politics
Poststructuralism
Socialisme ou Barbarie

MEMORY – see 'anamnesis', 'Christianity', 'forgetting' and 'history, historians'

MERLEAU-PONTY, MAURICE (1908–61) – see 'phenomenology', 'post-Marxism', 'thought without a body' and 'touch'

METANARRATIVE see **GRAND NARRATIVE**

MODERN, MODERNITY

Lloyd Spencer

Let us begin by using the terms 'modern', 'modernity', etc. in ways that summarise their usage in wider debates before turning to look at their significance for Lyotard. To begin with let us just remember the long period of history in which capitalism develops as a world system with global trade spreading local innovations. Science and the scientific method are established along with technological innovation, leading to social upheaval, the factory system and so on. All of this accompanies centuries of schism and struggle within Christianity which in turn leads to continual political upheaval, the emergence of new political structures and institutions. And all of this necessitates the development of a certain acceptance of pluralism, including the acceptance of secularism, as somehow constitutive of modern society.

Although diverse chronological and geographical mappings might be offered, modernity as a historical epoch is the summation of these changes. The 'Early Modern' period might be thought of as that very broad period of history including the Renaissance and Reformation in which these various changes first emerged and began to act upon one another to produce a cumulative and apparently irreversible historical dynamic which is sometimes referred to as modernity.

Modernity as an idea implies a kind of pluralism, a recognition of there being a diversity of contending viewpoints, perspectives, and eventually of different disciplines and sciences. This proliferation of perspectives takes place in opposition to the centralising force of the certainties offered by religion – at least as conceived by the modernisers. Proliferation of (often competing) perspectives is legitimated as serving the development of knowledge and learning conceived as a whole. Some kind of ultimate reconciliation of perspectives, some kind of wholeness, or comprehensive-ness, some kind of universality seems to be involved as a goal or ideal even in the developments of pluralism.

Modernity is, for Lyotard, to be grasped as a metanarrative. Indeed wherever, or whenever, one locates it, one could say that modernity comes into being with the idea that history has a shape and a direction (as it does very notably in the work of G. W. F. Hegel and Karl Marx). Modernity generates as its opposite the sense of the past as something old-fashioned, traditional, obscure; something in which we might be entangled, even enslaved. Modernity includes the sense of the future as a horizon of pos-sibility and of improvement and, as Jürgen Habermas puts it, that the future has already begun. Habermas for one feels that this is an 'unfinished project' which it is in humanity's interest to continue.

To be modern, according to Lyotard, is to seek legitimation in one or other form of metanarrative suggested by that sense of the future. Change and innovation are legitimated by being seen as part of the broader evolu-tion or development of human knowledge and self-understanding. The dynamism implied in the notion of modernity is one that is oriented towards a future enhanced by learning and greater understanding but, of course, also great control.

To be modern involves disentangling oneself from conventional think-ing and the authority of tradition. This sense of liberation from supersti-tion and obscurantism is a legacy of the struggles of philosophers (the *philosophes*) of the Enlightenment and the value they put on free thinking and independence from the authority of the Church and the *dictat* of arbitary political power. During the Enlightenment modernity became an explicit and central theme, became, one could say, a conscious and much-contested goal.

Modernity, or modern temporality, becomes an impulsion to 'exceed itself into a state other than itself . . . Modernity is constitutionally and ceaselessly pregnant with its postmodernity' (*I*, 25). Modernity minus underpinnings that are teleological or quasi-theological, stripped of the idea of a movement towards an ultimate end state, is already, in this sense, postmodernity.

It is worth reflecting on the fact that modernity itself becomes not just an ideal but also a challenging and sometimes frightening reality as the period of the Enlightenment comes to an end amid agricultural and indus-trial innovations, dramatic social change and a series of political upheav-als. Change becomes the norm. Being modern becomes more and more conventional. So much so that the problems of modernity and of being modern come to be addressed by an increasingly diverse range of modern-isms, each mapping modernity and outlining its challenges in its own way.

'Is this the sense in which we are not modern? . . . Are "we" not telling, whether bitterly or gladly, the great narrative of the end of narratives?' (*D*, 135). Having defined being modern as conceiving of humanity as having a goal, Lyotard poses the question of whether the abandonment of metanarratives which he proposes is not itself being offered as a new goal for humanity and thus the modern in a new guise:

Is postmodernity the pastime of an old man who scrounges in the garbage-heap of finality looking for leftovers, who brandishes unconsciousness, lapses, limits, confines, gulags, parataxis, nonsenses, or paradoxes, and who turns this into the glory of his novelty, into his promise of change? But this too is a goal for a certain humanity. A genre. (A bad parody of Nietzsche. Why?) (*D*, 136)

Lyotard's rather pessimistic view of history as a cycle of modernities and postmodernities becomes apparent at such points, although that does not mean he thinks we should be fatalistic in our outlook, rather that we should be aware how easy it is to be drawn into the grand narrative game, even when apparently rejecting it, and how necessary it is to stay vigilant against the prospect. It always has to be remembered that Lyotard is as capable of being critical of the postmodern as the modern, and that he will shy away from anything that becomes programmatic.

Passages

Enlightenment
Legitimation
Marxism
Modernism
Pluralism

MODERNISM

Lloyd Spencer and Stuart Sim

Modernism is an overarching label given to a tendency – an idea or ideal – which flourished across literature and the arts from roughly speaking the middle of the nineteenth century until it began to be challenged some time after the middle of the twentieth. By overarching it is meant that many more or less self-conscious movements in art and literature can be included under the modernist umbrella: Impressionism, Futurism, Cubism, Surrealism, all spring to mind as stridently and self-consciously

modernist movements. The opposition to academic, traditional or conservative norms of artistic (or literary) practice which is part of the
modernist impulse is clearly in evidence in the setting up of the first
Impressionist salon in 1874. Given the variety of styles and forms that this
opposition proceeded to generate over the course of its development, commentators now usually talk of 'modernisms'.

Modernisms characteristically involve technical or formal innovation
in order to express new content and respond to new challenges. In other
words, modernism poses the question of representation and the adequacy
of the inherited forms of representation. Lyotard has devoted books and
essays to several individual artists generally seen as 'modernist' including
Marcel Duchamp (*Duchamp's Trans/formers* ([1977d] 1990a)), Barnett
Baruch Newman ('Newman and the Instant', in *The Inhuman* ([1988c]
1991a)) and Jacques Monory (*The Assassination of Experience by Painting –
Monory* ([1984a] 1998)). Here there is no question of attempting to draw
distinctions between modernist and postmodernist (and there are many
passages in Lyotard's writings which treat these as intimately intermin-
gled). These treatments of modernist artists generally allow Lyotard to
think further some of the paradoxes of temporality (instant, event, chronol-
ogy) and the limits of representation or representability (and the notion of
the sublime). Newman's paintings raise the issue of 'Is it happening', for
example, and Duchamp's work is so designed as to resist critical interpretation, thus frustrating any attempt to pin any definitive meaning on them.

Lyotard sees both modernist and postmodernistic artistic practice as
being aware that there is something their efforts cannot capture, an unpresentable element in the sense that reality can never be completely captured
in a way that traditional, premodernist society believed. Modernity, he
argues, 'cannot exist without a shattering of belief, and without discovery of the "lack of reality" of reality' (*PC*, 77), and postmodernity shares
that characteristic. A critical distinction that Lyotard draws between the
former and the latter, however, is that modernists evince a nostalgia for
that lost cultural organicism, with its agreed system of rules and conventions which artists were trained to adhere to. Indeed, modernists are
viewed as being haunted by a sense of lack in this respect:

I shall call modern the art which devotes its 'little technical expertise' . . . as
Diderot used to say, to present the fact that the unpresentable exists. To make
visible that there is something which can be conceived and which can neither be
seen nor made visible: this is what is at stake in modern painting. (*PC*, 78)

There is, in other words, an 'aesthetic of the sublime' (*PC*, 77), an engagement with what transcends human understanding, which can be found at

work in the art of such as Kasimir Malevitch and his all-white paintings, and the linguistic experiments of James Joyce.

Postmodern art, in contrast, does not suffer from this 'nostalgia for the unattainable' (*PC*, 81). Its practitioners' concern instead is to make us ever more aware of the unpresentable, to endeavour to put this at the forefront of their art. Rather than a sense of regret at no longer being able to draw on rules and conventions, the postmodern artist accepts, and even celebrates, the fact that 'the work he produces cannot be judged according to a determining judgment, by applying familiar categories to the text or to the work. Those rules and categories are what the work of art itself is looking for' (*PC*, 81). Yet Lyotard also continues to emphasise the overlap between the two approaches, insisting that the postmodern is 'undoubtedly a part of the modern' and that '[a] work can become modern only if it is first postmodern' (*PC*, 79). It is also worth noting how much of his writing on aesthetic matters deals with figures who are generally classified as modernist – as in the case of Duchamp above, and, in music, composers such as Pierre Boulez and Luciano Berio.

It could perhaps be argued that Lyotard is not as critical as his contemporaries can be when it comes to modernism. Postmodernist artists have tended to turn their back on it and to regard it as having ossified into a style that, in its way, became just as rule-bound as the traditional styles it had rejected. Charles Jencks's attack on the 'International Style' in architecture (see *The Language of Post-Modern Architecture* (1984)) was motivated by just such a belief that practitioners were being constrained by a ruling aesthetic which was quite exclusive in its demands. The recent development of the notion of the 'altermodern', however, whereby there is a return to at least some of the spirit and ideals of modernism in its early days in order to break with what is felt by many to be the predictability that has crept into the postmodernist aesthetic (double-coding, pastiche, etc.) indicates that Lyotard's view of the modern and the postmodern as cyclical phenomena might be very much on the right lines in the aesthetic arena (for the altermodern, see Nicholas Bourriaud, *Altermodern: Tate Triennial* (2009)).

Passages

Aesthetics
Is It Happening?
Modern, Modernity
Rules
Sublime
Unpresentable

MOUFFE, CHANTAL (1943–) AND LACLAU, ERNESTO (1935–)
– see 'Marxism' and 'pluralism'

MUSIC

David Bennett

Avant-garde art-music was a key source for Lyotard's aesthetic theory. His essays include recurring discussions of Theodor Adorno's *Philosophy of New Music* ([1948] 1973) and commentaries on composers ranging from Franz Schubert, Robert Schumann, Gustav Mahler, Claude Debussy, Erik Satie and Edgar Varèse to John Cage, Pierre Boulez, Luigi Nono and Luciano Berio. His late essay 'Music and Postmodernity' ([1996a] 2009b) provides an important restatement of his theories of postmodernism as a watershed 'event' in cultural history as well as an exposition of his musical aesthetics.

Like Boulez (whom he admired), Lyotard scorned the stylistic eclecticism and pastiche often identified with 'postmodernist' music. While defenders of trends such as 'crossover music' (which fuses classical with popular styles) or 'world music' (which fuses Western and non-Western or indigenous styles) have celebrated them as a postmodern 'democratisation' of taste-cultures and a dismantling of cultural hierarchies, Lyotard and Boulez dismissed them as products of an anything-goes-if-it-sells ethos that confuses artistic value with market value. (As Lyotard puts it in *The Postmodern Condition* ([1979] 1984b): 'Eclecticism is the degree zero of contemporary general culture . . . It is easy to find a public for eclectic works. By becoming kitsch, art panders to the confusion that reigns in the "taste" of patrons' (*PC*, 76).) Lyotard's own preference was for music that is, literally, very hard to listen to.

In 'Music and Postmodernity', Lyotard follows Arnold Schoenberg and Adorno in suggesting that 'the history of Western music may be thought of globally as the grand narrative of the emancipation of sound' (MP, 38) from the inherited rules and customs of composition. Experimenting with new sound-technologies such as synthesisers, modern composers have progressively discovered what sound is capable of when those rules are stretched and broken. They have discovered that the laws of harmony, counterpoint, melodic progression, scales, modes, rhythm and so on are neither natural nor necessary to music but contingent — even what we call 'notes' are just arbitrary divisions of the sound-continuum. The only essentially musical element turns out to be what Lyotard calls 'sonorous matter' itself: 'the vibration of the air with its components, frequency, duration, amplitude, colour and attack, which acoustics, or the physics of sound, and psychophysiology analyse' (MP, 38). If there are no longer any foundational principles or truths in musical art, then contemporary composers feel the need to reinvent not just the style or form but the very rules of music for each work they compose. In the absence of foundations, a certain 'postmodernist' cynicism can creep into contemporary artistic practices, allowing market forces to occupy the role of artistic rules, defining art as anything the art-buying public is prepared to purchase ('the rule of the market for cultural objects then makes up for the absence of artistic rules' (MP, 39)).

Lyotard points out that musical modernists, from Debussy and Satie to Boulez and Cage, looked to oriental models (Indian, Chinese, Japanese musics) for ways of freeing sound from the narrative and expressive functions that it traditionally serves in most Western music. The narrative structure of much premodernist Western music dramatises tensions between theme and form, desire and discipline, individual and society, and shows how they can or, sometimes, cannot be harmoniously resolved. Lyotard describes the traditional narrative structure of Western musical forms (prior to atonal, aleatory or minimalist music) as 'recounting an odyssey, happy or unhappy, of a subjectivity', or 'narrating the drama of a subjectivity in disagreement with itself' (MP, 42). Liberating sound from form means emptying it of meaning or use-value, so that it no longer speaks to or for a subject; without address or destination, it becomes mere 'sonorous matter', and as such what Lyotard calls 'inhuman'. In so far as our ears are culturally programmed to filter mere 'sonorous matter' out of our perceptions of music (just as sound engineers filtered out the 'glitches' of audio-technology from music, before the practitioners of 'noise art' and 'glitch music' turned these accidental by-products into yet another medium of composition and 'expression'), then to be forced to sense this meaningless 'sonorous matter' is to be given an intimation of the limits of our own hearing and musical appreciation. Lyotard describes this as a sense of the 'inaudible' within the 'audible', arguing that, in any work of artistic value, there is always an element 'which defies ordinary reception or perception, and which will defy all commentary', 'it gestures towards a "presence" which is not presentable' (MP, 41). In *The Inhuman* ([1988c] 1991a) he characterises the encounter with formless 'sonorous matter' as the equivalent of 'listening to listening . . . lending the ear an ear' (*I*, 167), implicitly aligning his musical aesthetics with similar theories of defamiliarisation, estrangement and self-reflexivity in modernist art, such as Bertolt Brecht's or Viktor Shklovsky's. 'Our ears are deaf to what sound can *do*', he writes in 'Music and Postmodernity': 'we must give back to the act of listening the power to open itself to the inaudible' (MP, 40–1).

For Lyotard, the artistic value of any work consists not in its maker's intentions but in the 'event' of which the work is a trace or manifestation. The composer's task is neither to express her/himself nor to please an audience but 'to let the sound perform an act which seems to exceed the audible' (MP, 40), reopening the question of how and what we can hear, of what constitutes music and its appreciation. Such sonic 'acts' or 'events', which (like the sublime) exceed our powers of conceptualisation, do not lend themselves to a progressive narrative of musical history: 'The acts, which are neither the contents nor the forms of the work but its absolute power to move us, do not progress or improve during the course of history . . . The power to affect sensibility beyond what can be sensed does not belong to chronological time' (MP, 40). Despite this rejection of progress and teleology in music, Lyotard clearly favoured the perplexing and disturbing compositions of his high-modernist contemporaries, such as the 'deconstructive' composer Berio, over the music of their classical and romantic predecessors.

Passages

Aesthetics
Antifoundationalism
Event
Inhuman
Modernism
Sublime

NARRATIVE

Angélique du Toit

Narrative provides the vehicle through which we come to understand the world and ourselves by making communication within society possible. Shared narratives are the basis on which ideologies, cultures and traditions are based. Furthermore, narrative provides meaning to experiences and makes possible the creation of individual and group identities. Narrative is a powerful means by which to influence others through a certain way of thinking. It is multilayered and reflects the complexity of

interacting relationships of power. The narrative of a society is told from
the perspective of the rulers of the particular society. *The Postmodern
Condition* ([1979] 1984b) was a report on knowledge in the sciences and
technology in the most advanced societies in the developed world, and
in it Lyotard refers to postmodernism as a 'crisis of narratives' which
had emerged in the years prior to the publication of this book. The
crisis as he perceives it is associated with knowledge in these developed
societies.

Lyotard questions the scientific knowledge which has emerged and
which distinguishes itself from common knowledge or the knowledge
of the people. He challenges the idea that scientific knowledge represents the totality of knowledge, and argues that the narrative of scientific knowledge was dominated by one of emancipation and progress in
which the heroes were the scientists themselves. The scientific narrative
marginalised the knowledge of the people as primitive. Instead, Lyotard
claims that knowledge is more than the determination and application of
the criteria of what constitutes truth. Rather, it is a competence which
includes the ability of knowing how to live and listen. Irrespective of
the interpretation of knowledge, narrative is perceived as the quintessential form of knowledge. Lyotard also warns that knowledge will
become the most critical factor at stake in the worldwide competition for
power.

The debate identified by Lyotard on how knowledge is constructed and
consensus maintained continues to influence how society comes to understand the formation and dissemination of knowledge. He asserts that the
rules of science, literature and the arts have radically changed, going on
to suggest that these transformations have resulted in a crisis of the narratives that reflect the knowledge of these disciplines. Lyotard's interest
is in the way that narratives are used to legitimate and elevate themselves
to a status beyond mere stories. Legitimation refers to that which is taken
to make certain knowledge true and the social structures that support
and underpin such legitimation, and is both an epistemological as well as
a moral debate. Lyotard's criticism of legitimation is that it suppresses
and marginalises alternative perspectives and narratives. According to
Lyotard, science as an example does not restrict itself to discovering the
truth, but instead creates a metanarrative as legitimation of its own status.
He goes on to suggest that it is not possible to validate narrative knowledge
on the basis of scientific knowledge as the criteria by which to judge them
are different. Science no longer rises above its practice but descends to
the level of practice thereby to become immersed in it. The result is that
practitioners therefore assume responsibility for the legitimation of their
own practice, meaning that the function of narrative loses its great goals.

The crisis that Lyotard observes in scientific knowledge is attributed not to external factors such as the revolution of technology or the growth of capitalism, but instead to 'internal erosion of the legitimacy principle of knowledge' (PC, 39).

Postmodernism as put forward by Lyotard perceives each discourse as a language game with each one defined by its own knowledge criteria and with no discourse having superiority over the other. It is in essence the loss of the grand narratives established by the Enlightenment. Within the postmodern condition as proposed by Lyotard the modernist narratives or paradigms of knowledge no longer represent societies. An example is post-Christianity as many societies are of multifaith or no faith at all. This perspective supports the pluralism of narrative for which he argues. Instead, the narratives of science have assumed a power which imposes the adherence to 'correct narratives' discrediting alternative perspectives to knowledge. Essentially narratives can be perceived as stories that have developed throughout history to inform thoughts on various subjects such as science, freedom and capitalism.

For Lyotard, it is not surprising that the legitimation of what is perceived as truth by the scientific narrative should lead to a similar legitimation of what is perceived as just by the political discourse. Both communities establish laws which reflect the narratives of their particular discourses. The scientific community seeks to establish its legitimacy in performance. Lyotard argues that, instead of legitimating, the narrative of performance intervenes to alter scientific narrative, and as would be expected he takes a sceptical position to the underlying assumption of legitimacy. He makes the case for the *petit récit*, or little narrative, and the right of the individual to determine what is legitimate.

So instead of a grand narrative Lyotard argues for multiplicity and discursive segments all concerned with a different perspective on truth. He rightly challenges the paradigm which claims that knowledge is created for knowledge's sake in a society where most things are produced as commodities, including knowledge. Knowledge is also part of the hegemonic structures of the corporate environment which is based on the exercise of knowledge as power. In the postmodern society the traditional approach to learning and creation of knowledge has also changed radically with new ways of acquiring and disseminating knowledge, as generated by the revolution in technology and computerisation. Postmodernism does not support the belief that institutions and bureaucracies have the power to legitimate what is perceived as truth, and instead turns to pluralism and what Lyotard refers to as little narratives of dissent.

Passages

Knowledge
Legitimation
Performativity
Pluralism
Postmodern Science
Power

NARRATIVE OF EMANCIPATION

Stuart Sim

One of the key features of modernity as it has developed out of the Enlightenment movement has been the enthusiasm for what Lyotard calls 'narratives of emancipation', that is, narratives calling for liberation from the various evils besetting humanity. Closely allied to these are speculative narratives, the difference between the two being that the latter is more philosophically oriented, the former political – although there is no hard-and-fast dividing line between them, and in fact a fair amount of overlap to be noted. In both cases, they assume legitimating powers (over knowledge, for example), and Lyotard is always sceptical of their justification, and motivation, for so doing. Eventually, such narratives become a question of power and can give rise to social and political abuses when they are used to exclude other viewpoints.

For the Enlightenment *philosophes* the narrative meant liberation from the repressiveness of organised religion and the political system of the *ancien regime*, with its strictly observed and monitored social hierarchies that kept the bulk of the population in a state of subjection, the consequence being that only a small elite had any meaningful involvement in the political sphere. Essentially, what was being challenged by the *philosophes* was the forces of tradition, and that is a trend that has continued on into the modern world, which is very much oriented towards progress. Modern culture has developed a commitment to secularism and liberal democracy, as well as an abiding concern to improve the human lot through constantly rising living standards and the fruits of technological innovation, thus emancipating humankind from the evils of ill-health and poverty. Although it is undeniable that not everyone around the globe is sharing in these benefits of modernity (it has to be said that they remain more of a Western preserve, and not always equally experienced there either), they are nevertheless still being held up as ideals for humanity at large.

Lyotard is critical of narratives of emancipation in general on several grounds. First of all they make assumptions on behalf of others, something that Lyotard is never happy about, since it means difference is not being acknowledged. It is a characteristic move of both emancipative and speculative narratives to claim prescriptive authority, and to see this as being applicable to humanity at large. Narratives of emancipation invariably have such universalising intentions, regarding human beings as much the same everywhere and in need of the same rights. Marxism is a prime example of this tendency, believing that its theories hold for all humankind and that all societies without exception should be run on communist principles (although it should be noted that, given its philosophical roots, it might also qualify as a speculative narrative on the basis of the somewhat abstract notion of a 'dialectic of history' lying behind it). It is the avowed aim of classical Marxism, as expressed through the communist movement, to extend its doctrines over the whole globe and become the standard system of human government. Marxism-communism can see no virtue in other cultural systems, all of which it regards as ripe for emancipation from class struggle and the exploitative rule of the bourgeoisie: the legitimating power for the prescriptive this entails is simply assumed.

It is what is done in the name of narratives of emancipation once they establish themselves that most worries Lyotard, since this can mean suppression of dissenting minorities and even the use of terror against those who oppose the aims of any such narrative. Narratives of emancipation can turn into narratives of repression in all too many cases, as Marxism alone would prove in the instance of the Soviet regime, which treated dissent of any kind as treason and punished it accordingly. Even in the West there has been a distortion of the ideals of such narratives, which Lyotard argues are now interpreted mainly in terms of performativity, demanding ever-greater efficiency from the population to serve the needs of the system, thus effectively instituting a new form of subjection. Lyotard insists that we have now seen through this process, arguing that 'the grand narrative has lost its credibility, regardless of what mode of unification it uses, regardless of whether it is a speculative narrative or a narrative of emancipation' (PC, 37). Regrettably enough, however, there is ample evidence around to suggest that the narrative of emancipation, with 'humanity as the hero of liberty' (PC, 31), still exerts a considerable hold over our culture and is capable of evoking a populist response – as witness the various wars being waged in the name of extending the reach of liberal democracy, or the relentless campaign to make neoliberal economics the international norm through the globalisation of trade.

Passages

Dialectics
Enlightenment
Legitimation
Marxism
Modern, Modernity
Speculative Narrative

NAZIS, NAZISM – see 'aesthetics', 'anamnesis', 'Auschwitz', 'bearing witness', 'difference', 'forgetting', 'Heidegger, Martin', 'idiom', 'incommensurability, incompatibility', 'Is it happening?', 'Jews, Judaism', 'law', 'philosophy', 'phrase, phrasing', 'postmodernism' and 'terror'

NEOLIBERALISM – see 'capitalism', 'development', 'enthusiasm', 'narrative of emancipation' and 'pluralism'

NEWMAN, BARNETT BARUCH (1905–70) – see 'art', 'Is it happening?', 'literature' and 'modernism'

NIETZSCHE, FRIEDRICH (1844–1900) – see 'agonistics', '*dispositif*', 'modern, modernity', 'nihilism' and 'tensor'

NIHILISM

Keith Crome

The word 'nihilism' derives from the Latin *nihil*, which means 'nothing'. Gaining currency in the second half of the nineteenth century, the term was used then, as it often still is, to denote the belief that there is nothing of any worth or sense. Linked to what was understood to be an increasingly prevalent denial of the value of tradition and authority on the part of Europeans, it was employed to characterise such heterogeneous doctrines as positivism, atheism and anarchism.

The phenomenon was first clarified philosophically by Friedrich Nietzsche. Nietzsche saw the denial of the value of traditional authorities, the flowering of atheism and the rise of positivism as symptoms of

European nihilism. However, for Nietzsche nihilism was not simply a matter of belief, and it could not be reduced to a doctrine or set of doctrines. Rather, Nietzsche understood Western culture to be inherently nihilistic, and he viewed nihilism as the historical process shaping the fate of the West. He defined that process as one in which the highest values come to devalue themselves, by which he meant that those values that historically provided European humanity with its aim and purpose had lost their binding power and force, leaving a life which, lacking direction or truth, seeks nothing beyond its empty self-perpetuation.

In his first published article, 'Nés en 1925' (1948), Lyotard echoed Nietzsche's account of nihilism. Speaking about the situation confronting his generation, he declared that Europe, the 'so-called civilization of progress', is 'suffering its fate' by completing its own negation and consequently 'no longer knows how it should behave and therefore cannot understand itself' (*PW*, 86). For Lyotard, then, as for Nietzsche, nihilism formed the inescapable problem of his age; and although he subsequently wrote relatively little about nihilism directly as a topic, this was not because the issue was of little concern to him, but because, of the utmost concern, it pervaded his thought through and through. Thus nihilism constitutes the horizon against which Lyotard's writings should be understood in the sense that they offer not an abstract theoretical definition of it, but a series of strategically motivated confrontations with it.

For Lyotard, nihilism realises itself in the predominance of what in *The Postmodern Condition* ([1979] 1984b) he calls the logic of 'performativity' and, in *The Inhuman* ([1988c] 1991a) the ideology of development, which seeks to treat every being as a utility contributing to the efficient functioning of the techno-scientifically programmed social system, optimising its performance. Within such a system the human being is itself reduced to a mere *manipulandum*, its contingency and freedom effectively 'neutralised' (*I*, 69) as Lyotard puts it, by the demand for predictability.

As Lyotard understands it, the historical paradox of this annihilation of human freedom through the imposition of the logic of performativity is that, while it is tied to the expansion of capitalist techno-science, its origin is neither economic nor social, but metaphysical, arising in essence from out of the application of the principle of reason ('nothing is without reason' or 'everything has a cause' (*I*, 69)) to human relations. It is a paradox inasmuch as the principle of reason was intended to assure reason of its mastery of the world by ultimately rendering everything knowable (and thus effectively like itself), and in this way enable the realisation of human progress and freedom. It is a historical paradox, and not a merely logical one, in the sense that there can be no good arguments against the principle of reason, so that the problem it poses cannot be grasped and solved at a rational level, but only at a concrete, historical level by bringing contemporary subjectivity to crisis.

In order to induce such a crisis Lyotard stages his confrontations with nihilism in terms of a radical *aesthesis*, which he presents under a number of different headings, such as the figural, the libidinal or the sublime. What is at stake is the inscription of an affective event or intensity that cannot be situated as an effect, and which is therefore intrinsically recalcitrant to the principle of reason, refusing the mastery of the intellect. Lyotard thus seeks performatively to provoke a sensitivity to what is other than knowledge, a responsivity or possibility to that which, because it is an affect in excess of every effect, and thus not a positively apprehensible fact, can only be thought as a nothingness. Ultimately, then, Lyotard views nihilism as a historically constituted insensitivity to events, the annihilation of the nothingness that is the 'there is' of existence itself.

Passages

Development
Inhuman
Performativity
Reason, Rationality
Techno-Science

OBLIGATION

Anthony Gritten

Like many post-war thinkers, Lyotard spent much time considering justice, obligation, ethics and the good life. In France obligation received its most insistent and influential working through in the work of Emmanuel Levinas. Lyotard's phrasing of the concept is shot through with an abiding concern to acknowledge the kinds of social issues and problems that bring obligation into urgent focus.

Obligation (rather than 'an obligation') is a para-phenomenological event. Calling its addressee to attention, its presentation is too early and too late, ahead of ontology, discourse, self-governance, worlds and subjects, and it is already forgotten before it has ever been known. It is in this sense that the apparent circularity of Lyotard's statement that 'A phrase is obligatory if its addressee is obligated' (*D*, 108) should be understood. Obligation puts its addressee in the position of being open to the touch of the Other, exposed before law, representation, or concept. Lyotard's position diverges from Levinas's position on obligation (ethics as first philosophy) and the position identified by Jürgen Habermas as one of performative contradiction.

Obligation thus requires response, commentary, phrasing. It must be given its due, as one of any number of language games that are possible with phrases. Giving obligation its due means: listened to, obeyed. 'For obligation is a modality of time rather than of space and its organ is the ear rather than the eye' (*I*, 81). This means that the phrasing of obligation, the linking of further phrase-events, ethical or otherwise, does not follow automatically from obligation itself, but is unveiled in hearing, in what Lyotard terms 'passibility'. Lyotard follows Immanuel Kant in arguing that obligation cannot be deduced from or reduced to ontology, and that 'must', unlike 'ought', does not presuppose an ontology. Obligation, then,

should not be confused with *Redlichkeit* [uprightness], or probity in regard to *Rede* [speech]. The latter does not obligate: *It is necessary to link* is not *You ought to link*. It does not even suffice to say that there is no choice: one is not held by an occurrence the same way one is held to an obligation. (*D*, 116)

Ahead of ontology, obligation is an event of feeling for its addressee (rather than an event of thought, which implies a subject having the thought). For subjectivity to emerge from this minimal event of feeling and *nachträglichkeit*, and for it to avoid differends, there must be a working through with further phrases, *durcharbeitung*. Working through the feeling of debt produced by obligation, a feeling both joyful and anxious, requires a willingness to remain flexible, tolerant and svelte. This skill that is never acquired is not a matter of a universal and generalisable duty fulfilled by a universal subject, but is rather the addressee's activity of linking on to the particular phrase at hand, and of acknowledging that, for justice to be real, if never fully present, the addressee must continue to attempt to work through obligation, despite the lack of finality to this project, despite the lack of peace or pleasure in acknowledging the law and responding to obligation.

Passages

Addressee, Addressor/Sender
Ethics

Justice
Law
Links, Linkage
Phrase, Phrasing

OTHER – see 'anamnesis', 'Christianity', 'difference', 'differend', 'ethics', 'Jews, Judaism', 'law', 'obligation' and 'probity'

$$\boxed{P}$$

PAGANISM, PAGUS

Thomas Docherty

In 1992, Lyotard participated in a conference on 'The Philosopher in the city'. His paper, 'Zone', considered the intimacy of philosophy and the city, suggesting that, historically, 'Philosophy is not *in* the city, it is the city in the process of thinking' (*PF*, 19). However, the contemporary philosopher is relegated to the edges of the city and of civic life. This argument essentially returns to his earlier consideration of what he called 'paganism' in 1977. In both *Rudiments païens* (1977c) and *Instructions païennes* (1977a), he addressed the relation of philosophy to the polity. These texts sprung from disappointment with the actualities of French politics (especially of the Left); but they addressed a more fundamental concern: the relation of philosophy to the political, to the polity.

The word *pagus* gives French its word for the country: *le pays*. Lyotard finds the concept of the *pagus* useful because it helps him identify a region that has not been assimilated by a consensual politics. The *pagus*, a border *of* the polity without being totally *in* it, is the position from which a critique of the polity can be made. In *The Differend* ([1983] 1988a) Lyotard identifies 'home', the *Heim* as that area that neutralises 'dispute' among incommensurable 'regimens of discourse' (*D*, 151); by contrast, the *pagus* is where such incommensurability is fully recognised. Thus, while the polity homogenises thought under the sign of one totalising regime, the *pagus* releases the possibility of multiple differends.

'At home', politics become monotheological. 'Paganism' acknowledges that many gods have to be appeased, even when the gods demand contrary things of the human subject. Paganism is thus 'impious' (*IP*, 10):

it describes a situation where 'pagans' can no longer subscribe to the totalising story told by Marxism, yet still demand a form of justice. The *pagus* thus becomes instrumental in helping Lyotard formulate the anti-totalising philosophy of his postmodernism, and his establishment of the complex demand for forms of justice 'without criteria', a justice made by judgements that have no foundational philosophy for their legitimation. Instead of there being but one monotheology of justice (piety), there are many.

The *pagus* becomes identified with the character of the *métèque*, one who does not enjoy citizenship because she or he is a 'foreigner' domiciled in the polity. Lyotard identifies this position as that ascribed to 'women, children, foreigners, slaves' (*RP*, 219); and paganism is what will acknowledge the rights of such human subjects and, indeed, will learn from their heterogeneity with respect to the polity.

The pagan, then, does not subscribe to a single code (of political Right or Left), but rather finds herself having to negotiate political complexity. No master-code can prescribe her voice or identity; rather, she is multiple. In paganism, there can no longer be a demand for a single homogenised identity that would effect a seamless continuity among all aspects of the pagan's life: by definition, the pagan is complex, perhaps even self-contradictory, but all the more political and ethical for that.

Passages

Antifoundationalism
Judgement
Justice
Philosophical Politics
Pluralism
Totality, Totalisation

PARALOGY

Keith Crome

The term paralogy is of Greek origin, and in its ordinary acceptation meant 'false reasoning'. In the treatise *On Sophistical Refutations* (Aristotle 1955), Aristotle gave the term a more precise sense. For Aristotle, paralogisms are a type of sophistic argument, that is, an argument that simulates a genuine argument but which in fact does not conform to the rules of logic, and that is consequently deceptive. Aristotle's aim in examining paralogistic reasoning is to enable the philosopher to guard against it. Most philosophers have followed Aristotle's lead, regarding paralogisms negatively. In the *Critique of Pure Reason* (1999 [1781]), for example, Immanuel Kant identifies a series of paralogistic arguments found in traditional, rational metaphysics concerning the nature of the soul. Apparently true, but in fact illusory, such arguments illegitimately convert the sense of the self that accompanies all our thinking into a substantial entity, treating it as if it were a real thing or object. However, while the deceptions of these paralogistic arguments can be guarded against, Kant argues that they cannot be dispelled, for they are an inevitable and natural part of human reason.

Although Lyotard employs the concept of paralogy in a number of works, his most important use is in *The Postmodern Condition* ([1979] 1984b). For Lyotard, as for Aristotle and Kant, a paralogism violates accepted rules of argumentation. Unlike Aristotle and Kant, however, Lyotard does not regard such a violation negatively, and for him paralogy is not something to guard against. Recasting and extending Kant's insight that the paralogisms are inherent to reason, Lyotard conceives paralogy positively as the principle of reason, identifying it as the driving force behind contemporary science and knowledge.

Lyotard develops his positive conception of paralogy, which transforms it from one mode of argument among others into the grounding and legitimating principle of scientific argumentation, by adopting a framework for the analysis of scientific discourse derived from the Wittgensteinian notion of language games. According to this approach, statements are analysed as utterances defined by certain rules that specify their pragmatic properties and the use that can be made of them. Pointing to the fact that contemporary science recognises and accepts as legitimate propositions that challenge the rules and axioms of classical science and logic (for example, Kurt Gödel's identification of the existence of a proposition within the system of arithmetic that is neither demonstrable nor refutable), Lyotard argues that postmodern knowledge progresses, and conceives itself as progressing, paralogistically, giving credence to utterances that destabilise the accepted order of scientific reason by instituting new rules for its language games.

Lyotard extends this positive account of paralogy to all language use. Viewed pragmatically, the supposed unity of language dissolves into a multiplicity of language games, each with its own rules and ends. Not only do these many games intrinsically resist reduction to one transcendent system of meaning, no one game being homologous with another, but every move made within a game – every speech act – is in principle paralogistic, having the capacity to modify the rules of that game. Ultimately, this paralogistic potential is nowhere better realised than in the constant harassment of accepted diction by popular idioms.

Passages

Language Games
Phrase, Phrasing
Postmodern Science
Pragmatics
Reason, Rationality

PASSAGE – see 'archipelago', 'genre' and 'probity'

PCF (FRENCH COMMUNIST PARTY) – see 'May '68, *événements*', 'Marxism', 'narrative of emancipation' and 'post-Marxism'

PEREGRINATION

Stuart Sim

Lyotard consistently argues against there being a predictable pattern to events. The future always remains unknown territory, and we delude ourselves in thinking otherwise. We can react to events but we can never claim actually to control how they unfold, in the manner that metanarratives tend to assume. Lyotard applies the same principle to his analysis of his career as a philosopher. This is marked out by chance as much as anything and, rather than there being any grand plan behind his development as a thinker, he conceives of it as a series of peregrinations that could have taken a different turn if events had worked out that way: 'The delusion that we are able to program our life is a part of an ancient fidelity to something like a destiny or destination' (*P*, 3). Recognising the delusion does not mean that we should give in to apathy, however: political engagement is still expected of us.

Lyotard describes the various careers he considered as he was growing up: to become a monk, painter, historian, or novelist, for example. Marriage and fatherhood intervene and he drifts into teaching philosophy in Algeria in the 1950s. The latter connection leads to him becoming a commentator on Algeria for the Socialisme ou Barbarie group that he was a member of in the 1950s and 1960s. He is soon wrestling with the contradictions of the Algerian revolution, which becomes a source of disputes inside the group, uncertain as to its Marxist credentials. Here again, he decides that to see some sort of destiny, such as a Marxist one, being worked out is a delusion:

one cannot 'give a meaning to an event or imagine a meaning for an event by anticipating what that event will be in reference to a pre-text' (*P*, 27). It is a familiar Lyotardian line: that a pattern cannot be imposed on events, whether political or personal. Eventually, he finds himself caught up in 'a *différend* with Marxism' (*P*, 45) that takes his career off in yet another direction – ultimately to the vicious attack on Karl Marx and Marxism in *Libidinal Economy* ([1974] 1993a) and the development of a post-Marxist sensibility.

Peregrination is yet another aspect of Lyotard's critique of determinism. He remains a firm believer in the openness of the future, and communicates a constitutional dislike of the idea that we are ever stuck in some predetermined groove, such as the dialectic of history that Marxists claim is propelling us towards the utopian ideal of a classless society. Lyotard will always resist such notions, which assume a degree of human control over both others and the environment that he insists it is impossible to achieve. Existence is far more chaotic than that, thus more amenable to the workings of small-scale, limited objective, little narratives than grandiose metanarratives with inflated ideas of their own power and importance. Most people's lives from this perspective constitute a series of peregrinations that we make up as we go along, depending on the arbitrary turn of events.

Passages

Algeria
Event
I Don't Know What
Libidinal Economy
Marxism
Socialisme ou Barbarie

PERFORMATIVITY

Neal Curtis

Performativity is most extensively discussed in Lyotard's 1979 report on knowledge, entitled *The Postmodern Condition* ([1979] 1984b), but can be found in numerous other essays, two of which will be mentioned here. Central to *The Postmodern Condition* as an analysis of the status of research and teaching under late capitalism is the idea that the previous (meta) narratives that gave legitimacy to research and teaching have been lost.

Lyotard argues that research in both the sciences and the humanities is no longer supported by the Idealist belief that knowledge is a good in itself, or the Republican belief that knowledge will make us free. These two narratives that emerged out of the eighteenth-century revolutions but came to maturity in the nineteenth century are no longer applicable in an age where capitalism has matured and increasingly dominates every aspect of social life, including the legitimation and hence production of knowledge. In the second half of the twentieth century knowledge is legitimate only if it optimises the current system's performance, or optimises 'the global relationship between input and output' (*PC*, 11) in ever-expanding networks of information and commodification. For Lyotard this equates to a transformation in the nature of knowledge. No longer is knowledge aiming towards an as-yet-unanswered question regarding the nature of the good society; instead the question is taken to have been answered by the marketisation of society; and the function of knowledge now is to increase the operational efficiency of this specific but universalised socio–economic system. Here the relationship between suppliers and users of knowledge assumes 'the form already taken by the relationship of commodity producers and consumers to the commodities they produce and consume' (*PC*, 4). All knowledge must now produce a surplus value contributing to economic growth. Philosophers become cultural entrepreneurs whose books are good because they sell well, while scientific knowledge is good if it produces technological spin-offs that in turn produce a surplus value in the capitalist cycle of exchange. Rather than science being experimental in the speculative sense, it becomes another 'force of production' (*PC*, 45).

Lyotard's turn towards small narratives is in part an attempt to avoid theory's incorporation 'into the programming of the whole [where] the desire for a unitary and totalizing truth lends itself to the unitary and totalizing practice of the system's managers' (*PC*, 12). Partial and limited knowledge, and sensitivity to singularity, is a form of resistance to performativity. Two other good discussions of this principle are 'Domus and the Megalopolis' in *The Inhuman* ([1988c] 1991a) and 'Marie goes to Japan' in *Postmodern Fables* ([1993a] 1997). In the first essay the regularity of the *domus* or family home is contrasted to the system of the megalopolis. While being ordered and operating according to a law, every *domus* contains a secret, in contrast to the megalopolis as a fully technologised social form that demands everything be rendered transparent, quantified, archived and communicable, a system closed off to the singularity of the event, perhaps even premised on its prevention. In 'Marie goes to Japan' the pessimism of the earlier essay is expressed even more strongly and fatally. Performativity is presented here as a 'stream of cultural capital' (*PF*, 3), 'which means the capitalization of all cultures in the cultural bank'

(*PF*, 8). Predating Michael Hardt and Antonio Negri's critique of the politics of difference in *Empire* (2000), Lyotard argues that 'what cultural capitalism has found is a marketplace for singularities' (*PF*, 7). The task for thought after this radicalisation of performativity is a very difficult one indeed, given that what was formerly resistant has now been fully appropriated.

Passages

Knowledge
Legitimation
Performativity
Resistance
Speculative Narrative

PHENOMENOLOGY

Derek M. Robbins

Phenomenology ([1954] 1991b) was Lyotard's first book, written while he was teaching in a lycée in Constantine, Algeria, and published in paperback in the series of small, introductory texts – Que Sais-je – by the Presses Universitaires de France. During his lifetime, the book went through twelve editions. The tenth edition of 1986 was translated into English and published, in 1991, by the State University of New York Press. On occasions, Lyotard amended the bibliography, but he did not edit his text. Even though his later work was to show signs of the influence of Ludwig Wittgenstein and to become concerned with exegesis and interpretation of Immanuel Kant's *Critiques*, the book on phenomenology remained, muted but immutable, in the background. It represented the French response to the work of Husserl at a particular, mid–century moment, but it is also an important source for understanding the subsequent development of Lyotard's own thinking.

The nineteenth century had seen a revival of interest in the study of Logic in Western Europe, but there was conflict between those who insisted on the formal characteristics of reasoning and those who took the study of logic to be indissociable from the psychological study of thought processes. This became a conflict between philosophical idealism and empiricism. Husserl was one of those who, at the turn of the century, sought to overcome this opposition by analysing formal logic positivistically. Hence his early *Logical Investigations* ([1900/1]

1970) – logical enquiries which predated the influence of his disciple, Martin Heidegger, which became dominant after 1930. In the 1930s and early 1940s, there were two main tendencies in the French reception of Husserl's thought. The first was a tendency to consider Husserl's work as a form of modern scholasticism. The alternative response to Husserl's work seemed to involve seeking to constitute existentialism out of phenomenology. This pushed further the ontological interpretation of phenomenology advanced by Heidegger. Emmanuel Levinas, Jean-Paul Sartre, Maurice Merleau-Ponty and Paul Ricoeur are the French thinkers most associated with the existentialising of Husserl which followed on from the publication of Heidegger's *Being and Time* in 1927. Ricoeur published a translation of Husserl's *Ideen I*, with a detailed translator's introduction, in 1950. His philosophical exegesis was an attempt to distinguish Husserl's transcendental idealism both from Cartesian a priorism and from Kantian transcendental idealism. Ricoeur argued that

Husserl's 'question' . . . is not Kant's; Kant poses the problem of *validity* for possible objective consciousness and that is why he stays within the framework of an attitude which remains natural. . . . Husserl's question . . . is the question of the origin of the world . . . it is, if you like, the question implied in myths, religions, theologies and ontologies, which has not yet been elaborated scientifically. ('Introduction', Husserl 1950: xxvii–xxviii)

Ricoeur's exposition of Husserl opened up the possibility that Husserl's work could help in attempting to analyse the foundations of Kantian a priorism. Phenomenology was not to be understood as another philosophy but as a method for analysing all modes of thought, including that of philosophy.

The bibliography to the first edition of Lyotard's book indicates that he was aware of these strands of phenomenological thought. He recognised that any response to phenomenology demanded that it should be understood as a movement rather than as a fixed philosophical position. He tried to outline the 'common style' of phenomenology after 'having rendered to Husserl that which is Husserl's: *having begun*' (*Ph*, 34). He located the development of Husserl's thought in the context of late nineteenth-century trends, highlighting that Husserl wrote *against* psychologism and *against* pragmatism. The first part of the book, devoted to Husserl, concluded that, according to Husserl, 'the truths of science are founded neither in God, as Descartes thought, nor on the a priori conditions of possibility, as Kant thought, but on the immediate experience of evidence by which individual and world find themselves in harmony from the beginning' (*Ph*, 64). This conclusion was followed by a short 'note on Husserl and Hegel'. Lyotard acknowledged that it was Hegel who had originally given 'phenomenology' its meaning, but he argued that the crucial distinction between the two thinkers was that 'Hegelian phenomenology *closes* the system' while 'Husserlian description inaugurates the grasping of the "thing itself" before all predication' (*Ph*, 68). In other words, to use Lyotard's later terminology, Hegel's dialectic was wrongly subordinated to a historical grand narrative. In this early text, therefore, we can find Lyotard's latent hostility to totalising systems of thought. The challenge for the phenomenological movement was to resist becoming appropriated by systematic philosophy.

Lyotard's account of Husserl was influenced by the work of Merleau-Ponty, but, in *Discourse, Figure* ([1971] 2010), he was anxious to distance himself from what he regarded as Merleau-Ponty's excessively cognitive interpretation. Through the 1970s, Lyotard pursued a quest to articulate the primacy of the libidinal or experiential. The search took him away from phenomenological philosophy, but it led him towards a phenomenological understanding of Kant's transcendentalism. Most apparently in *The Differend* ([1983] 1988a), Lyotard sought to deconstruct the idealist legacy of Kant and to construct a libidinally based, critical philosophy, derived from close scrutiny of Kant's *Critique of Judgement* ([1790] 2000). Although Lyotard did not subsequently return to close exegesis of the work of Husserl, his first book announced his methodological commitment to transience, and it influentially outlined the implications of the phenomenological style of thinking for research in the human sciences, notably in relation to Psychology, Sociology and History. It was his phenomenological approach to the work of Kant, apparent in *Just Gaming* ([1979] 1985), *Enthusiasm* ([1986a] 2009a), and *Lessons on the Analytic of the Sublime* ([1991b] 1994) which enabled him to articulate the later moral and political philosophy which, perhaps, was Lyotard's greatest achievement.

Passages

Dialectics
Enthusiasm
Existentialism
Heidegger, Martin
Philosophy

PHILOSOPHICAL POLITICS

Stuart Sim

Lyotard is much exercised by the plight of those marginalised by the formal political process, and argues that it is the role of philosophers to help them find a voice. Such a situation traditionally arises when a differend occurs and the stronger party imposes its will on the weaker (a colonial power on the colonised, for example, or powerful employers on their employees). The weaker are then forced to defend their cause in a system set up to enshrine the values of the stronger and, not surprisingly, discover they can make very little impression on those judging, who are effectively agents of the power structure behind the system. Lyotard feels this is where philosophers should step in, calling their intervention 'philosophical politics'. He conceives of this as an activity 'apart from the politics of "intellectuals" and of politicians' (*D*, xiii), both of whom are motivated in the main, he contends, by self-interest and a desire for power.

Philosophers who choose not to involve themselves in philosophical politics and collude with those in authority instead are betraying their calling in Lyotard's opinion. He goes so far as to argue that 'they cease to be philosophers' and 'become what one calls intellectuals, that is, persons who legitimate a claimed competence' (*PW*, 95). Seen from this standpoint philosophy is a subversive activity which should never allow itself to be appropriated by power structures. Unfortunately, that is what so often has proved to be the case over its history, Lyotard complaining that '[f]or a long time, in the West, philosophers have been exposed to the temptation of the role of the intellectual', and that 'there are not many, since Plato, who have not succumbed to this temptation' (*PW*, 95). To speak on the side of authority, which is almost never justified in its assumption of power over others, is to help uphold a metanarrative: anathema to someone of Lyotard's outlook. Lyotard accepts that to adopt this attitude is to be in a minority within his profession, but believes this is the only principled line to take and that philosophy should at heart be a dissenting activity.

A good example of Lyotard's notion of a philosophical politics can be found in his writings on Algerian affairs in the 1950s and 1960s, when the war of liberation was taking place against the French colonial regime. Lyotard studiously refuses to side with either 'authority' involved in the struggle, being critical of both the French and the Algerian revolutionary force (the FLN). He expresses doubts about the latter's commitment to the Algerian populace, for example, suspecting that they may be more interested in the prospect of gaining power for themselves. Neither is he convinced by their argument that it is a Marxist class war taking place. In Lyotard's view that is to impose a framework on events that is alien to the nature of the country and the situation it faces. For his part, he chooses to support, and do his best to articulate, the needs of the population in general, his argument being that 'the problem of helping Algerians to live is conceived and solved in terms of an individual or a small collectivity, a village, a family, a quarter' (*PW*, 302). It is one of his characteristic arguments against totalisation, which narrows the struggle down to what it means at a local or individual level: 'The unemployed person wants work; the woman wants bread for her son; the combatant wants to be honored for having fought; the student wants books and professors; the worker wants a salary; the peasant wants seeds; the shopkeeper wants to restart business' (*PW*, 302). There is a clear disjunction to be noted between the perception of those applying the theory and those on the receiving end. Only by distancing himself from authority can a philosopher make such points and reveal the emergence of differends.

Philosophical politics sets itself the task of identifying differends, whereas formal politics is generally concerned to suppress differends, with those in power imposing their own genre of discourse on everyone else, such that the latter can hardly see how they are being dominated and exploited. If opposition can only be phrased in the language and rules of the oppressors then that means they will invariably hold the upper hand in any debates or negotiations that occur. Lyotard saw this as all too typical of the way that metanarratives – such as Marxism – worked, and regarded it as the duty of philosophers to make this as widely known as possible.

Passages

Algeria
Differend
Intellectuals
Marxism
Philosophy
Politics

PHILOSOPHY

Stuart Sim

Philosophy has traditionally played a larger role in the French educational system than it has in most countries (certainly in the Anglo-Saxon world anyway), and it is very much to the fore in the work of the generation of poststructuralist-postmodernist thinkers who came to prominence in the country's intellectual life in the later twentieth century. This is the generation of such figures as Lyotard, Jacques Derrida, Michel Foucault and Gilles Deleuze, and it has left an indelible mark on the fields of critical and cultural theory. Lyotard is a less maverick figure in terms of philosophical history than most of his contemporaries, and his work ranges across the major topics and debates of the discipline in an assured and professional manner (as in his commentary on Immanuel Kant, *Lessons on the Analytic of the Sublime* ([1991b] 1994)). He is also in many ways the most explicitly political thinker of this particular generation, and he will always seek to find a political dimension in philosophical enquiry. Indeed, he regards that as an obligation all philosophers should feel themselves to be under, as in his call for the development of a 'philosophical politics' whereby philosophers put themselves to work on behalf of the disadvantaged and the exploited in society in an attempt to ameliorate their situation.

Lyotard does have something of a love-hate relationship with his subject, however, as well as with the majority of its practitioners. He is not one to make grandiose claims for its importance in the overall scheme of things, as he makes clear at various points over the course of his career. Thus his throwaway remark about himself in a television programme in 1978, 'he is a professor of philosophy at the University of Vincennes; hence he does philosophy. No one has ever been quite sure what that consists of' (*PW*, 91). The programme itself hardly constituted an advertisement for philosophy as a sober academic exercise, with the producer deliberately playing tricks with the audience, such as making the soundtrack out of synchronisation with the image, and Lyotard talking about himself rather pretentiously in the third person. Nevertheless, the short sequence contains some important insights into Lyotard's vision of what professional philosophy should be. He quickly homes in on some very practical concerns, such as, 'Can economic relations between people work well only if they produce and buy the greatest possible number of manufactured products . . . ?' (*PW*, 92). Philosophers ought to engage with such 'common questions', he asserts, and that means particularly 'questions of authority' (*PW*, 93). Having raised the issue of authority, Lyotard proceeds to make a sharp distinction in the philosophical community between those who serve authority and those who don't. To be in that former category is to 'cease to be philosophers' (*PW*, 95), and unfortunately enough that seems to represent the majority of the profession in Lyotard's unforgiving opinion. Only a minority over the history of Western philosophy have been able to resist the temptation to become complicit with those in power, and Lyotard firmly aligns himself with that minority. As for the majority, '[t]hey become what one calls intellectuals, that is, persons who legitimate a claimed competence' (*PW*, 95), and Lyotard has little time for those involved in the process of legitimation.

Lyotard's early book *Phenomenology* ([1954] 1991b) is a fairly standard piece of philosophical writing, and it became a much-reprinted textbook over his lifetime. From his time in *Socialisme ou Barbarie* in the 1950s onwards, however, his writing leans more and more to the political – perhaps not surprisingly, given the critique of Marxism the movement was committed to conducting. Lyotard's most philosophical work in his later career is *The Differend* ([1983] 1988a), which includes dialogues (or 'notices', as he dubs them) with many of the major figures in Western philosophy from the classical period up to the present. Even here, however, the political aspect is very much to the fore, with Lyotard's primary concern being to show us how philosophy can help us to deal with disputes, particularly differends, 'where the plaintiff is divested of the means to argue and becomes for that reason a victim' (*D*, 9). The starting point of the book is the problem of the Holocaust and Lyotard's disdain for those revisionist historians who deny that the event ever occurred, so we are made very aware this is a piece of philosophical enquiry with an explicit political agenda. Philosophy is being allied with the cause of history's victimised, and Lyotard is adamant that it should help us to 'bear witness' to the fact of injustice and enable us to reduce its incidence in our society.

Similarly, when Lyotard engages with the work of Martin Heidegger in *Heidegger and "the jews"* (1988b [1990b]), political concerns are driving the argument yet again. Even if he shies away from making specific connections between Heidegger's philosophy and his politics (as many of his contemporaries in France did during the rancorous 'Heidegger Affair' of the late 1970s), Lyotard does detect a totalitarian bias in Heidegger's thought that could well dispose adherents towards support of a totalitarian political system such as Nazism revealed itself to be. The philosophy is made to be ideologically accountable, in the manner that we come to expect from someone so sensitive to the lure that authority can exert, its ability to turn philosophers into regime-bolstering intellectuals.

A philosophical politics is the logical outcome of Lyotard's set of interests, with philosophy being deployed to help the victims of differends find a voice with which to make their grievances publicly known. Philosophy is a very practical subject from that point of view, with a self-consciously anti-authoritarian, anti-totalitarian ethos. It is never a grand narrative but the means for challenging the credibility of the very notion of grand narrative: 'Philosophy is a discourse that has as its rule the search for its rule (and that of other discourses)' (*PW*, 21). And it is important to note that in

Lyotard's scheme any rules that are found are retrospective only, and do not commit us to anything going on into the future.

Passages

Differend
Heidegger, Martin
Phenomenology
Philosophical Politics
Rules
Socialisme ou Barbarie

PHRASE, PHRASING

Stuart Sim

The act of phrasing is a central concern of Lyotard's. We communicate with each other by means of phrases – or 'sentences', as Geoffrey Bennington has suggested is a better English equivalent to the French word *phrase* (although most translators of Lyotard nevertheless have opted for 'phrase'). Phrases operate according to the rules of their own particular regimen, and there are a range of these regimens in existence, such as 'reasoning, knowing, describing, recounting, questioning, showing, ordering, etc.' (*D*, xii). The critical thing about phrases is that they demand linkage; even silence is regarded as a link by Lyotard, since it still invites a link to be made to it, the chain itself neither ceasing nor breaking down at such points. All links have to conform to the rules that are laid down by their phrase regimen, however, which means that they cannot be translated into another regimen. Genres of discourse provide 'ends' for the linking of heterogeneous phrases, and again we are to note that the rules are specific to each case and that what applies in one genre will not in another: if that principle is flouted, then a differend is created. Each genre of discourse has its own rationale that should respect that of others and not be motivated by imperialist ambitions to take any of them over.

We are to recognise that something important is at stake when phrases are linked – the 'end', whatever it may be, of the given genre of discourse, to which we are contributing in our own personal way (or at the very least, commenting upon the validity of). Yet Lyotard also warns us 'that the linking of one phrase onto another is problematic and that this is the problem of politics' (*D*, xiii), where, as we know, imperialist ambitions are only too prone to assert themselves as metanarratives jostle with each other for leverage. How we might contrive to put together 'good' links, those that will enable us to make judgements without committing ourselves to the self-interested programme of a particular metanarrative, becomes one of the main themes of *The Differend* ([1983] 1988a).

Despite the necessity of phrasing, Lyotard disclaims any particular authority for himself, and by extension philosophy as a discipline, in the quest to locate the good links:

In writing this book, the A. had the feeling that his sole addressee was the *Is it happening?* It is to it that the phrases which happen call forth. And, of course, he will never know whether or not the phrases happen to arrive at their destination, and by hypothesis, he must never know it. (*D*, xvi)

The phrases themselves are being put into circulation by Lyotard for others to link onto as they decide is best, and no-one can, or should, claim control over the linking process – which is precisely what metanarratives illicitly proceed to do of course. Metanarratives are in consequence constant sources of differends, when 'something "asks" to be put into phrases, and suffers from the wrong of not being able to be put into phrases right away' (*D*, 13). If one had to sum up Lyotard's philosophical project, to say to what 'end' it was primarily directed, it would be to bring that state of affairs to a close and to liberate linkage from such nefarious practices.

Lyotard wants to see a constant supply of new narratives coming on stream, with all of us being able to exercise our right – indeed, our obligation as he understands it – to add our own phrases to the spreading network. Phrasing, even in its silent mode, becomes an expression of our humanity, and it would be one of the most damning criticisms to be made of any narrative project that it would want to eliminate phrasing altogether, as Lyotard claims is the ultimate objective of techno-science in its surge towards the inhuman. The unpredictability of phrasing goes against the desire for optimum efficiency and performativity that drives the forces of both development and techno-science, and they will always remain suspicious of an activity whose outcome they cannot plot with precision. Phrasing is effectively a site of conflict in Lyotard's view therefore, and one about which we cannot remain neutral – not if we wish to halt the onward march of metanarratives or the expansion of the realm of the inhuman. Anything that prevents us engaging freely in phrasing, or that tries to efface the memory of particular chains of linkages as the Nazis so notoriously did with the Jews, is to be treated as the enemy.

Passages

Genre
Idiom
Is It Happening?
Links, Linkage
Obligation
Pragmatics

PLATO (428/427–348/347 BC) – see 'agonistics', 'differend', 'event', 'great Zero', 'justice', 'postcolonialism' and 'tensor'

PLURALISM

Stuart Sim

Pluralism is a logical outcome of the postmodernist worldview, with its refusal to accept that there is any such thing as a universally valid legitimation procedure that would privilege a particular system. That is taken to be a licence for the construction of a wide range of political narratives, none of which would have the right to claim domination over the others. This would also apply in realms other than the political, with the notion of intellectual authority, for example, coming in for scrutiny: no one theory or theorist could be considered to supply all the answers or to be beyond all possible doubt (Lyotard emphasises that this is what he thinks is now the situation in the scientific world). Neither could any kind of ethnic domination be defended under such a regime.

Lyotard wants to see a proliferation of narratives, arguing that this is the only way to break the stranglehold that grand narrative has gained over us: hence his support for what he calls 'the justice of multiplicity' (*JG*, 100), whereby all systems accept that others must be left free to operate according to their own rules. Narrative itself needs no legitimation: compiling narratives is an entirely natural human activity, one of the primary ways we have of making sense of our world – 'the quintessential form of customary knowledge' (*PC*, 19), as Lyotard perceives it. Problems only arise when one narrative claims precedence and seeks to sideline its rivals. Unfortunately, that describes much of the course of human history, with various cultural systems coming to believe that they alone are in possession of some ultimate truth, or that they represent the highest possible stage of human development: neither monotheisms nor empires much like opposition.

Support for pluralism in the political realm is a fairly standard response throughout the postmodern community, as in the case of such thinkers as Michel Foucault and the post-Marxists Ernesto Laclau and Chantal Mouffe. Foucault made a point of championing the cause of marginalised and oppressed groups throughout history: prisoners, the mentally ill, and homosexuals, for example. In each case, a norm of behaviour had been imposed on the population by those in positions of power, and those who did not conform were persecuted, either by social exclusion or imprisonment. Laclau and Mouffe argued that Marxism had failed to recognise the changing character of social protest around the globe, and the various movements this had given rise to, because of its inability to be flexible as regards its theoretical model. Rather than admitting that there might be gaps or contradictions in the model that would explain its failure to predict the course of recent history (and, in particular, the robustness of capitalism as a socio-economic system), it continued to demand that it had to be followed to the letter by any revolutionary minded group. Lyotard is part of this general shift away from a belief in universal theories and monoculturalism, and his ideas need to be seen within this context. He is an important player in a wide-ranging public debate, someone who was critiquing the rigidity of Marxism as early as the 1950s. The growth of multiculturalism as an ideal in Western society is further evidence of how this debate has served to change minds and attitudes.

Multiculturalism is not without its critics, however, and support for pluralism is often very superficial. Grand narratives have not, as Lyotard argued in *The Postmodern Condition* ([1979] 1984b), lost their appeal for us, and might even be seen to have been undergoing a revival in recent times. Neoliberal economics, the basis for globalisation, does not accept the validity of other economic theories (socialist or communist, for example) and campaigns against any government that tries to restrict the operation of the free market; neither does religious fundamentalism admit the claims of other religions, insisting that only one can be in possession of the truth and recipient of divine approval. There seems to be a deep-seated need among a large percentage of the globe's population for the security that grand narratives can bring, not to mention the power, that theorists like Lyotard have severely underestimated. Apart from anything else, such theories give clear-cut answers to problems, believing they have the criteria by which to determine right and wrong. Postmodernism's relativism and pragmatism are not to everyone's taste, although that does not detract from the value of efforts like those of Lyotard to draw attention to how little substance universal theories in reality have, and advocating the virtues of pluralism in their stead.

Passages

Legitimation
Little Narrative
Marxism
Narrative
Post–Marxism

POLITICS

Stuart Sim

It is not unreasonable to see Lyotard as the most politically conscious of his generation of thinkers in the poststructuralist-postmodernist movement in France; probably only Michel Foucault can be cited as having anything like such a strong bias in this respect. From his Algerian writings onwards politics occupies a central place in Lyotard's thought, and he demonstrates an abiding concern with relating philosophy to the main issues of the day, from the Algerian war of liberation through the *événements* to the rise of techno-science, globalisation and the information society. Over the course of his long career we are to note a steady movement away from Marxism and revolutionary theories predicated on absolutist worldviews to a commitment to a micropolitics based on flexibility of response and the exercise of individual initiative. Lyotard is a consistent opponent of the totalising imperative that underpins so much of both left- and right-wing political thought, serving to close down opposition to those controlling the narrative. Although one would still describe him as leftist in orientation in his later years, Lyotard is conspicuously non-doctrinaire in outlook, the kind of post-Marxist thinker to draw harsh criticism from the traditional left for whom post-Marxism amounts to a betrayal of the cause.

The Algerian writings chart a growing disenchantment with Marxist theory on Lyotard's part that is to reach its peak in *Libidinal Economy* ([1974] 1993a), where he dismisses the entire Marxist tradition with a torrent of insults and invective: 'We could say that it is through suspicion and intimidation, warned as we are by a militant past of, when laying a hand on Marx, even and indeed especially if it were to screw with him, we are closely watched by the paranoiacs calling themselves Marxist politicians and in general all the Whites of the left' (*LE*, 96). His political vision from then onwards excludes grandiose universal theories and advocates a grass-roots approach that resolutely avoids prescribing political solutions for the whole of humanity. The role of philosophers in this is to help the disadvantaged assert themselves, a project dubbed a 'philosophical politics'. If, in contrast, philosophers permit themselves to be co-opted into the traditional political set-up to provide support for the established interests, then they turn into mere intellectuals – a class for whom Lyotard has little time.

Lyotard ultimately conceives of politics as a struggle between little and grand narratives, encouraging a constant turnover of the former as a means of wrong-footing the designs of the latter and thus keeping them under stress. Little narratives are pragmatic constructs designed to fight specific abuses committed by the grand, and for Lyotard they will only be effective if they reject the temptation to turn into permanent institutions in their own right. Ideally for this thinker, politics would consist of inter-action between mutually respectful little narratives, with grand narratives consigned to oblivion. This is what he thought we were on the cusp of in the later twentieth century, arguing in *The Postmodern Condition* ([1979] 1984b) that grand narratives were increasingly being met with an attitude of incredulity by the general public. The way to keep that incredulity growing, he felt, was to open up the data-banks to public use, such that there was no longer an information deficit between little and grand nar-ratives. That would lead to a diffusion of the power that went along with having control of information and thus radically alter the political land-scape. Lyotard saw the promise of a new world of politics therefore, but the rise of religious fundamentalism in the interim period, as well as the spread of the globalisation ethic and the market fundamentalist views that inform it, has put paid to that vision for the time being.

Politics comes to the fore in pretty well all of Lyotard's later writings, building on the call for little narrative resistance made in *The Postmodern Condition*. The controversy over the Holocaust, for example, spurs him to write *The Differend* ([1983] 1988a) and *Heidegger and "the jews"* ([1988b] 1990b), contesting the claims of the deniers who were becoming increas-ingly vocal in the 1980s, in what is a very pointed example of his commit-ment to philosophical politics. *Just Gaming* ([1979] 1985) deals at length with the issue of justice, as Lyotard defends his casuistical theories on how this should operate (on a 'case-by-case' basis, without preconceptions on the part of the judges, or reference to overarching ethical theories) against the probing questioning of Jean-Loup Thébaud. The increasing influence over our lives exerted by techno-science and development leads to the apocalyptic sentiments expressed in *The Inhuman* ([1988c] 1991a), where the human race is pictured as facing the twin threats of the ultimate death of the sun and the inhuman policies likely to be devised by the techno-scientific project to meet that eventuality. In each case the argument is driven by a political agenda.

Politics as it is actually practised, however, invokes a pessimistic response from Lyotard, for whom it appears a battleground between competing genres of discourse. It is not itself a genre of discourse, although that is how participants generally view it, taking their own principles – 'deliberative consensus' or 'divine right' (*D*, 141), for example – as definitive of what politics should be about. For Lyotard, however, '[w]hat politics is about and what distinguishes various kinds of politics is the genre of discourse, or the stakes, whereby differends are formulated as litigations and find their "regulation"' (*D*, 142). Once a genre of discourse manages to assert itself in this way, it claims the right to judge, and that will be to the disadvantage of all other genres with their different stakes and ends. Lyotard's own conception of politics is very different: 'politics is not at all a genre, it bears witness to the nothingness which opens up with each occurring phrase and on the occasion of which the differend between genres of discourse is born' (*D*, 141). Whereas traditional politics exploits the emergence of the differend to seize power, philosophical politics sees its responsibility as 'detecting differends and finding the (impossible) idiom for phrasing them' (*D*, 142). The strong link that Lyotard wants to establish between philosophy and politics is very much evident at such points.

Passages

Algeria
Idiom
Incredulity
Philosophical Politics
Resistance
Totality, Totalisation

POSTCOLONIALISM

Eleanor Byrne and Stuart Sim

Lyotard's most sustained encounter with issues of postcolonialism comes in his Algerian writings for the journal *Socialisme ou Barbarie* from the mid-1950s to early 1960s. In his editorial introduction to Lyotard's *Political Writings* (1993b) Bill Readings remarks of Lyotard that he has no pretension when focusing on anti-imperialist struggles, as in the case of the Algerian war of independence against France, to set himself up as the voice of the colonially oppressed. Rather, 'he writes not of "the Algerian War", but of "the Algerians' war" – a war that is not his, cannot be his but that nonetheless calls out to him, demands a testimony that can never be adequate, a response that can never redeem his debt or obligation' (*PW*, xix). Throughout these writings (published later in book form in France as *La Guerre des Algériens* (1988a)) Lyotard keeps airing his doubts as to whether the political system that eventually replaces French colonialism will be any more attentive to the needs of the Algerian people. What the Algerian War of Independence represents to Lyotard is the collapse of modernist imperialism, and he supports it on that basis, but he is distrustful all the same of the motives of the revolutionary leaders – presciently enough as later events have shown. Many anti-colonial struggles of that period did indeed lead to authoritarian, and often corrupt, regimes coming to power, and to someone like Lyotard that represented a lost opportunity to institute a new social model free from grand narrative dogma. The Algerian writings also catalogue Lyotard's growing recognition that Marxism is no more capable of providing that new model than any other Western-derived grand narrative.

Throughout his later writings Lyotard campaigns for paganism, with its lack of any overarching grand narrative, as a basis for the desired new model, and the postcolonial critic Homi K. Bhabha deploys this concept in his discussion of the contemporary postcolonial and post-imperial nation in his essay 'DissemiNation', arguing that:

The nation is no longer the sign of modernity under which cultural differences are homogenised in the 'horizontal' view of society. The nation reveals, in its ambivalent and vacillating representation, an ethnography of its own claim to being *the* norm of social contemporaneity. The people turn *pagan* in that disseminatory act of social narrative that Lyotard defines, against the Platonic tradition, as the privileged pole of the narrated. (Bhabha 2005: 214)

Yet where paganism does exist in the contemporary world it is always under threat, as Bill Readings makes clear when he invokes the concept with regard to Australian Aboriginal culture, arguing that this remains so radically different to Western culture, in such a state of profound differend, that it cannot be subsumed under any Western grand narrative (including Marxism). 'Lyotard's paganism', Readings contends, 'calls for a rethinking of the notion of community under a horizon of dissensus rather than of consensus' (Readings 1992: 184).

The modern nation-state, however, is very much structured on the notion of consensus, employing notions such as the existence of a universal human nature to support this – signalled by the assumption of 'we' (representing the people) in documents like the French Revolution's 'Declaration of Rights' of 1789, as Lyotard discusses in *The Differend*

([1983] 1988a: 145). It is a notion that is also put to use, more conten-
tiously, to underpin the West's imperialist, colonialist ambitions. While
colonialism might have been overcome (a few pockets excepted), universalising ideas of that nature, and the 'narratives of emancipation' they
enshrine, are still highly influential in the new world order, for all that
Lyotard claimed in *The Postmodern Condition* ([1979] 1984b) that grand
narratives were in terminal decline. It might also be pointed out that
the effect of globalisation has been to create a neocolonialist relationship
between many underdeveloped nations and the Western capitalist system,
bearing out Lyotard's warning about the multinationals' inherent capacity
for 'imperilling the stability' (*PC*, 5) of such states.

Passages

Algeria
Differend
Dissensus
Marxism
Narrative of Emancipation
Paganism, Pagus

POSTHUMANISM

Stuart Sim

Although there are aspects of Lyotard's work that reasonably enough
could be described as humanist overall in sentiment, he seems determined
to distance himself from that tradition. This is consistent with the trend
within twentieth-century French thought, stretching from structuralism through poststructuralism, to denigrate humanism and treat it as an
outmoded worldview associated with some of the more suspect legacies
of the Enlightenment project (such as Theodor W. Adorno's suggested
connection between the Enlightenment mindset and outrages like the
Holocaust, which had a profound influence on poststructuralist thinkers).
We can note a posthumanist sensibility developing in French intellectual
life that can at times take on an anti-humanist dimension. The structural
Marxist philosopher Louis Althusser was one who proudly proclaimed his
anti-humanist credentials, identifying humanism with bourgeois capitalist
ideology, and there is at the very least an ambivalence among poststructuralist thinkers about humanist concerns such as the importance of self-
development and self-realisation. For Michel Foucault, for example, this

insistence on the individual as the central focus of culture was a transitory phenomenon of no great significance in the general historical scheme of things, and it would duly fade away leaving little trace.

The rediscovery of classical Greek culture in the Renaissance period gave a boost to the development of modern humanism, with the notion of humankind as 'the measure of all things' coming to the forefront. The Enlightenment built on this by challenging the authority of religious belief, encouraging individuals to trust in the power of human reason instead of theological doctrine. Along with this turn to reason comes a growing commitment to the implementation of human rights as a way of protecting the individual from the arbitrary exercise of political power. Eventually, humanist values are integrated into liberal democratic ideology, and thus come to form the basis for the modern, secular world order. Postmodernism has offered a critique of this order, claiming that over time it has turned into an oppressive system unwilling to countenance opposition to its aims. Most notably, it has taken issue with its cult of reason, and we find thinkers like Lyotard pointing up the limitations of reason at every opportunity. In rejecting the modernist paradigm, and calling on us to question humanist ideals and what they are being used to sanction (the exploitation of the developing world, as a case in point) postmodernists are clearly adopting a posthumanist stance.

One could argue that Lyotard's concept of the little narrative has a humanist air about it, because it champions the idea that individuals count for more than the forces of authority in their society. In fact, Lyotard is a spirited defender of the little against the grand, and will always want to oppose the will of the latter (as in the case of Marxism and its claims to universal validity), seeing it as inimical to our development into svelte, politically radical individuals, able to respond creatively to events. When it comes to choosing between individuals and theories, Lyotard will always choose individuals.

The work where Lyotard sounds closest to the humanist tradition is *The Inhuman* ([1988c] 1991a), his most sustained attack on the socio–economic ethos of our time – capitalist 'development' underpinned by a reason-led techno–science. Lyotard rails against a culture where development has been given its head and human beings are becoming progressively more subordinate to the corporate will. The forces of development are concerned solely with extending their empires; they prize efficiency above all else, and are more than willing to reduce humans to mere cogs in the machine if that is necessary to achieve this. For Lyotard, this is to install the inhuman right at the heart of our culture, and we ought to be combatting such a project. His reaction sounds at least proto-humanist, and one could easily find common ground between him and the humanist movement against a system in which machines and computers are considered to take precedence over human beings. Neither side would wish to see the inhuman emerging victorious.

Posthumanism is largely concerned with the questionable uses of humanist values in the services of Western imperialist ideology, and Lyotard certainly aligns himself with that position. He is not an anti-humanist in the Althusserian mould, however, and there is clearly an identification with the cause of the individual in his work, in the sense that he is very much opposed to the oppressive effect of belief systems in people's lives. It is best to regard him as a defender of the human, rather than humanism in its most widely understood, ideologically loaded, sense.

Passages

Development
Enlightenment
Inhuman
Little Narrative
Poststructuralism

POST-MARXISM

Richard G. Smith

In accordance with the prevailing intellectual climate in France after the Second World War Lyotard's early career and writings were concerned with Marxism. In his first book, *Phenomenology* ([1954] 1991b), he concerned himself with the potential of, and the inherent incompatibility of, phenomenology (the ideas of such thinkers as Edmund Husserl and Maurice Merleau-Ponty) for advancing the social and political philosophy of Marxism. Subsequently, in the seventeen years before the publication of his next major work – *Discourse, Figure* ([1971] 2010) – Lyotard's writings, and activities, fell within the orbit of Marxism and socialist revolution. From 1954 to 1964, Lyotard, was a member of – and wrote for the in-house journal of – the Marxist collective Socialisme ou Barbarie (Socialism or Barbarism), a grouping and publication whose aim was both to advance the Marxist critique of reality and to provide a critique of bureaucracy, particularly in relation to Stalinism and the French communist party (PCF). Taking over responsibility for the 'Algerian section' of the journal in 1955 Lyotard wrote primarily on the Algerian situation (see *La Guerre des Algériens* (1988a)): the issue of French colonial occupation, the bloody war for independence that broke out in 1954, Algeria's early years as a sovereign state after independence in 1962 and so on. However, what is notable about Lyotard's writings on Algeria is that they express considerable dissatisfaction with the ability of Marxist theory to match up with the reality of the political situation in Algeria. Indeed, through the 1960s, Marxist theory offered, for Lyotard, little purchase on the Algerian situation; his belief in Marxism was being eroded by the unfolding of events in Algeria, events that seemed divorced from the framework of ideas and concepts proposed by Karl Marx and his followers. His loss of faith was subsequently further compounded by the hijacking, and betrayal, by the PCF of the *événements* of May '68, revolts – undertaken through an alliance of students and workers – in which Lyotard had been actively involved, organising demonstrations at the University of Nanterre.

Disillusioned with both the PCF and official Marxism, Lyotard had by the late 1960s drifted away from Marxism altogether to adopt an anti-Marxist position. In both his doctoral thesis, *Discourse, Figure* ([1971] 2010), and *Libidinal Economy* ([1974] 1993a), Lyotard famously changes his philosophical position – engaging with, while also distancing himself from, the ideas of Jacques Lacan and Freud – irrevocably to part company with Marxism. Dismissing those attempts in France that, led by Althusser in the 1960s and 1970s, sought a new interpretation of Marx as 'scientific', Lyotard wrote that:

We no longer want to correct Marx, to reread him or to read him in the sense that the little Althusserians would like to 'read *Capital*': to interpret it according to 'its truth'. We have no plan to be true, to give the truth to Marx, we wonder what there is of the libido in Marx. (*LE*, 97)

Lyotard now burned all his bridges with Marxism, alienating his friends and colleagues among the French left, to mark a definitive break and sketch out another way of thinking that was akin to the poststructuralism of Gilles Deleuze and Felix Guattari's *Anti-Oedipus*, published just two years earlier, in 1972. Lyotard does not critique Marxism on its own terms, but rather undermines its concepts and claims (such as false consciousness) through a focus on the libido – the uncontrolled, uncontrollable and underexploited excess of forces, energies, drives, desires and potentiality – at work in both Marx and capitalism itself. Thus, through an intersection of Marx and Sigmund Freud, political economy becomes libidinal economy, the 'system named Marx' becomes the 'desire named Marx', and philosophy moves beyond rational explanation, and thinkers such as Marx, to become a 'theoretical fiction' that is attentive to how any situation and structure is one where a multitude of feelings and desires, intensities and affects, are at play, always exceeding any attempt at interpretation that would only dampen their intensity.

Lyotard intensifies his attack on Marxism, by this point just one of the large-scale 'universal' systems of thought he had rejected as a 'grand narrative', in an essay entitled 'A Memorial of Marxism: Pierre Souyri'. Published in 1982, in the French journal *Esprit*, and in English as an afterword to *Peregrinations* (1988b [1990]), Lyotard presents a personal account of his friendship with Pierre Souyri (d. 1979) – the Marxist historian and author of *Révolution et contre-révolution en Chine*, whom he first met in the 1950s at a union meeting, and with whom he was a member of both Socialisme ou Barbarie (Socialism or Barbarism), and Pouvoir Ouvrier (Worker's Power) until 1966. In his essay, Lyotard explains that he drifted away from Souryi to the point that their positions became incommensurable:

Our *différend* was without remedy from the moment that one of us contested or even suspected Marxism's ability to express the changes of the contemporary world. We no longer shared a common language in which we could explain ourselves or even express our disagreements. (*P*, 49)

In other words, it is not that Lyotard simply disagreed with Souyri – his friend and colleague who, following dialectical materialism, was of the view that 'The problems we confront are, in my eyes, neither ill-posed nor insoluble within the framework of Marxist concepts' (*P*, 48) – but rather that, for Lyotard at least, their respective theoretical positions had become incommensurable, lacking even a common vocabulary and language, so that dialogue and debate was rendered pointless. Thus, Lyotard's memorial to Souyri has a wider symbolism as a testament to not only his arrival at a differend with Marxism but also his recognition that, rather than having a privileged status outside its own sphere of competence, Marxism is just one differend in a world full of differends.

Passages

Algeria
Differend
Libidinal Economy
Marxism
Poststructuralism
Socialisme ou Barbarie

POSTMODERN, POSTMODERNITY

Richard G. Smith

While Lyotard's oeuvre spans many topics – in aesthetics, philosophy, politics and so on – he is best-known for his highly influential and controversial formulation of postmodernism as presented in *The Postmodern Condition* ([1979] 1984b). Moving on from a libidinal philosophy – in *Libidinal Economy* ([1974] 1993a) – that was concerned with the event and the limits of representation, Lyotard shifted his interests, by the late 1970s, to paganism (for example, see *Just Gaming* ([1979] 1985) and 'Lessons in Paganism' (in *LR*, 1989)) and a concern for difference, multiplicity and pluralism, through the formulation of a postmodern philosophy centred around 'language games', non-universal justice, and the concept of *The Differend* ([1983] 1988a). Indeed, the primary focus of Lyotard's later works is on postmodernism (overshadowing the term 'paganism'), as through a number of publications – such as, *The Postmodern Explained to Children* ([1986b] 1992), *Toward the Postmodern* (1993d), and *Postmodern Fables* ([1993a] 1997) – he clarifies and develops his diagnosis of, but not resignation to, the postmodern condition of fragmentation and pluralism.

The Postmodern Condition: A Report on Knowledge was commissioned by the Quebec Conseil des Universitiés and was published as a report on 'the condition of knowledge in the most highly developed societies' (*PC*, xxiii). It was through this report that Lyotard gained international fame for, among other things, his definition of the philosophy of 'postmodernism' as, in part, a rejection of those modern discourses – such as the physical and human sciences – that can only legitimise themselves through recourse to a 'meta- or grand narrative':

> I will use the term *modern* to designate any science that legitimates itself with reference to a metadiscourse . . . making an explicit appeal to some grand narrative, such as the dialectics of Spirit, the hermeneutics of meaning, the emancipation of the rational or working subject, or the creation of wealth . . . I define *postmodern* as incredulity toward metanarratives. (*PC*, xxiii–xxiv)

Lyotard argues that changes in society and culture in the second-half of the twentieth century have led to a collapse of faith in the 'grand narratives' – also referred to as 'master-discourses', 'super narratives' or 'metanarratives' – of modernity, to produce a crisis in postmodern societies as to what constitutes knowledge. That is to say that the 'postmodern condition', or 'postmodernity', Lyotard describes, is one that, first and foremost, recognises that confidence in 'world philosophies' – such as, liberalism, Christianity, Hegelianism, science, Marxism and so on – with their 'great stories' – such as, the progress of history towards social enlightenment and emancipation, the narrative of Christian salvation, the transcendence of history through class struggle or divine intervention and so on – has severely waned. This has been due to both actual events (the development of nuclear and chemical weapons, science's contribution to ecological disaster, the persistence and growth of world poverty despite the techno-logical breakthroughs of advanced capitalism and so on), and the techno-logical changes – such as 'computerisation' – that have transformed what constitutes knowledge and information in advanced economies.

'Our working hypothesis', writes Lyotard, 'is that the status of knowl-edge is altered as societies enter what is known as the postindustrial age and cultures enter what is known as the postmodern age' (*PC*, 3). That is to say that, a consequence of the widespread loss of confidence in those broad metaphysical contexts – be they artistic, cultural, economic, political, religious, scientific or social – that served to situate (ground) and justify (legitimate) modern knowledges, activities and cultural practices is that, in the 'post' era, the 'truth-value' of all knowledge has been provincialised, unable to transcend social, institutional or human limitations. Thus, the postmodern condition is one that is replete with a multitude of 'discur-sive species' or 'language games' – micro-narratives, little-narratives, or small stories – that, rather than adding-up to a single centralised modern project, a unified and timeless totality of 'complete knowledge', are now operating as distinct self-legitimising minoritarian spheres of knowledge.

The corollary of Lyotard's 'incredulity toward metanarratives' is that all knowledge, including science, is shown to be a 'little narrative' with no outside or beyond: any particular knowledge – be it, for example, a scientific experiment or a religious text – can no longer transcend its par-ticularity (to claim that it has universal or timeless value) through recourse to a meta-discourse outside its own sphere of competence, such as truth, order, and reason, or progress, emancipation and justice. In other words, no metanarrative is possible, only narrative, for knowledge is always limited by the fact it is produced within a 'language game' that it cannot transcend: each specialism (even within 'science') speaks its own language, sets its own agendas, produces its own particular truths and can only legitimise itself.

While *The Postmodern Condition* was the work that established Lyotard's reputation as the postmodernist par excellence, the real philosophical basis for that predominantly sociological work was, in fact, outlined a few years later in his book on the concept of *The Differend* ([1983] 1988a). In that work 'language games' become 'regimens of phrases' and 'genres of discourse' as, rather than simply resigning himself to the relativism of a heterogeneous postmodern patchwork culture of 'little narratives',

Lyotard strives for dissensus and a non-universal justice (judgement without criteria) so that the differend is no longer suppressed (that is, neither returned to a centre, origin or meaning in a metanarrative nor silenced in a 'language-game'), but is freed from consensus. Those who have been silenced in any particular 'language game' (because their position contravened its established rules of argumentation and validation) are enabled through the differend to unleash the potential of experimentation (a new 'paralogical' narrative): a breaking of the rules, or the invention of new rules, in any 'language game', so as to open up new ways of thinking and acting that displace the status quo/consensus in any particular field of knowledge to allow the pursuit of the as-yet unknown.

Passages

Differend
Knowledge
Language Games
Little Narrative
Paganism, Pagus
Paralogy

POSTMODERN SCIENCE

Stuart Sim

In *The Postmodern Condition* ([1979] 1984b) Lyotard puts forward the notion of there being a distinctively 'postmodern' science which 'is producing not the known, but the unknown' (*PC*, 60). He draws his evidence from areas like catastrophe theory (and the work of such scientists as Benoit Mandelbrot, famous for his work on fractals), which seems to demonstrate that there are aspects of physical processes lying beyond human control and involving a significant degree of paradox in their operation. Undecidability and indeterminacy are recurrent features in the workings of the natural world: catastrophe theory and even more particularly its successors chaos theory and complexity theory picture that world as governed by a series of processes marked by a combination of randomness and determinism – which can only appear paradoxical and bewildering to the layperson. Ultimately, postmodern science reveals that there is an element of the sublime about scientific enquiry, that there are limits to what can be known.

Against Lyotard's claims, it could be argued that scientists are not so much concerned with generating the unknown as delving deeper into it to make sense of its workings. For most scientists, the unknown is only a stage on the road to greater knowledge, and few are willing to accept unknowability as a ruling principle in their work. One generation's unknown is so often a later generation's common knowledge: dark matter and dark energy, as cases in point, may seem mysterious entities now, but they may not always be. However, there are others in the scientific world who do insist that we must accept the existence of unbreachable limits to human knowledge, with John D. Barrow, for example, exploring what these might be in his book *Impossibility* (1998). One such limit is that we cannot ever know anything about those areas of the universe which are too far away from us for light to have reached us from there (or possibly ever to do so, given an expanding universe).

Lyotard is attracted to undecidability and indeterminacy as reinforcements of his worldview, believing that the future is essentially open and that our actions can change the state of the world: revolutions can occur, metanarratives can be challenged successfully. The *événements* represent the kind of spontaneous 'event' that he claims can never be entirely foreseen by the ruling authorities, and constitute a vindication of his belief in human freedom. Lyotard is consistently critical of theories which claim inevitable outcomes for social or political processes (as does Marxism, for example), and emphasises instead the unpredictability of human affairs: to think otherwise would be to lapse into a fatalism which could only benefit the ruling authorities. Postmodern science, with its many apparent paradoxes, enables Lyotard to argue against determinism in general, and also provides further evidence for the existence of the sublime – the area which, by definition, lies forever beyond the boundaries of human knowability. Paradox always works against totalising systems of thought, and Lyotard is throughout his career an anti-totalising thinker concerned to prove that individual actions do matter and that we should not permit systems to dictate how we live.

Passages

Catastrophe Theory and Chaos Theory
May '68, *événements*
Sublime
Totality, Totalisation
Unknown

POSTMODERNISM

Thomas Docherty

Although the term 'postmodernism' long predates Lyotard, his work gives it a very specific inflection and one that is at odds with the prevailing customary and journalistic usage. The predominant view is the 'periodising' view whereby it describes an art and culture 'after' a modernism of 1870–1945. Lyotard, however, regards the postmodern not as a period but as a mood or an attitude, one that is as likely to be found in François Rabelais or Laurence Sterne as in Marcel Duchamp or Gertrude Stein, say (1984b: 84–5). The mood in question is one governed by a crisis in judgement and thus in justice.

In *The Postmodern Condition* ([1979] 1984b), he pithily defined this mood as one governed by an 'incredulity toward metanarratives' (*PC*, xxiv). The 'modern', indebted to the foundational philosophy of René Descartes, is characterised by a thinking that legitimises a given particular judgement (a local narrative) by its conformity to a rule that is already given by a more general state of affairs (the metanarrative), such as the dialectics of Spirit (G. W. F. Hegel) or the historical movement of class struggle (Karl Marx) or a generalised notion of a univocal historical progression towards emancipation (Enlightenment). The postmodern abandons such simple justice or validation of judgement.

Here, Lyotard is indebted to Theodor W. Adorno, who saw the potential totalising tendency in foundational philosophies, especially those advanced in the name of the Enlightenment. Such totalising thought eliminates the particularity of the specific historical or aesthetic 'event', construing the event instead simply as a 'sign' whose meaning is guaranteed or explained by an appeal to its governing metanarrative. In 1985, with Thierry Chaput, Lyotard mounted an exhibition of *Les Immatériaux*. The exhibition questioned the whole Cartesian programme of thought in which the subject identifies itself as 'the master and possessor of nature' (1985a: 17). This was to be 'a postmodern drama. There is no hero in it, no overarching single story' (1985a: 5). Instead, the spectator is called on to reawaken her sensibilities by navigating multiple possible routes through the exhibition, thereby constructing multiple, even contradictory, narratives about its plural meanings. Where the modern 'loved grand systems and totalities', postmodernism realises that 'the reason that governs knowledge is not the same reason that governs living. We must multiply the modes of rationality' (1985a: 5).

Here certain key postmodern characteristics emerge: (1) suspicion regarding the metanarrational 'project of modernity' that gives the subject

autonomous mastery of her own freedom and possibilities; (2) the opening
of multiple local narratives that do not depend for their legitimation upon
an appeal to a foundational philosophy; (3) the challenge to the human to
construct and release multiple narratives, multiple identities; and (4) the
rigorous critique of legitimation and of judgements.

It is not the case that Lyotard questions reason as such; rather, he
argues that modernity sees 'the insinuation of the will into reason', and
thus, the reason in question is not 'purely' reasonable. Further, the
Enlightenment prefers one rationality – Cartesian method or the abstractions of mathematics – proposing it as the *only* viable rationality. The result
is that modernity's 'progress' towards emancipation is, in fact, ambivalent:
it is a progress marked by advances in the abstractions of *technology* which,
while certainly becoming more sophisticated and complex, do not necessarily entail corresponding advances in human freedom. Lyotard's postmodernism acknowledges this technological complexity and asks that we
match it in our thinking about the complexities of emancipation.

Following the historical crises of the mid-twentieth century, Lyotard
becomes wary of any thinking that proposes itself as totalising. Indeed, he
considers such thought to be governed by Terror (a word with great significance for one shaped both by the trajectory of the French Revolution
and by mid-century Nazism). In response, he argues that we must 'wage
a war on totality' (*PC*, 82); and the consequence of this is that we attend
to difference. First, such difference becomes the very structure of our
own identity: we are shaped by the multiple and potentially contradictory
local narratives that we use to make sense of the events of life. Second, it
follows from this that we have a problem concerning the establishment
of the social as something founded upon consensus: a proper attention to
difference sees us multiply the possibility – and in fact the necessity – of a
certain dissent, a differend. The proper – postmodern – attitude towards
knowledge is one where we pursue the unknown, not to master it with one
universally agreed explanation, but rather to multiply differences.

There are consequences here. Postmodernism regards truth in more
pragmatic terms: 'what is better in the way of belief'. Thus we avoid allowing one local voice to become a universal, totalising 'wilful' force called
Truth. Further, the event that is an artwork provokes a differend: a call to
judgement among disparate multiple voices, but a judgement that eschews
the possibility of consensual Truth.

The final consequence is the most far-reaching. Provoking a crisis in
judgement, postmodernism provokes a corresponding crisis in political
justice. Lyotard's postmodernism requires that we 'judge without criteria': we can have no appeal to any pre-existing system of rules, any code
transcending the local, that would legitimise the result of our judgement.

There is now a massive problem facing us: we must judge (even to eschew judgement or to delay it is already an implicit act of judgement); yet we have no criteria against which to measure the right validity of our judgement. We can only know 'after the fact' what to make of our judgement. Thus, the philosopher – even the postmodern subject – is in the position now of the artist: she 'works without rules in order to formulate the rules of *what will have been done*' (*PC*, 81). Once the judgement is made, we will be able to formulate its rules; but these rules cannot themselves become foundational. In turn, they must be abandoned. In this way, we have a 'future anteriority' that characterises the postmodern mood; and – the greatest claim of all – postmodernism becomes the very condition of the possibility of modernity. If we wish to be modern, or contemporary, we must accept the anxiety of the postmodern mood.

Passages

Art
Judgement
Little Narrative
Modern, Modernity
Modernism
Totality, Totalisation

POSTSTRUCTURALISM

Richard G. Smith

Lyotard is widely associated with postmodernism, standing as the leading analyst (not advocate) of the postmodern condition. However, he is also often identified (in the Anglophone academy at least) as one of the main progenitors – along with such thinkers as Giorgio Agamben, Roland Barthes, Jean Baudrillard, Hélène Cixous, Gilles Deleuze, Paul de Man, Jacques Derrida, Michel Foucault, Felix Guattari, Luce Irigaray, Sarah Kofman, Julia Kristeva, Jacques Lacan and Emmanuel Levinas – of poststructuralist philosophy. That is to say that Lyotard's way of thinking and style of writing bears many of the hallmarks of poststructuralist thought and so is often placed alongside those thinkers who, from the 1960s, drifted away from the then-dominant intellectual discourse of structuralism towards a collective philosophical programme that was for difference, multiplicity, figuration, the arbitrariness of the sign, the decentredness of the subject, non-presence, the remainder, the undecidable, the irreducible singularity of the event, the constructivism of language and theory, the demise of 'grand narratives' and so on.

In accordance with other poststructuralist thinkers Lyotard displays a fierce hostility to closed or totalised systems: 'Let us wage a war on totality' (*PC*, 82). In *Libidinal Economy* ([1974] 1993a) Lyotard concerns himself with 'dissimulation', that is to say with how any given system, linguistic or otherwise, conceals within itself other systems, singularities, affects and intensities that are inconsistent, not only with the system but also with each other. In other words, the mantra of structuralism that content (appearances, events) is reducible to form (structures), that below-surface logics have a causal efficacy over surface events, is displaced in Lyotardian poststructuralism. Akin to Deleuze's 'lines of flight', Lyotard is attentive to the 'limits of structuralism', to how the more a system attempts to circumscribe its elements to stave off change the more it creates 'lines of flight' that escape any given system of meaning. That is to say that Lyotard does not just ask signs to speak as would a semiotician, but rather also places the terrain of signs into motion: 'signs are not only terms, stages, set in relation and made explicit in a trail of conquest; they *can also* be, indissociably, singular and vain intensities in exodus' (*LE*, 50).

As with a number of other poststructuralist thinkers – such as Baudrillard, Deleuze, Derrida and Foucault (but also Alain Badiou and Martin Heidegger) – Lyotard's philosophy includes a conceptualisation of the event (*événement*) and the singularity. Lyotard's philosophy of the event is locatable as a part of his 'war on totality' (universality, systems of meaning, the principle of identity and so on) in favour of difference, plurality, particularity, experimentation, dissension and the new. For Lyotard, an event is an occurrence that is not consistent with any pre-given system's attempt to place it, organise it, within a meaningful logical structure and closed system of meaning. The event cannot be bound in and explained away, but rather resists, escapes and overwhelms those theoretical systems (such as dialectical materialism) that attempt to account for the event's uniqueness and intensity as a singularity, through recourse to a pattern or narrative of undifferentiated unity whereby any effect is always attributable to a cause.

Like other poststructuralists – such as Deleuze and Derrida – Lyotard is a philosopher of difference. Wary of structuralism's categories, and categorisation of the world, Lyotard is attentive to the injustice, violence or even 'Terror' that such totalising metatheories do to difference as they simplify the complexity and heterogeneity of differential space and time to assert such metaphysical illusions as identity and permanence. In his works *Just Gaming* ([1979] 1985) and *The Differend* ([1983] 1988a) Lyotard insists on the impossibility of doing justice to any event (even one as horrifying as Auschwitz), precisely because any imposed system of meaning and categorisation inevitably leads to both the event's diminishment and disappearance (as its complexity is reduced) and injustice, because debate is closed down and the Other is subordinated to a dominant narrative and discourse. In other words, there are events that cannot be named, cannot be represented, precisely because they are differential and so cannot be done justice to when stamped on by a simple identity. Thus, akin to Baudrillard's hyper-real with no critical distance, or Derrida's famous claim that '[t]here is nothing outside of the text [there is no outside-text; *il n'y a pas de hors-texte*]' (Derrida [1967a] 1976: 158), Lyotard's contention is that while one is always within narrative one is also never beyond it: 'The first thing to avoid, comrades, is pretending that we are situated elsewhere. We evacuate nothing, we stay in the same place, we occupy the terrain of signs . . . It speaks to you? It sets us in motion' (*LE*, 50, 51).

Passages

Auschwitz
Difference
Differend
Event
Libidinal Economy
Totality, Totalisation

POUVOIR OUVRIER – see 'drift, drifting', 'Marxism', 'post-Marxism' and 'Socialisme ou Barbarie'

POWER

Angélique du Toit

It is impossible to understand the position of Lyotard on power without a discussion of the term 'grand narrative'. A persistent theme of his work is the opposition to universal truths or metanarratives and the authoritarianism associated with them: we need 'no longer have recourse' (*PC*, 60) to these in his opinion. It is true to say that Lyotard leads the revolution against universal theories, exhibiting a disdain of authority in whichever disguise it may present itself. He argues fiercely against many of the claims inherent within the Enlightenment and sets out to undermine the fundamental principles which underpin the broad claims associated with this historical phenomenon. His deep-seated suspicion of authority can be defined as a scepticism of perceived wisdom and cultural norms.

The essence of Lyotard and his work is his opposition to the power associated with bastions of authority, whether they be political authority or the grand narratives of science. Power is not a quality reserved for a select few, but rather it is a body of knowledge which allows an individual to define the world in a way of their choosing – hence his call to 'give the public free access to the memory and data banks' (*PC*, 67) of our information society. He challenges the claims of these grand narratives in their monopoly of a perceived ultimate truth which suppresses any dissenting voices. Instead he argues for the multiplicity of communities of meaning, the innumerable separate systems in which meanings are created and disseminated. Furthermore, he argues for the incommensurability of such systems and their ability to exist side by side. Postmodernism posits that it is through relationships that those claiming power are granted such power: permission is given by those engaged in the relationship through their acceptance of imposed power.

Political power has centred on the ability of governments and other political groups to insist on obedience from society without an understanding as to what discourse informs the justification of obedience. It is an obedience not from a descriptive position, but one of prescription. Lyotard's distrust of the grand narratives promoted by the 'priests' of philosophy and science is grounded in a suspicion that their narratives are the stories of the ruling classes in an attempt to legitimate their power. Postmodern thinkers such as Lyotard have at their core a rejection of the assumed power of authority and urge their resistance in whichever form they may present themselves. His thinking is characterised by a deeply held scepticism of authority and its rules and the power it exerts over the individual. In fact, he encourages the individual to be a constant source of annoyance to any form of grand narrative.

Lyotard argues for the right of every individual to have an equal voice in situations of conflict. The individual voice or little narrative has, according to Lyotard, the right to control her own destiny, thereby reclaiming the power to decide. A criticism of the works of Lyotard and other postmodern philosophers is that they do not offer a clear-cut alternative philosophy. Instead, they only urge opposition and a shift of power from the 'grand narrative' to the ability of the individual or 'little narrative' to oppose the force of the ideologies represented by such grand narratives.

In *The Postmodern Condition* ([1979] 1984b) Lyotard refers to the assumption that knowledge has become the dominant force of production in recent times. He goes on to suggest that it will be a key contributor in the division between developing and developed countries, arguing that the striving for knowledge will be a major factor in the worldwide competition for power. The race for information in gaining domination over other nation-states is likely to replace the need for control over raw material, cheap labour and territory which were the focus of power battles in the past. The battle for knowledge reflects the erosion of the erstwhile power of the State in control of the production and distribution of knowledge and the commercialisation of knowledge in favour of economic power. In the last few decades we have witnessed the erosion of the power held by the State through increased power exercised by multinational corporations through their dominance of knowledge creation.

Increasingly, investment decisions are being taken by such corporations and continuing the disempowerment of nation-states, and the meltdown of the banking sector is an example of the impotence of governments to control or influence such decisions that have threatened the stability of economies worldwide. The technological revolution that makes the internet and other forms of communication available to all is a powerful force in removing the ownership and control of knowledge and learning from the State. Lyotard argues in *The Postmodern Condition* that whoever controls knowledge exerts power and authority.

The opposition to universal truths as put forward by Lyotard and others is depicted in the term, the differend, and represents the condition which arises from a dispute between two discourses operating under different sets of rules. Traditionally, one discourse will exert its power and come to dominate the other, thereby producing a 'solution' to the dispute resulting in the suppression of the other. But this is a process to be resisted, and Lyotard illustrates the need for maintaining and protecting the differend through an event such as Auschwitz which is not clearly explained by theories of the time. Such events have the power to raze any deterministic truths. Bearing witness to the differend would prevent the establishment of political power and domination wherever and in whatever form it strives to exert itself. Lyotard also turns his scepticism against the techno-scientist whom he argues is bent on dehumanising and destroying mankind, citing this as yet another attempt to exert control over the differend.

Lyotard does not necessarily provide an answer to the question of how the sharing of power is to be achieved, but his support of the differend is akin to that of a moral duty. One could also argue, however, that the term differend, and the passion with which Lyotard defends it, is analogous to a grand narrative in itself with its associated beliefs and assumptions. The belief in equality could be subjected to the same criticisms as would be levied against any other universal truths or beliefs.

Passages

PRAGMATICS

Georges Van Den Abbeele

Pragmatics is a subfield of linguistics that analyses the interactions *between* interlocutors in the context of communication, as opposed to the study of utterances in terms of their form (morphology), meaning (semantics), internal organisation (syntax) or sound structure (phonology). Pragmatics, especially as developed by linguists such as Oswald Ducrot, François Recanati or Alain Berrendonner, also expands certain tendencies in the philosophy of language, especially speech-act theory (J. L. Austin) and Ludwig Wittgenstein's concept of language games, that emphasise what language does as much as what it says.

Wittgenstein inspires Lyotard's first foray into the question: *Just Gaming* ([1979] 1985), where he analyses ethical situations from the point of view of language games, specifically the dubiousness of deriving prescriptive utterances from descriptive ones (or an 'ought' on the basis of an 'is'). Lyotard later rejects the concept of language games, and in a series of works culminating in *The Differend* ([1983] 1988a), he develops his own brand of pragmatics as a philosophical and situational analysis of discursive interaction.

Specifically, Lyotard's pragmatics posits a dynamic interplay between the four instances (addressor, addressee, sense and reference) constituted by the universe of a sentence, or *phrase*. In communicational terms, this can be expressed as someone saying something about something to someone. The formula is deceptively simple, however. It should not be construed as implying pre-existing subjects using language as if it were a mere tool for users situated entirely outside it. This is the reason why, in his *Diacritics* interview, he rejects the concept of language games as 'repeating the constant arrogance of Western anthropocentrism' (Van Den Abbeele 2004: 249). For Lyotard, the pragmatic relation, or 'phrase-regimen' (prescription, cognition, inquiry, definition, etc.), is constitutive of the instances themselves, including the addressor and addressee.

The difference between sense and reference applies Gottlob Frege's well-known distinction whereby different expressions refer to the same thing but with different meanings, as in the example of 'morning star' and 'evening star' both referring to the planet Venus. The difference between *destinateur* and *destinataire* is often rendered in standard communicational theory by 'sender' and 'receiver', a terminology that both loses the symmetry posited by the French terms and again supposes an instrumentalised view of communication whereby an utterance is unproblematically transmitted from someone who sends it to someone who receives it. The French terminology, and the homophonically equivalent addressor/addressee, does not assume reception as a fact, only that the sender addresses or 'destines' something to someone, who may or may not get it at all.

The difference is important in understanding the subtlety of Lyotard's complex use of this simple schema of the phrase (which, incidentally, he is quick not to limit to language or discourse in any narrow sense, nor its participants to human beings). Where the analysis gets interesting is in the interaction, not between interlocutors but between *phrases*, or what he refers to, via the metaphor of the chain, as 'linking on'. The specific rules or protocols that determine *how* one phrase is linked on to another is called a genre of discourse (narrative, dialogue, philosophical speculation). Despite such organisational strictures, the phrase is never a static object, and one phrase necessarily implies, entails or links on to another. That linkage is not so much a *logical* necessity (which would correspond only to a certain genre of discourse) as an *ontological* one: there must necessarily come to pass a phrase that links onto what has been phrased, or else it is the death of discourse itself. While the classic communicational or dialogue model posits the addressor and addressee changing places with each phrase while altering the sense attributed to a reference that remains stable and consistent, the pragmatics Lyotard deploys studies all kinds of possible interactions between the four instances of the phrase universe, where any one of these can be marked as another instance in the ensuing phrase: addressor can become reference, sense can become addressee, in endless concatenations. The only limitations are those imposed by various phrase regimens or genres of discourses or grand narratives that legitimate only certain linkages between phrases and not others. It is at this point, however, that the analytical concerns of pragmatics dovetail with those of politics, ethics and justice. Lyotard's pragmatics thus opens up an entire philosophy and politics of phrases, from the analysis of *how* any given phrase links onto another all the way up to that of the great narratives that have structured history. As he writes in *The Differend*, 'the social is implicated in the universe of a phrase and the political in its mode of linking' (*D*, 198).

Passages

PRESCRIPTIVES see DESCRIPTIVES AND PRESCRIPTIVES

PROBITY

Anthony Gritten

Probity, increasingly important to Lyotard in later writings, is a quality of judgement that is central to the kind of attitude that Lyotard tries to encourage as part of the good life. It is closely related to phronesis, prudence and reflective judgement, and Lyotard's phrasing of the concept is influenced by Aristotle and Immanuel Kant, though it differs in significant ways from both.

Probity is not a quality of judgements in which the telos is mastery of the event, but a quality of judgements in which lightness of touch, patience and attention to detail, are present and predominant. It is a quality of judgement embodied in the attitude (and ideology) that the singular request of the case here and now demands attention in order for justice to arise, that sensitivity to the multiple contingencies of each and every individual case is an important quality both of the just judgement and the good life to which it contributes. Just as the free-floating attention of the psychoanalyst is anchored by the demand to accord equal attention to every utterance of the analysand, however empty they may appear, and just as the mother's attention is focused in a unique way upon the demands of her child, so judging with probity involves a general suspension of the aggressive grasping that characterises cognition. It involves opening the mind to the events which touch it, to unknown events which it can apprehend but not comprehend, and acting as a passage for the feelings which arise from these events. This giving over of the mind requires courage, since it is difficult to apprehend the delicate nuances, tender resonances and generally timbral nature of the event such that these qualities are phrased justly in each judgement.

In this respect, then, judging with probity involves bending a third ear towards the event and listening in to what happens. It is thus central to artistic practice, and Lyotard frequently turns to art in order to argue that aesthetic judgement carries an important secret: that of the manner (rather than method) in which critical thought operates. The artist's aim is to become receptive enough to encounter events, and this means becoming svelte: light, patient and attentive. In the artistic search for new affects, feelings, phrases and judgements, probity is a quality of activity.

Unlike obligation, probity is embodied in events with respect to which there is a degree of freedom in the phrasing. Like cognition, judging with probity requires situational knowledge, but, unlike cognition, it is also a matter of embodied, reflective judgement. Indeed, because for Lyotard justice is an Idea in the Kantian sense (rather than an experience), judging with probity is a matter of exercising judiciousness in dispute, and making do pragmatically without criteria. This does not mean that probity is simply a matter of coping without facts, but rather that the rules connecting sensible data to concepts and the manner of judging have to be created for and in each individual case (rather than adopted wholesale from prior experience). In this respect, probity is a quality of judgement that does not lend itself to articulation and generalisation into an ethics *qua* system or method, and it is not embodied in judgements that claim to separate subject and object. Rather, it is witnessed and developed in the living of a certain kind of *ars vitae*, a way of life in which judgements are enacted and exercised (not merely learnt) as a means of valuing both time and the singularity of the other.

For some commentators, Lyotard's phrasing of probity omits the components of education and habit that characterise Aristotle's conception. It is certainly true that probity is at heart a pagan behaviour, since the only guide to judging with probity is what is immediately at hand (the nearest it comes to being a method is in being a largely comparative affair). However, there is much in the later Lyotard to suggest what kinds of education and habit Lyotard would incorporate into probity: all those activities and beliefs that slow down passing, that make decisions with less haste and more thought, and that thus bear witness to the differend. As he phrases these virtues in *The Inhuman* ([1988c] 1991a): 'I do not like this haste. What it hurries, and crushes, is what after the fact I find that I have always tried, under diverse heading – work, figural, heterogeneity, dissensus, event, thing – to reserve: the unharmonisable' (*I*, 4). It is this, the unharmonisable, that judging with probity seeks to acknowledge, and to phrase.

Passages

PSYCHOANALYSIS

Tony Purvis

The foundational concept in psychoanalysis is the unconscious, and so any discussion of Lyotard's intervention in the field will address this term with some degree of alignment, if not synonymy, with psychoanalysis. The closely related term in Sigmund Freud and in Lyotard is that of desire, as also in Jacques Lacan. Lyotard is writing at a time in which the theoretical and political implications of Lacan's return to Freud were still on the critical agenda. It is no surprise, then, that Lyotard uses similar language to that of a psychoanalysis indebted to Lacan's structuralist contributions to the field.

It is the figurations of desire, and its intensities, more than language, however, which preoccupy Lyotard's discussion of the unconscious/psychoanalysis. Unlike the structuralist Lacan, Lyotard inflects psychoanalytic theory with the notions of figure and libidinal intensity. In that Lacan's most important reading of Freud is summarised in the former's suggestion that the unconscious is structured like a language, so Lyotard links our understanding of psychoanalysis to the operation of figures, which subsequently become dis-figured, rather than condensed, through desire.

The unconscious, as the concept is formulated in Freud, is closely tied to his theory of repression. Freud argues that we are not conscious of what we desire because the culture requires subjects to repress their desires. This is the argument which Lacan endorses in his own return to Freud. Desire in that sense is on the side of the unconscious in classical psychoanalytic theory. Lyotard's work, because it is keenly interested in the operation of desire in culture, is also aware of the extent to which culture is lived at the level of unconscious desires or in a libidinal economy.

It is in *Discourse, Figure* ([1971] 2010), however, that Lyotard first outlines his case. Freud's analysis of patients demonstrates how the

unconscious is most closely exposed via the analysis of dreams, slips of
the tongue and bungled actions. For Freud, dream thoughts are hidden
messages and codes that require analysis and interpretation. It is these
aspects of dream-work which interest Lyotard, and particularly through
the operations of condensation and displacement. However, Lyotard's
theory of the unconscious goes further than Freud's by way of a reversal of
the aforementioned logic of the dream-work. Lyotard suggests that condensation (metonymy) *does not* compact the material of the dream; and nor
is desire actually disguised. Patients are already speaking their desires/
the unconscious with great intensity as far as Lyotard is concerned. The
unconscious, in other words, *is* desire, but not in a disguised form at all. It
is a force whose intensity is manifest not by way of condensation but via
disfiguration.

Lyotard's reading of Freud's case histories suggests that psychoanalysis
does not produce a cure for the patient after analysis. To that extent, he
concurs with Freud in affirming that a psychoanalysis does not come to an
end. However, he also departs from classical Freudian theory. Lyotard's
rendering sees psychoanalysis/the unconscious in terms of new concen-
trations and energies. His key contribution to an understanding of Freud
and thus psychoanalysis suggests that the talking cure is as much a libidinal as it is an economic operation. The curing at work in psychoanalysis,
argues Lyotard, is one which seeks to confine and redirect so-called
blocked energy towards language. However, Lyotard's important inflection of psychoanalysis suggests that this can only happen via a move from
libidinal economy to political economy. In classical psychoanalysis, the
royal road to the unconscious is through the dream. Lyotard adds to this
the crucial dimension of desire. The work of desire *is* the dream, and it
operates by an active disfigurement of desire itself. For Lyotard, psychoanalysis, synonymous now with the unconscious, endlessly connives with
desires to produce yet more figures.

Passages

Desire
Dream-work
Figure
Libidinal Economy

R

REASON, RATIONALITY

Stuart Sim

The Enlightenment is instrumental in instituting what might be called a cult of reason in Western culture. As far as the major figures of Enlightenment thought were concerned (the *philosophes*, for example), reason was to be the antidote to the superstition of religion, as well as the dead weight of tradition that underpinned authoritarian political systems, and they campaigned for an enhanced role for it within the social order. The older designation for the Enlightenment period, the 'Age of Reason', gives an indication of how the term came to be identified with the social and political changes that ushered in the modern era from the eighteenth century onwards. Commentators now question just how rational the century in reality was, even in intellectual circles such as the *philosophes*, and it is quite easy to put together a very different picture of it than the Age of Reason tag suggests, one in which superstition still played a large role and in which a cult of feeling countered the influence of Enlightenment ideas (as in the rise of Romanticism as an aesthetic movement). Yet there is no denying that reason came to take on great symbolic significance in Western society, being considered, for example, the motivating force behind socio-economic progress – the primary concern of modernity as a cultural formation.

Postmodern thought takes issue with the Enlightenment project, which means that it sets itself against the cult of reason and its insistence that it holds the key to humanity's development. Again and again, thinkers like Lyotard draw our attention to where reason fails and its limitations are starkly revealed: hence his obsession with the sublime, that classic instance of the unknowable as far as humanity is concerned. Postmodernists paint an altogether less complimentary picture of the human animal, and in so doing problematise the ideological basis of contemporary Western culture, with its belief that rational solutions can always be devised for any problems that arise. Science, from the modern Western perspective, is a quintessentially rational activity, and feeds directly into the world of technology, which provides the means to improve our lifestyle and command over the environment. Lyotard's position is that this combination, techno-science in his terminology, is in fact bad news for humanity and holds out the prospect of a form of slavery, with humankind increasingly under the control of the techno-scientific establishment and subservient to its will. For Lyotard, techno-science propels us into the realm of the inhuman. Not that he finds contemporary scientific research exactly an advertisement for rationality, since the world it is discovering seems anything but rational in its organisation (illustrated by the succession of paradoxes thrown up by chaos theory, complexity theory and quantum physics, for example).

The anti-Enlightenment attitudes adopted by Lyotard and the poststructuralist-postmodernist school in general have led to charges of irrationalism being levelled against them by such critics as Jürgen Habermas, who regards these attitudes as politically reactionary and potentially anti-democratic in their implications. Habermas is unashamedly pro-modernity, regarding it as an 'unfinished project' for all its admitted shortcomings. It would be more true to say, however, that such as Lyotard are not so much irrational as against what reason and rationality have come to stand for in our world: an uncritical acceptance of the grand narrative of socio-economic progress, as a case in point, which involves suppression of social groups who for whatever reason do not buy into the dominant ideology being propounded by their rulers.

In a more general philosophical sense, Lyotard is simply to be seen as carrying on the tradition of the sceptics in pointing out where reason's limitations have to be acknowledged – as in the case of being unable to establish logically sound foundations for discourse. The argument here is that even philosophy is not as rational an activity as it would like to think it is, and that the condition of certainty it seeks to achieve through the deployment of reason (as in the case of René Descartes) is an impossible goal. Rationalists believe in the existence of absolute truths against which we can measure our statements and codes of behaviour, but Lyotard the sceptic and pragmatist remains firmly unconvinced: 'What I say is true because I prove that it is – but what proof is there that my proof is true?' (*PC*, 24). At best, he will admit to a 'relative certainty in matters of truth' (*JG*, 99), but that would hardly count as a defence of reason for a confirmed rationalist.

Passages

Antifoundationalism
Enlightenment
Modern, Modernity
Paralogy
Poststructuralism
Scepticism

REFERENT

Stuart Sim

The nature of reference has exercised philosophers considerably over the years, and Lyotard enters into this debate at some length in *The Differend* ([1983] 1988a). At stake in the debate is the relation between terms (including, for example, names) and the objects, events, etc., they signify. Theories of reference need to explain how that process of signification works so as to make meaningful connection between terms and objects possible.

Lyotard has more than just a professional philosophical interest in establishing how to prove the reality of the referent. He is concerned to challenge those revisionist historians (such as Robert Faurisson) who deny the fact of the Holocaust on the grounds of insufficient evidence. In Faurisson's line of argument there would have to be eye-witness reports from deportees as to the existence of gas chambers, and then to these being used to kill people in camps like Auschwitz, and as these are not forthcoming he claims the Holocaust is a myth: lack of verification is taken to mean lack of a referent. Lyotard's acid rejoinder to the demand for such empirical proof is that 'it can be answered that no one can see one's own death', further insisting that 'no one can see "reality" properly called' (*D*, 33). There is, however, a sequence that can be put in motion to verify referents and thus counteract the revisionist school: 'there is someone to signify the referent and someone to understand the phrase that signifies it; the referent can be signified; it exists' (*D*, 16). The problem is that Faurisson is engaging in a different genre of discourse, one which 'does not have a stake in establishing reality' (*D*, 19). For Lyotard, this makes him guilty of bad faith.

Adopting the notion from Saul Kripke, Lyotard points out the importance of the 'chain of communication' when it comes to referents. These develop over time and enable various speakers to make statements about the referent, building on the chain that exists. In the same way, we are to recognise that there is a chain of communication leading back to Auschwitz and the Holocaust. Neither of these therefore require the testimony of an eye-witness in order to substantiate their reality, since 'reality is not established by ostension alone' (*D*, 40). Lyotard is exceedingly careful not to be drawn into a debate set up on the revisionists' terms, based as these are on the primacy of ostension. Instead, his line is that a 'referent is real' if it is the same whether 'signified', 'named' or 'shown' (*D*, 43), and in Auschwitz's case this is so. A further stipulation is that the reality has to be reaffirmed every time around: it does not have the character of a universal truth (something from which Lyotard will always shy away).

It is entirely characteristic of Lyotard to feel the need to link the philosophical and the political in this explicit manner. He is a thinker who invariably sees a political dimension to philosophical enquiry, refusing to remain in the safety of the abstract realm.

Passages

Auschwitz
Discourse
Genre
Links, Linkage
Philosophical Politics
Pragmatics

REPRESENTATION – see 'anamnesis', 'event', 'grand narrative', 'history, historians', 'idiom', 'incommensurability, incompatibility', 'judgement', 'libidinal economy', 'little narrative', 'May '68, *événements*', 'modernism', 'postmodern, postmodernity', 'sublime' and 'unpresentable'

RESISTANCE

Stuart Sim

The notion of resistance to traditional power structures is central to Lyotard's philosophy, although it has to be said he can be somewhat vague as to how this should be prosecuted. He is not one to advocate violence (he argues against the use of terror or terrorism at several points in his work), but one can wonder how this can be avoided if grand narratives respond aggressively to significant resistance to their authority – as we know they are prone to do, especially if it is of the radical kind that Lyotard seems to favour. (One thinks of the *événements* in this connection, when there was a concerted, if somewhat chaotic, attempt to bring down the French government.)

Little narratives are based on the principle of resistance, being designed to challenge larger forces within society – the government or the many corporations that go to make up the collective power base of the grand narrative (as well as its received intellectual authorities). Lyotard makes a particularly impassioned plea for little narrative resistance against both development and techno-science in *The Inhuman* ([1988c] 1991a):

[W]hat else remains as 'politics' except resistance to the inhuman? And what else is left to resist with but the debt which each soul has contracted with the miserable and admirable indetermination from which it was born and does not cease to be born? (*I*, 7)

This resistance is necessary, otherwise we risk reaching a stage where development and techno-science might consider they no longer have any need of the human at all, progressing from an inhuman to a non-human world. Once again, however, we can only speculate on how far we should go in the process of resistance. Marxists would of course recommend armed resistance, but what Lyotard calls his '*différend* with Marxism' (*P*, 45) means he has lost faith in the value of that type of response: 'the politics which "we" have inherited from revolutionary modes of thought and actions now turns out to redundant' (*I*, 7), as he rather despairingly notes, so we need to find other ways of taking the fight to grand narrative.

Lyotard does give us a more specific idea of what form resistance might take in *Instructions païennes* (1977a) when he encourages us to

alternate between harassing the State and harassing capital. And if it is at all possible to do so, use one to attack the other . . . [U]se laws and institutions against the abuses committed by entrepreneurs, organise tenants' associations, shopfloor struggles, ecological campaigns. (*LR*, 152)

He is not worried that such a campaign is unlikely to overturn the grand narrative quickly, preferring to work henceforth on a gradualist basis: 'We have to take our time' (*LR*, 152), as he counsels. Again, the more radically minded leftist movements would regard this as an inadequate response, all but tantamount to selling out to the enemy, as would radical fundamentalist groups in the non-Western world (Islamist, for example), who also feel that violence is the only effective way of demonstrating the seriousness of one's opposition.

We should not be too hard on Lyotard for leaving resistance such a vague concept, however, as this is likely to be the position anyone finds themselves in after rejecting Marxism, with its seductively easy solution on how to conduct revolutionary politics: a solution which in the main led to authoritarian and repressive regimes that did not really improve the lot of the world's oppressed very significantly over the course of the twentieth century. A disenchanted revolutionary always faces something of a dilemma in this respect, in laying himself open to charges of collusion if he suggests working within the system in order to change it: opponents can always claim that the system can contain such dissent, which poses no really substantial threat to its overall power. The argument back from someone like Lyotard has to be that it is false to think there is a simple answer to socio-political problems, and that no one theory has the legitimacy to enforce its will on the mass: that is just to replace one grand narrative with another. Lyotard's pragmatic turn to the little narrative is an acknowledgement that totalising approaches on the Marxist model historically have proved to be unsatisfactory, and that the complexity of human affairs requires a more nuanced response – even if this does not deliver the instant change that radical revolutionaries invariably want. What is needed instead is practical action with realistic objectives that involves people at a grass-roots level and makes a demonstrable difference in their everyday lives – and thus their political consciousness.

Passages

Ethics
Little Narrative
Paganism, Pagus
Power
Techno-Science
Totality, Totalisation

RICOEUR, PAUL (1913–2005) – see 'phenomenology'

RULES

Stuart Sim

Rules lay down the procedures to be followed in a wide range of human activities and are supposed to apply equally to all participants. Given that they pre-exist in most cases – as in games, for example, where the rule-book is passed on from generation to generation – they have a tendency to take on the force of law over time, even if it is agreed that they can on occasion be modified. For Lyotard, the conventional aspect is critical, since the notion of being indefinitely bound by regulations is anathema to someone so opposed to prejudgement, and who lays so much emphasis on the need to respond flexibly to events as they occur. We are to regard rules as applying within language games, but having no force outside each particular game, and Lyotard clearly thinks they should be treated lightly in every instance to keep them from inhibiting spontaneity or the development of a svelte character.

The degree of lightness we should ideally exhibit becomes evident when we turn to Lyotard's conception of artistic creation in a postmodern period. Postmodern writers and artists are those who have moved past existing frameworks and are striking out into new territory where they eschew the use of 'preestablished rules' or 'familiar categories' (*PC*, 81). Instead, '[t]hose rules and categories are what the work of art itself is looking for', so that creative artists 'are working without rules in order to formulate the rules of what *will have been done*' (*PC*, 81). Rules are purely retrospective therefore, with Lyotard arguing that the creative process itself is to be understood as being in the nature of an event, in which case the artist would be shackled if he or she were made to operate according to any pre-existing aesthetic scheme. Postmodernism seems to offer a whole new sense of freedom to artists, who should not feel themselves to be constrained by the rules set down by tradition or the artistic and critical authorities. Equally, they should not feel bound by their own previous efforts either: each time around they should be assuming something like a *tabula rasa*. Lyotard's vision of justice is very similar: judges should start afresh in each case, avoiding reference to previous practice.

Lyotard views the postmodern and the modern as cyclical phenomena, so this is not necessarily an attack on set aesthetic schemes of the kind to be found throughout history (neoclassicism being a particularly good example, or more recently socialist realism), but he does seem to be expressing a distinct preference for the freedom of the postmodern ethos. The radical nature of his thought comes through most strongly in his dislike of the prearranged – in philosophical thought no less than in the realms of art or politics. Rules must not be permitted to cramp the creative impulse, and rules are precisely what those in control of social and political systems seem determined to impose on us wherever possible – and to make us regard as sacrosanct, rather than provisional or pragmatic in the fashion of Lyotard.

Passages

Aesthetics
Justice
Language Games
Modern, Modernity
Svelteness
Touch

$$\boxed{S}$$

SARTRE, JEAN-PAUL (1905–80) – see 'existentialism', 'intellectuals', 'Jews, Judaism', 'phenomenology' and 'writing'

SCEPTICISM

Stuart Sim

Postmodernism as a movement of thought is highly sceptical in its orientation, espousing an attitude of suspicion towards authority in its various forms as well as received wisdom in general. It is critical of totalising systems of belief, seeing these as lacking any foundation (antifoundationalism is effectively the default position for the postmodern thinker), and thus open to challenge if they venture to assume any authority over us – which of course they traditionally do in the guise of ideologies and religions. We might characterise postmodernism as a particularly radical version of scepticism that is concerned to draw our attention to where belief systems fail to add up, and are in fact marked by contradictions and unsubstantiated assumptions that they are trying to hide.

Scepticism is well entrenched within the Western philosophical tradition, going right back to its beginnings in classical Greek culture. One of the most powerful strains of it is to be found in Pyrrhonism, which emphasises the relativistic nature of judgement in a manner that becomes standard among the sceptical community right up to our own day. As the leading chronicler of Pyrrhonism, Sextus Empiricus, points out, in order to make judgements about the truth or falsity of beliefs then we need to possess criteria which already have been validated for this purpose; but this only pushes us into an infinite regress which undermines the whole exercise (what validates those criteria in their turn and so on). This is the basis of relativism: that we can never establish a starting point from which to make judgements, that there are always unsubstantiated assumptions in play at some point (as Lyotard puts it in typically blunt fashion, 'according to what rules can we debate the rules to adopt for the debate?' (*P*, 52)). For such as Sextus and the Pyrrhonian tradition that is reason enough to back away from belief: at the very least to be as modest as one can in claims as to what one knows with any sense of certainty. The main target is those who are dogmatic about their beliefs (as postmodernists will argue those who defend metanarratives tend to be, with Marxists particularly guilty of this fault), and dogmatism will remain the enemy of scepticism throughout its history.

Lyotard shares the sceptical turn of mind of the postmodern movement in general, and there is a definitely antifoundational character to his thought: 'There is no metalanguage, and by metalanguage, I mean the famous theoretical discourse that is supposed to ground political and ethical decisions that will be taken as the basis of its statements' (*JG*, 28). It is one of his main criticisms of Marxism that it assumes something like a tribunal of history that provides justification for its theories, and the political practices following on from these, when no such thing does, or indeed ever could, exist. In reality, Marxism is simply one among many genres of discourse, none of which can be considered as superior to the others, and none of which have a monopoly on making value judgements about political or ethical matters: each has its own set of rules, but they do not hold for other genres. Unlike sceptics such as the Pyrrhonists, however, Lyotard is still very much exercised by the need to make value judgements, even if we have no absolute criteria on which to rely. He is not willing to let events such as the Holocaust escape judgement, and there is an unmistakably moralistic quality to his thought that can be missing in many other relativists. In his case scepticism is not being deployed to close down debate (as so often can be the practice with sceptics, notably those of a Pyrrhonian persuasion), rather it is to be seen as the problematical background against which we must continue to search for ways to achieve some kind of justice in human affairs.

As a politically engaged thinker deeply disturbed by the extent of the abuse of power in our culture, Lyotard is not willing to let things rest when relativism comes on to the scene, even if there is no metalanguage to appeal to for confirmation of our judgements. The point is to keep striving to make judgements in some manner or other that we can find a general measure of agreement on among our fellows (on the horror and injustice of the Holocaust, and the maltreatment of Jews over the course of European history which laid the groundwork for this particular event, for example), and Lyotard is a pragmatist on that score. To back away from having a position in such cases, as in conveniently 'forgetting' what happened to the Jews in the Holocaust, is indefensible in his eyes. The 'case-by-case' method becomes one of his preferred methods of arriving at judgements. Each case is to be taken on its merits without reference to any previous cases, and the decision will form no template for the future either. The method would seem to depend heavily on the good will of the judges involved, who would be expected to be as impartial as possible: '[t]he judge . . . will be considered just only by his actions, if it can be seen that he judges well, that he is really just' (*JG*, 28). While one can see many potential problems with such a procedure (it certainly leaves a lot to personal temperament), what it does indicate is that Lyotard is firmly committed to the notion of justice, which he does not regard as being contingent on the principle of a metalanguage. Scepticism does not absolve one of the obligation to be as just as one can under all circumstances.

Ultimately, scepticism becomes a weapon against the totalising imperative to Lyotard, a way of demonstrating that metanarratives can never be justified, nor the authority they lay claim to either. The onus this lays on us is to reconstruct society on pluralist lines, where various narratives can flourish, without losing sight of the need for it to have a basis in, and commitment to, justice.

Passages

Antifoundationalism
Judgement
Marxism
Pluralism
Relativism
Totality, Totalisation

SENTENCE – see 'addressee, addressor/sender', 'agonistics', 'phrase, phrasing' and 'pragmatics'

SEXUALITY

Tony Purvis

Reference to Lyotard's understanding of sexuality in many critical studies of his work is sparse. Yet Lyotard is a key theorist of sexuality, even if this is in part a result of what he fails to say about the topic directly. It is argued here that Lyotard is a queer theorist *avant la lettre* in that his early work constitutes a theory of sexual queerness before it is a theory of sexual identity per se. A closer inspection of some of his critical vocabulary, however, tells something of how the sexual serves as a backdrop to the libidinal and political dimensions of his output as well as his anticipation of what is now called queer theory.

Lyotard is again indebted to Sigmund Freud's work, and not simply for the latter's theory of the unconscious. Freud's view, that the child is born without a sexual identity or a sexual orientation, is crucial to Lyotard's discussions in *Libidinal Economy* ([1974] 1993a). Drives and desires, while they may or may not be prior to culture, are none the less prior to how sexual orientation is figured in adulthood. Nor is there in Freud's theory any psychic unity attached to the child. Rather, there emerges a psycho-analytic language which hesitatingly speaks of fluidity, dispersion and the sexual more than sexual identity.

It is the fluidity and the perversity of desire which attracts Lyotard. Freud famously writes about the child's sexual perversity in relation to an account of desire which is described as as 'polymorphous'. It is *Libidinal Economy* which theorises and embraces the potential of such polymorphous-perverse shape-shifting. For Lyotard, the body – if it can ever be assigned a sexuality in any simple way – is wholly libidinal. Such libidinality means that orientations of desire are prior to – or at least more significant than – how sexuality and its orientations are constructed in the culture. Sexuality is important to Lyotard, but it is not an identitar-ian model which is being espoused. Rather, it is through the figure of the Möbius band that Lyotard frames his revised theory of polymorphous perversity.

Sexual orientation and desire are not attached to a single object or person. Nor is sexual desire conceived as a desire for a 'person' so much as it is a force which blurs how we might imagine anatomical sexing, the body and gender. If there is no continuity among these three categories, then Lyotard's work is prescient to the extent that it suggests he is moving beyond categories which structure and limit sexuality, a move embraced by queer theory some fifteen years later. Moreover, and for Lyotard this is central, sexual desire is not *personal* at all. Anything can or could be the object of desire in Lyotard's theory of the political and libidinal economies.

His experimental thinking in *Libidinal Economy* is, in itself, impor-tant. He writes of the 'immense membrane of the libidinal body', of 'heterogeneous textures' and of zones which 'are joined end to end in a band which has no back to it, a Möbius band' (*LE*, 2). Alert to the ways in which psychoanalytic desire is often framed in binary terms (masculinity/ femininity, male/female, hetero/homo) Lyotard uses instead 'libidinal' as a way of thinking through the dimensions of the sexual. The Möbius band, 'far from being 'smooth' is 'covered with roughness, corners, creases, [and] cavities' (*LE*, 3). With this kind of language, Lyotard, far from multiplying sexual norms, importantly attempts to disfigure them.

Passages

Body
Desire
Great Ephemeral Skin
Libidinal Economy
Psychoanalysis

SINGULARITY – see *'dispositif'*, 'event', 'idiom', 'judgement', 'May '68, *événements*', 'performativity', 'poststructuralism' and 'tensor'

SOCIALISME OU BARBARIE

Derek M. Robbins

Socialisme ou Barbarie was a group, with an associated journal, which was established by Cornelius Castoriadis in 1949. Born in Constantinople and a student of law, economics and philosophy in Athens, Castoriadis had come to Paris after the Second World War, where he joined the French section of the Trotskyist Fourth International. He and others – notably Claude Lefort – became disillusioned with the Fourth International. *Socialisme ou Barbarie* was a splinter group. In its journal's opening number (March 1949), Castoriadis argued that 'Today the "Fourth International" uses a spurious faithfulness to the letter of Marxism as a substitute for an answer to the important questions of the day' (Castoriadis 1988: 77). The most important 'question of the day' was how to preserve the agency of the working classes when, in both capitalist and communist countries, they are represented by gigantic trade unions and political parties which are 'cynically playing the role of direct agents of the ruling class and of the capitalist State, or of the bureaucratic capitalism that reigns in Russia' (Castoriadis 1988: 77). Castoriadis concluded with a sentence which clearly indicated the basis of the alternative expressed in the title of the group and the journal and of their prescriptions for the future: 'Only one force can arise today to challenge the continuing decay and increasing barbarism of all regimes based upon exploitation: that of the producing class, the socialist proletariat' (Castoriadis 1988: 106).

In late 1972, Castoriadis wrote a 'general introduction' to a collection of his early essays entitled *La société bureaucratique* in which he indicated that the first of several theoretical lessons learnt after the Second World War, articulated in 1953–4, was that the 'independence of ruling strata vis-à-vis their own population' (Castoriadis 1988: 12) as well as in relation to the populations of the opposing dominant world blocs had been overestimated. In an article published in *Socialisme ou Barbarie* in 1954, entitled 'Situation de l'impérialisme et perspectives du prolétariat' (The Situation of Imperialism and Proletarian Perspectives) Castoriadis argued that 'the fundamental characteristic of the contemporary era' was the struggle between the American and the Russian blocs to dominate and exploit the rest of the world. In spite of their different ideologies, both blocs were indistinguishable in the colonial context in wanting to suppress any kind of domestic uprising which might impinge upon their attempts to secure international supremacy (Castoriadis 1988: 256).

In 1982, Lyotard wrote a Preface to a posthumously published book on revolution and counter-revolution in China up to 1949 by a former associate in *Socialisme ou Barbarie* – Pierre Souyri (Souyri 1982). Lyotard added this article to the American and French editions of *Peregrinations* (1988b [1990]) because it supplemented the account of his intellectual development given in those Wellek Library lectures – detailing his involvement with Socialisme ou Barbarie. Souyri and Lyotard had joined the group together in 1954. As a result of his experience as a teacher in Algeria from 1952 to 1954, Lyotard became the Algerian 'correspondent' for the journal. Twelve of the articles written by Lyotard between 1956 and 1963 during the Algerian war of independence were published together in 1989 in his *La guerre des Algériens*, and eight of these were included in his *Political Writings* (1993b). Lyotard's texts gave tangible detail about the specifics of the North African situation to support the group's general views on local bureaucracies and its dissatisfaction with the stance of the Communist Party on colonialism.

Lyotard and Souyri both became members of a subgroup of Socialisme ou Barbarie – entitled Pouvoir Ouvrier (Worker Power) with an associated monthly publication – in 1959, and this developed into a full secession from the main group in 1964. (Castoriadis disbanded the main group during the winter of 1965–6.) In 1966, Lyotard resigned from Pouvoir Ouvrier, having lost confidence in the capacity of Marxist thought to deliver social change. Souyri never gave up on his Marxist convictions and regarded Lyotard's resignation as a betrayal. Using the language which he was developing in the early 1980s, Lyotard's article of 1982 on Souyri treated the analysis of their intellectual differences as a case-study analysis of their 'differend', thereby absorbing the differences of their relationships to the Marxist grand narrative into a broader political and ethical agenda which would build on dissensus rather than imposed ideological consensus. This transition in Lyotard's thought commenced with his resignation from Socialisme ou Barbarie which had been a dominant influence, and it continued through his involvement with the events of May 1968, as reflected in *Dérive à partir de Marx et Freud* (1973a), leading, at the end of the 1970s to the publication of *The Postmodern Condition* ([1979] 1984b).

Passages

Algeria
Differend
Dissensus
Marxism
Postcolonialism
Post-Marxism

SOUYRI, PIERRE (1925–79) – see 'Marxism', 'post-Marxism' and 'Socialisme ou Barbarie'

SPECULATIVE NARRATIVE

Stuart Sim

Two of the major forms that grand narratives take in the modern era to claim the right of legitimation are the narrative of emancipation and the speculative narrative, the difference between these being that '[o]ne is more political, the other more philosophical' (*PC*, 31). That is, narratives of emancipation are concerned with achieving human liberty and ensuring our freedom from tyranny, whereas speculative narratives are undertaken in the name of some abstract higher ideal such as knowledge, scientific truth or something even more amorphous such as G. W. F. Hegel's notion of the 'World Spirit'.

Lyotard dates the rise of the modern speculative narrative from the founding of the University of Berlin in the early nineteenth century and its expressed commitment to the principle of learning (and particularly scientific learning) for its own sake – although this was seen by the founders in the wider context of the need to improve the moral and spiritual condition of the Prussian State. The spirit of speculation is held to be central to the university ethos (and has remained officially so throughout the Western higher education system into our own time), even if, as Lyotard notes, it is not quite an end in itself as long as it is perceived to have a role in a larger political project. Behind this idea, however, lurks the desire to create a 'unity to learning' (*PC*, 33), which is yet another dubious project of totalisation in Lyotard's opinion.

Science has increasingly become the dominant speculative narrative of our time, and universities have become heavily implicated in the process. Scientific research is a major part of the university's brief, and at least on the face of it scientific departments are dedicated to the search for truth. Lyotard considers that questionable enough, but thinks the reality is far less idealistic than it is presented, arguing that in most cases the search has turned into a self-justifying activity within a self-enclosed system: 'Statements are treated as their own autonyms and set in motion in a way that is supposed to render them mutually engendering: these are the rules of speculative language. The University, as its name indicates, is its exclusive institution' (*PC*, 35).

Speculative narratives based on science have been badly hit, however, by the rise of what Lyotard calls 'postmodern science', with its tendency, in his interpretation, to keep 'producing not the known but the unknown' (*PC*, 60), thereby in effect undermining itself as a legitimating process. The rules of speculation no longer seem to be working, and are failing to provide the feedback loop that the system needs to protect its claim to authority: instead, it is confronted by more and more paradoxes that it cannot explain.

We find ourselves in the postmodern condition when neither the emancipatory nor the speculative narrative can maintain their aura of credibility (Marxism, which made use of both, has suffered accordingly). As far as Lyotard is concerned, we must accept that justification in the name of some postulated higher unity is always suspect and generally has an underhand political motive.

Passages

Legitimation
Narrative
Narrative of Emancipation
Postmodern Science
Totality, Totalisation

STALINISM – see 'aesthetics', 'May '68, *événements*', 'post-Marxism' and 'terror'

STRUCTURALISM – see 'deconstruction', 'deictics', 'difference', 'posthumanism', 'poststructuralism', 'psychoanalysis', 'thought' and 'writing'

SUBJECT

Karen Langhelle

Throughout his career, Lyotard has consistently sought to challenge modernity's reliance on a subject-centred philosophy. Whereas the pre-moderns believed that a divine entity could furnish the ground for knowledge, with modernity comes the view that the only recourse we have to epistemological certainty is through the thinking subject, as exemplified in the first-person narrative of the Cartesian *Cogito*. To Lyotard, it amounts to a metaphysical illusion to conclude that because *I think* there must therefore first be a unified subject capable of processing experience and synthesising thought. The only thing that resists radical doubt is the fact that there has been the phrase, *I think:* to doubt that there has been a phrase means voicing this doubt in the form of phrase.

Perhaps the greatest consequence of Lyotard's rethinking of the unified subject is that it 'inevitably lead[s] to the abandoning of the linguist-communication structure (I/you/he/she) which . . . the moderns endorsed as an ontological and political model' (*LR*, 317). Initially, Lyotard would rely on the notion of narratives not only to describe the subject-centred structure of language but also to challenge it. Modernity's privileging of the sender position allows for a concept of narrative that 'legitimate[s] knowledge as the effective performance of rational communication' (Readings 1991: 67). Positioned outside the narrative, the subject-sender uses it as a tool to reach a point of consensus with an anonymous receiver, this point being the constitution of a 'total subject' (humanism's 'man' or Marxism's 'proletariat'). Against this view, Lyotard pits the example of the Cashinahua's 'savage' narrative, where the subject-sender 'situates himself in the two forgotten poles . . . of Western thought' (*JG*, 33), as both part of the narrative as a reference as well as its receiver-listener.

However, it is in *The Differend* ([1983] 1988a) that Lyotard most successfully formulates his distinctly postmodern view of the subject as one of dispersion and displacement. Here, a phrase is not a message passed from one unified subject to another, both of which are external to it. Instead the phrase presents a universe in which are marked to varying degrees the four poles of addressor and addressee, referent and sense. This phrase universe is not something presented to the subject; rather, the subject is situated in the universe of the phrase. As such, the subject's identity can have no more permanence than the deictics that mark it: like *I*, the subject 'appears and disappears with this universe, and thus with this phrase' (*D*, 33). Nor can proper names be said to prove a continuity between a 'subject of uttering' and the permanence of a self: names may be 'rigid designators' of reality, but they are ultimately empty, since any number of meanings may be attached to them. The subject, therefore, is the temporary effect of a phrase and for this reason cannot be said to provide a stable ground for the knowledge of reality. Rather than constituting the experience of the subject, reality thus entails the differend, insofar as it is only the result of a particular linking of phrases.

Passages

Addressee, Addressor/Sender
Deictics
Knowledge
Modern, Modernity
Phrase, Phrasing
Referent

SUBLIME

Pamela Sue Anderson

Lyotard's conception of the sublime develops in critical relation to both Immanuel Kant's feeling of the sublime and Kant's establishing of what has been thought to constitute the 'modern' in philosophy, especially in aesthetics, morality and metaphysics. As Lyotard explains, Kant describes the unrepresentable aspects of 'the real sublime sentiment' as 'an intrinsic combination of pleasure and pain: the pleasure that reason should exceed all presentation, the pain that imagination or sensibility should not be equal to the concept' (*PC*, 81; cf. Kant [1764] 1973: 45; and [1790] 2000: 128–31). Lyotard, then, argues that Kant's aesthetic of the sublime is modern in contrast to a 'postmodern' sublime which 'puts forward the unpresentable in presentation itself' (*PC*, 81).

Following after the French reception of G. W. F. Hegel's philosophy, Lyotard also describes Kant's account of the sublime as a failure in Hegelian terms, that is, as a subject who sacrifices the 'I' for the universal, or the absolute, in ways which are overly abstract, not adequately embodied. In historical-political terms, Hegel links the Kantian sublime with the bad infinity as analogous to the sacrifice of the individual to absolute freedom in the terror of the French Revolution. But Lyotard disagrees with any Hegelian or post-Hegelian reading of Kant insofar as it claims to usher in the end of modernity, as if in a temporal progress the postmodern follows after the modern. For Lyotard, it is the reverse: to become modern the sublime has first to become 'postmodern'. The latter is 'understood

[as] not modernism at its end but in the nascent state, and this state is constant' (*PC*, 79). Ironically for Hegel, his absolute sublime suffers the loss of not only the concrete 'I' but also human difference.

Lyotard contends that the modern response to Kant's feeling of the sublime as falling 'outside the horizons of presentation' stresses 'the powerlessness of the faculty of presentation', and yet this leaves a 'nostalgia for presence' (*PC*, 79). In Kant's *Critique of the Power of Judgement* (2000 [1790]), the sublime is unlike beauty which can be, in principle, linked to an ideal, but unrealised universal consensus; this happens, for Kant, when a particular generates a new universal. In this well-known (Kantian) account, the universal communicability of the sublime derives not from the understanding and not from sensibility in any immediate manner; rather the sublime's universality involves ideas which come from reason and are related to a higher faculty of the supersensible. And here the sublime seems to be contra-purposive for our power of judgement, unsuitable for our faculty of presentation, and as it were doing violence to our imagination, but is nevertheless judged all the more sublime for that (Kant [1790] 2000: 129).

In Lyotard, the postmodern 'irrupts' within the sublime once the focus is on 'the power of the faculty to conceive' (*PC*, 79); and so, the powerlessness of the imagination takes hold in the failure of representation. This unrepresentable aspect of the sublime has made Kant's 'Analytic of the Sublime', in the *Critique of the Power of Judgement*, of major significance for Lyotard's interpretation of the uncontainable moments of excess which constantly irrupt – and interrupt – modern philosophy. In his *Lessons on the Analytic of the Sublime* ([1991b] 1994), Lyotard contends that the demand for universal communicability fails when it comes to the sublime which undercuts itself in escaping all 'universality' and 'univerzalisation' (*LAS*, 239). What remains distinctive for Lyotard's sublime is its connection to '*un différend*', a difference, on which 'the fate of thought depends and will depend' (*PC*, 80): that is, a conflict between genres of communication. Lyotard's differend involves a conflict which, in political terms, is not resolvable; and hence, what is at stake is described in terms of 'incommensurability' (*PC*, 79). Lyotard describes the irreconcilability of terms as the chasm between competing Kantian faculties of reason and understanding, and 'imagination or sensibility' (*PC*, 81) and understanding, in the moment of the sublime.

In other words, the sentiment of the sublime takes place when the imagination fails to present an object which might, if only in principle, come to match a concept: 'We can conceive the infinitely great, the infinitely powerful, but every presentation of an object destined to "make visible" this absolute greatness or power appears to us painfully inadequate' (*PC*, 78; cf. Kant [1790] 2000: 129).

The postmodern sentiment of the sublime, then, becomes the pleasure in irreconcilable conflict over this unpresentable in presentation. Such conflict is crucial for those feelings of the sublime to occupy a position in a social network of 'messages . . . in perpetual motion' (*PC*, 16). In turn, the movement of these messages generates the distinctive disorientation characterising the postmodern (cf. Battersby 2007: 37–8).

So, Lyotard exposes the manner in which Kant's critical philosophy is perpetually interrupted by the sublime as uncontainable moments of excess; and yet, Lyotard also argues that the terror of modernity's absolute universality is (rightly) disturbed; that is, any absolute unity, or totality, is (and should be) continually disrupted by postmodern difference. Due to incommensurable 'absolutes', accompanying a multiplicity of language games, the postmodern sublime cannot privilege consensus; rather, Lyotard looks for a means to mobilise difference. Over and against philosophers from Kant to Hegel and Karl Marx, who suppose a metanarrative progresses toward truth and justice, Lyotard argues for a multiplicity of heterogeneous, incommensurable language games with their own immanent criteria. Anyone who rejects this must be, according to Lyotard, thinking from a totalitarian or rigidly doctrinaire standpoint.

Lyotard's later essays, in *The Inhuman* ([1988c] 1991a), demonstrate that the sublime of avant-garde painters is also 'an event, an occurrence' in the 'here and now' (*I*, 90–3). Ultimately, this is meant to create a positive picture of the sublime, even in the pain of bodily differences, in postmodern art and philosophy as 'the joy obtained in the intensification of being' (*I*, 93). Otherwise, the danger is the loss of the human: the sublime would disappear without time and organic bodies.

Passages

Difference
Differend
Incommensurability, Incompatibility
Modern, Modernity
Unknown
Unpresentable

SVELTENESS

Stuart Sim

Svelteness is for Lyotard a condition of heightened adaptability that individuals should aspire to, a method of remaining responsive to events rather than being controlled by them. As outlined in the essay 'Svelte Appendix to the Postmodern Question' in *Tombeau de l'intellectuel et autres papiers* (1984b), it is to be conceived of as 'wakefulness', indicating that, as Lyotard points out Stendhal had recognised earlier, 'the ideal is no longer the physical force of ancient peoples; it is flexibility, speed, metamorphic capacity (one goes to the ball in the evening, and one wages war the next day at dawn' (*PW*, 28). The svelte individual is not burdened by ideological baggage and is able to move between situations, and roles, with ease (in Italian, svelte means slenderness, and it is used that way in the fashion industry). Lyotard goes on to contend that it will only be when we have many more such individuals in society that we will start to achieve any justice in our politics.

Such a notion meshes well with Lyotard's conception of the little narrative, which is not designed for the long term but instead the short-term objective (confronting a particular social or political abuse, for example). Little narrative should have no desire to continue on once such an objective has been realised: in other words, its ideology should be as 'slender' as possible. Svelteness means to be always on the lookout for new opportunities, rather than to be concerned with creating a permanent power base that would seek to oppress others – the beginnings of the grand narrative principle, and what should be avoided at all costs.

Lyotard sees svelteness as being in an intriguing conflict with capitalism, which he pictures as driven by an 'infinity of the will' (*PW*, 28–9). Svelte individuals are more interested in 'learning, knowing, inventing, circulating' than plain 'working' (*PW*, 29), which serves the cause of capitalism and must be mediated to prevent it taking over our lives. Capitalism is pictured as an anarchic force, which the state tries its best to tame, although its desire to go on expanding can only be contained to a certain extent. Svelteness becomes a political statement against both capitalism and the state, introducing more of a human dimension into what can be a 'very ugly' (*PW*, 26) process that can bring out some of the worst aspects of human nature.

Lyotard is critical of how capitalism is turning information into a marketable commodity (one of the most striking features of late twentieth-century culture in his view), and encourages us to resist this, arguing that we ought 'to critique the shallow notion of information, to reveal an irremediable opacity within language itself' (*PW*, 27). Svelteness, which he asserts is 'most of all a quality of language' (*PW*, 28), is integral to that project of resistance; a means of demonstrating that language cannot be tied down in the way that the capitalist system is claiming, that our individual production of information, too, is characterised by a subversive flexibility, speed, and metamorphic capacity.

Passages

Capitalism
Knowledge
Language Games
Little Narrative
Politics
Resistance

T

TECHNO-SCIENCE

Stuart Sim

Techno-science represents for Lyotard one of the most powerful forces in our world, and can be interpreted as the conjunction of the multinationals and scientific enquiry. Scientific exploration nowadays is heavily funded by the corporate sector and, in those cases where it is not, it is eventually taken over by the sector if it has the potential to lead to commercially viable technological adaptation. Techno-science is at the cutting edge of advanced capitalism, concerned with exploiting science for profit. The transformation of scientific discoveries into technological products has been one of the defining features of modernity as a cultural system, and Lyotard feels that the process is in danger of getting out of hand as the corporate sector increasingly drives scientific exploration in order to strengthen the degree of control it has built up over humanity. The fear he has is that technology will be turned against us and become an end in itself rather than a means to serve our needs.

In *The Inhuman* ([1988c] 1991a) Lyotard speculates that the techno-scientific establishment is striving to improve its computer systems so that they will outlast the death of the sun 4.5 billion years or so into the future. It is doing so because such systems are far more efficient than humanity, as well as more controllable. He paints a nightmare scenario of humanity eventually being eclipsed altogether by computer systems, his argument being that the techno-scientific project in general is designed to put the inhuman at the centre of our culture, with all the unfortunate implications this would have for us as a species. Techno-science would be inclined 'to abandon, or even actively to destroy, those parts of the human race which appear superfluous' (*I*, 76) to its goals.

Techno-science is effectively a grand narrative for Lyotard and like all grand narratives he wants it to be met with resistance, but the extent of its power in our culture makes it a formidable enemy. The main problem is that we have become accustomed, it could even be said addicted, to constant technological improvement, regarding this as an essential element of our culture – almost part of our birthright. We expect new gadgetry to be coming on stream on a regular basis to enhance our lifestyle and give us greater control over our environment, and could be said to be in collusion with techno-science in that sense. The more we come to rely on that technology, however, the more we find ourselves becoming subservient to the corporations which commission and manufacture it, and Lyotard is warning us that such power could very easily be used against us in future if techno-science found it expedient to do so.

What Lyotard has identified in techno-science is the tendency of modernity to become obsessed with systems and efficiency (as it did in the first instance with industrialisation) and to reduce human beings to the status of servants of the system. Techno-science is merely the latest expression of advanced capitalism in that respect.

Passages

Inhuman
Modern, Modernity
Posthumanism
Power
Thought Without a Body

TENSOR

Ashley Woodward

The tensor is an interpretation of the sign Lyotard develops in *Libidinal Economy* ([1974] 1993a) and attendant essays. The tensor is distinguished from the semiotic sign, but is not another kind of sign, set up in opposition: it is an interpretation of all signs from a different perspective, one which includes the semiotic but also adds 'a dimension of *force* which escapes the logic of the signifier' (*LE*, 64). In short, the tensor is '[a]t the same time a sign which produces meaning through difference and opposition, and a sign producing intensity through force [*puissance*] and singularity' (*LE*, 54).

Lyotard contends that the semiotic sign (as understood by, for example, Charles S. Peirce, Ferdinand de Saussure, Umberto Eco and Jacques Lacan) is religious and nihilistic in the sense elaborated by Friedrich Nietzsche. In its simplest sense, the sign replaces something for someone. This replacement may be thought of in two ways. First, the sign may be understood as signifying a signified, the 'meaning' it stands for. Lyotard characterises this as a kind of Platonism, because signs are seen as mere appearances which signify Ideas. In this sense, semiotics is nihilistic because it negates the significance of any material, bodily, sensuous or affective givens by asking: of what concept is this a sign?

Second, signification may be understood as being constituted by signs alone, meaning being endlessly deferred in a system of references. In Saussurean linguistics, meaning in this system is regulated by structural differences. For Lacan, the terms in this system are kept disjunct by a great, absent signifier. According to Lyotard, '[n]ihilism in its entirety stands here: meaning deferred, and lack slips into this deferral' (*LE*, 70). This religious nihilism of the sign is clearly indicated by the twelfth-century Victorin theologians, for whom Creation must be understood as a system of signs in which God has encoded messages, but who believe we shall never be in full possession of the code which would allow us to decipher them. Nietzsche characterises religion as nihilistic because it places meaning and value in a transcendent world beyond our reach, and the parallel with the semiotic theory of the sign here is clear.

Lyotard poses the tensor in response to this nihilism. The term 'tensor' implies intensity and tension. This tension needs to be thought in three dimensions: between intensity and meaning; between different desires and libidinal drives; and between the different meanings these desires can give rise to. Lyotard insists that the tensor is not simply polysemantic. In its dimension as intense singularity it has no assignable meaning as such. The potential meanings of the tensor are not delimited by the relatively rigid semiotic structures of signification, but are shaped in more fluid ways by the plastic forces of desire. While all signs are in principle tensors, Lyotard offers the proper name as an apt example because logicians such as Bertrand Russell and Gottlob Frege have had difficulty explaining it in terms of a logico-linguistic structure. Lyotard focuses his discussion around 'Flechsig', the name of Judge Schreber's former doctor in the well-known case discussed by Freud (*LE*, 54–60; Freud 1953–74: vol. 12). In Schreber's delirium, the name 'Flechsig' becomes the site for a host of incompossible desires and meanings in tension with each other (for example, both love and hate).

Lyotard advocates a reception of the tensor sign which is distinguished from the semiotician's decoding: 'It speaks to you? It sets us in motion'

(*LE*, 50–1). Instead of assuming that one is being spoken to through signs and attempting to decipher the message, the libidinal economist attempts to be receptive to the energy of the sign and to channel and transform it in new ways. It is a creative, active response aimed at constructing 'other things, texts, images, sounds, politics, caresses, etc.' (*LE*, 51). In the arts, the tensor invites us to feel and be inspired by the energy of the painter's brush stroke or the dancer's gesture, without immediately 'dematerialising' these things by trying to see beyond them to some conceptual meaning they supposedly represent. Politically, the tensor allows a way of understanding and responding to the attempts of existing institutions and ideologies to co-opt events for their own ends: it indicates that events, understood as tensors, exceed any such ends and that their energy can be exploited in new, unexpected ways, opening up possibilities for political change. In Lyotard's later work some similar themes are taken up through a treatment of the proper name as a rigid designator, and the feeling of the sublime is called a tensor sign (D).

Passages

Great Ephemeral Skin
Great Zero
Libidinal Economy
Nihilism
Sublime

TERROR

Stuart Sim

Terror is an important part of the armoury of grand narratives, one of their key strategies for enforcing compliance with their vision of unity. The act of legitimation itself carries with it a threat of violence if we do not accept its writ or the objectives it establishes for us. In our own era this has become focused on the optimisation of the system's efficiency: 'The application of this criterion to all of our games necessarily entails a certain level of terror, whether soft or hard: be operational (that is, commensurable) or disappear' (*PC*, xxiv). Neither variety of terror is ever justified, and Lyotard is a vigorous opponent of coercion in whatever form it takes – whether undertaken in the name of 'freedom' or something altogether more sinister, such as Nazism or Stalinism (and the latter, as he darkly notes, 'is not the monopoly of the communist parties' (*PW*, 68)).

Soft and hard terror might be taken as roughly equivalent to Louis Althusser's Institutional State Apparatus, with its use of psychological and sociological pressure on individuals, and Repressive State Apparatus, with its outright use of violence. They indicate the lengths to which the grand narrative of the state is willing to go to maintain its hold over the population; the difference in Lyotard's case being that he regards this as intrinsic to all grand narratives, not just those on the side of capitalism and bourgeois democracy. The attitude in each and every instance will be '[a]dapt your aspirations to our ends – or else' (PC, 64). We are to be constrained into the language game that the grand narrative wants us to play, and if that game is based on a bourgeois democratic idea like freedom then we will simply have '[t]error in the name of freedom' (JG, 92). There is the added complication that the terror most likely will come to take on a life of its own, and freedom to mean little more than submission to a domineering grand narrative – such as that of Western imperialism. Lyotard also speaks of 'the white terror of truth' (PW, 240), and clearly regards rationality and rationalism as forms of terror designed to restrict what we can think (and again, we can see how these have been co-opted in the cause of Western imperialism).

Terror is to be regarded as an everyday part of our lives, therefore, with Lyotard claiming that the social bond 'is traversed by terror' (JG, 99). Our existence is largely governed by fear, and that of course is very much to the advantage of the grand narrative. As a corrective to a society run on such principles, Lyotard recommends one based instead on 'the justice of multiplicity', which would 'prohibit terror, that is, the blackmail of death toward one's partners' (JG, 100). Under the aegis of the justice of multiplicity, little narratives would thrive and the fear that characterises such a society as our own would evaporate – which is about as close to a utopian vision as Lyotard will ever allow himself.

Passages

Justice
Language Games
Legitimation
Little Narrative
Reason, Rationality

THÉBAUD, JEAN-LOUP – see 'antifoundationalism', 'descriptives and prescriptives', 'dissensus', 'game theory, gaming' and 'judgement'

THOUGHT

Stuart Sim

Lyotard's attitude to thought recalls that of the structuralist movement to language. It is for him something that we act as a channel for, that we move in and out of, rather in the way that theorists like Barthes contended language spoke through us: 'thoughts are not our own. We try to enter into and belong to them. What we call the mind is the exertion of thinking thoughts' (*P*, 6). Thoughts are compared to clouds, an amorphous, ever-changing entity that can neither be pinned down nor plotted with any accuracy. Lyotard recommends that we should go with the flow of thought without deluding ourselves that we are in any way in control of its overall trajectory.

We are born into thought, therefore, and cannot regard ourselves as the creator of any particular aspect of it as a system. Instead, we are making use of what is already there in the fashion of a *bricoleur*: 'I suggest that each thinking consists in a re-thinking and that there is nothing the presentation of which could be said to be the "premiere"' (*P*, 8). Lyotard picks up here on a recurrent theme of poststructuralist thought, the impossibility of ever locating precise origins. In Jacques Derrida's case this was symbolised by the figure of the *mise en abyme*, which offered merely an infinite regress of an image; Benoit Mandelbrot's fractals registered the same experience, meaning that we could never have a complete picture, or understanding, of any given entity. For Lyotard, in similar vein, '[e]very emergence of something reiterates something else, every occurrence is a recurrence' (*P*, 8–9), and we cannot identify where this process begins. He suggests that we find our way around in the clouds of thought we encounter as Ludwig Wittgenstein claimed we did in the pre-existing language games we are also born into: 'groping around in the stream of phrases' (*P*, 6) without being guided by any set rules. Any such rules would at best be conventional anyway (as Wittgenstein insisted), and the process of orienting ourselves cannot be seen as predictable or predetermined.

Above all, Lyotard wants to emphasise 'the lightness of thoughts' (*P*, 5), which is in keeping with his overall commitment to flexibility in regard to ideas and politics – the attitude of svelteness he so admires. We should never allow ourselves to be trapped in one way of thinking or belief system, otherwise we are likely to start acting in an authoritarian and totalitarian manner that is to humanity's collective disadvantage. The more we recognise the fluidity of thought then the more we can inhibit the development of grand narrative. Grand narrative amounts to an attempt to regulate thought, which to Lyotard is a pointless and self-deluding activity. Neither is philosophical discourse immune from this impulse, with Lyotard warning us that 'what is threatening in the work of thinking (or writing) is not that it remains episodic but that it pretends to be complete' (*P*, 6). In thought, as in knowledge, completeness must always lie beyond our reach.

Passages

Clouds
Fractals
Language Games
Rules
Svelteness
Totality, Totalisation

THOUGHT WITHOUT A BODY

Daniel Whistler

'Can Thought Go on Without a Body?', the first chapter of *The Inhuman* ([1988c] 1991a), is key to understanding Lyotard's later thought. Not only is this essay the major source for garnering his opinions on technology, solar catastrophe and the mind–body relation, by dramatising these opinions in a dialogue between 'He' and 'She', but also it marks one of Lyotard's most intriguing excurses into questions of gender.

'Thought without a body' orients much of Lyotard's later work. 'A Postmodern Fable', for example, introduces the 'cosmic' dimension of the problem. This can be summed up in two statements: first, 'The Sun is going to explode' (*PF*, 83); second, 'something ought to escape the conflagration of the system and its ashes' (*PF*, 84). It is *what this 'something' will be* which interests Lyotard. The overriding question concerns 'what human beings will have become' (*PF*, 84) when they escape the Sun's explosion. Can human thought be conceived as surviving the solar catastrophe, when the human body is ineluctably restricted to the specific energy sources of the Earth?

Entwined with this 'cosmic' concern is a political one which Lyotard stresses in his Introduction to *The Inhuman*. The scientific system directed towards saving 'humanity' from this solar catastrophe is a 'grand narrative' which must be resisted. This is 'the inhumanity of the system which is currently being consolidated under the name of development' (*I*, 2). It is, moreover, to another 'inhuman' element Lyotard turns for such

resistance: 'a familiar and unknown guest' (*I*, 2–3) within the mind that
stimulates thought. In 'Can thought go on without a body?', Lyotard goes
on to discuss whether this second 'good' inhuman is, in fact, only possible
through the very physical embodiment of thought which the first 'bad'
inhumanity of the system is trying to eliminate in the name of escaping the
solar catastrophe.

On first glance, 'Can thought go on without a body?' presents a differend between two different genres of thought: the technological versus
the philosophical, the male versus the female. 'He' opposes himself to
'you philosophers' and adopts, instead, a technological discourse which
conceives of thought as a form of 'software' that can be 'programmed' into
different 'hardware' (whether the human body or an artificial body): 'so
the problem of the technological sciences can be stated as: how to provide
this software with a hardware that is independent of the conditions of life
on earth. That is: how to make thought without a body possible' (*I*, 13).
For 'He' (at least initially) science must create forms of hardware that can
withstand the solar catastrophe and so allow thought to continue without
a body.

'She', in contrast, resolutely rejects not only the possibility of the separation of thought and body but also the terms in which 'He' frames the
debate. 'She' is committed to the uniqueness of thought's embodiment in
flesh. Bodies cannot be exchanged, because the particularity of the individual's flesh is what gives rise to thought. In what follows, She provides
a subtle phenomenological description (indebted to Maurice Merleau-
Ponty, among others) of the role of flesh in stimulating thought. Gender in
particular is the paradigmatic example of such bodily difference (*I*, 21–3).
On this reading, each genre of discourse has a corresponding inhumanity
and a corresponding catastrophe, but the two remain incommensurable,
and 'He' and 'She' talk forever at cross-purposes.

However, such an account does not do justice to the complexity of
Lyotard's thinking here. To take the most basic example: 'He' is not
fully committed to the disembodiment of thought, but raises a number of
objections to the separation of thought and body. For example, thought
is not structured around binary logic but the ambiguities of perception.
Acknowledgment of this forces 'He' to retract his earlier positions: 'It's
obvious from this objection that what makes thought and the body inseparable isn't just that the latter is the indispensible hardware for the former'
(*I*, 15–16).

It is therefore important to recognise the continuities that exist between
the two voices, as well as their differences. Instead of a differend, the
correct model on which to interpret this essay is one of a gradual retreat
from the software/hardware model to one which does full phenomeno-

logical justice to the indeterminacies of the relation between thought and body. This is not to say Lyotard refutes the technological position with a phenomenological one: the solar catastrophe remains crucial for the late Lyotard. However, he uses the essay, 'Can thought go on without a body?', to begin to generate a way of thinking about the mind–body relation which remains committed to the fleshy differences which give rise to thought.

Passages

Body
Inhuman
Posthumanism
Resistance
Techno–Science
Thought

TIME

Stuart Sim

As its subtitle indicates, time is a major preoccupation of Lyotard in *The Inhuman: Reflections on Time* ([1988c] 1991a), where he addresses the problem faced by the human race in the eventual, and inevitable, death of the sun. Lyotard's warning is that techno–science might respond to this by moving past the human to put its faith in computerised systems, which in theory would have the ability to outlast the sun's demise as a source of light and heat. He feels this is a process which is already under way in our culture and that it will lead to the marginalisation of the human race, a trend he exhorts us to combat in order to prevent the triumph of the inhuman. The relationship we construct to time becomes a critical part of that campaign of resistance.

The Inhuman suggests an interesting tension in Lyotard's concept of the event. He continually returns to the liberating quality of the event throughout his writings, seeing this as proof that metanarratives cannot predetermine what will happen no matter how much they may strive 'to subordinate the present to what is (still) called the "future"' (*I*, 65). Responsiveness to the event, and the opportunities it can present, acts as an antidote to the power of metanarratives, revealing the limitations of their power to control. The openness of the future is an encouragement to little narratives everywhere therefore, a sign that there is always hope in taking on the might of the metanarratives in their lives, thus preserving 'the contingency and freedom proper to the human project' (*I*, 69). Yet the future is not ultimately open if we cast our minds ahead to the death of the sun. At some point, we shall no longer be able to turn events to account, and the human project will be staring at extinction. All of us have to confront this prospect in our own individual lives, but the death of the sun signals something far more apocalyptic: 'Human death is included in the life of human mind. Solar death implies an irreparably exclusive disjunction between death and thought: if there's death, then there's no thought. Negation without remainder. No self to make sense of it. Pure event. Disaster' (*I*, 11). The task this leaves us with is 'how to make thought without a body possible' (*I*, 13). Techno–science and development are dedicated to expansion and can only regard solar death as a challenge to be overcome, perhaps by means of an advanced generation of thinking-machines. But Lyotard cannot really convince himself that such a separation can be made, refusing to concede that machines are ever thinking, as we understand the term.

Until we reach the fateful point when the contingency and freedom of the human project collapses, however, we exist in time and that disposes us to make sense of the events within it by means of periodisation. For Lyotard this is a delusive activity, and he speaks of

the pointlessness of any periodization of cultural history in terms of 'pre-' and 'post-', before and after, for the single reason that it leaves unquestioned the position of the 'now', of the present from which one is supposed to be able to achieve a legitimate perspective on a chronological succession. (*I*, 24)

It is in the interests of metanarratives like modernity to have us believe that we do indeed have such a perspective, of having evolved over time into a much more successful culture – a culture programmed for perpetual material progress through the agency of techno–science and development, to the extent that we no longer need concern ourselves much with the past (as capitalism, for example, does not). Neither is postmodernity outside this process; in fact, 'the postmodern is always implied in the modern . . . Modernity is constitutionally and ceaselessly pregnant with its postmodernity' (*I*, 25). It is as if modernity believes it has conquered time, with Lyotard noting that '[d]evelopment imposes the saving of time' in the cause of ever–faster and more efficient production; but as he also insists, '[t]o go fast is the forget fast' (*I*, 3). Forgetting is one of the cardinal sins for Lyotard, who demands that we must always bear witness to our actions (as plainly did not happen in so many cases in respect of the Holocaust). Whatever promotes forgetting is also promoting the cause of the inhuman.

What we are engaged in, Lyotard argues, is the 'rewriting' of modernity, an activity which requires a constant 'working through' by us where there has to be 'the deployment of time between "not yet", "no longer" and "now"' (*I*, 35). None of the computerised systems constructed by development have any sense of those categories, merely constituting a menu which development manipulates to its own ends. Deploying time, indeed having an awareness of time, is to be regarded as a defining aspect of the human, thus part of our resistance to the inhuman scheme proposed by development. The tragic aspect to all this, however, is that we have only limited time in which to resist.

Passages

Development
Event
Inhuman
Modern, Modernity
Performativity
Resistance

TOTALITY, TOTALISATION

Stuart Sim

For thinkers committed to difference, pluralism, pragmatism and epistemological relativism, the totalising imperative can only be regarded as the enemy, and it comes under constant attack from poststructuralists and postmodernists, for whom totality will always remain an alien concept. The depth of Lyotard's antipathy to the concept can be gauged from his recommendation that we should 'wage a war on totality' (*PC*, 82) if we genuinely want difference to go on playing a significant role in our social and political lives. From his early career, and the doubts he voices about the validity of Marxist methodology, onwards, Lyotard never wavers in his opposition to totality and everything that it has come to represent in Western culture – philosophically and ideologically.

The system-building imperative is very strong throughout the Western philosophical tradition, and both poststructuralists and postmodernists have been at some pains to expose its deficiencies. Their primary concern is with what such systems exclude, such as any reference to the arbitrariness of their foundations of discourse. As latter-day sceptics, they espouse a relativist line on epistemological theories, pointing out that their assumption of totality does not hold up. There simply is no starting point that can unproblematically provide a basis for discourse, with Lyotard arguing that all we have in reality is a series of narratives (as well as the ability to keep on creating new ones) that have to be judged pragmatically in terms of their effects, rather than their, to him non-existent, truth-value: 'they are legitimated by the simple fact that they do what they do' (*PC*, 23). Universally applicable legitimation must always remain a mirage, and Lyotard takes it as one of his major tasks as a philosopher to demonstrate this as well as the damage that has been done by believing otherwise. Ideologies that regard themselves as in possession of such principles of legitimation tend to take it as their right to impose themselves on others: imperialism starts from just such an assumption, and in its Western form is still a critical factor, often a very disruptive one, in global politics.

Marxism has been a particular target of Lyotard, whose writings for the *Socialisme ou Barbarie* journal over the course of the Algerian revolution chart a growing disenchantment with the totalising bias of the theory. Marxism presents itself as a universal theory, holding the answer to all the problems of humanity whenever and wherever these arise. Dialectical materialism is taken to be a natural law of existence and completely beyond any doubts as to its truth, as is the assumption that human history is to be viewed as a perpetual class struggle which it is Marxism's destiny finally to resolve. For Lyotard, however, Marxism has at best a limited applicability to the Algerian situation, which is not amenable to a 'one-size-fits-all' solution of the kind that Marxism insists upon. Lyotard finds it difficult to envisage the Algerian population as a totality, seeing them instead as a disparate group of individuals with their own special needs consequent on the position they occupy within society. Prophetically enough, he foresees problems if the Marxist model is persevered with in this case, suggesting that it will lead to political authoritarianism.

Grand narratives in general work in terms of totality, convinced their system is best and that all who disagree with this are an enemy who must be marginalised, or even silenced. Capitalism rejects the claims of communism, and vice versa, and theocracies reject both as well as those of any other religion. Pluralism is rarely given a chance in such systems, and even the apparent official support for multiculturalism in the West in recent history has proved fraught with problems, arousing considerable opposition from those who demand an integration that would effectively eradicate cultural difference, as well as from those who think that such integration is impossible anyway and would rather retain the original monoculturalism.

Lyotard insists that the notion of totality is ideologically motivated, serving the cause of those in positions of power. Neither can he find any justification at all for it philosophically, his line of argument being that there is always something that lies beyond our ability to know or experience – such as the realm of the sublime. From this stance, any thinker who feels he or she has a foolproof method of grounding knowledge is deluded. Although not the first to reach such a conclusion – it is a staple of sceptical thought, particularly of his contemporary Jacques Derrida – Lyotard makes more political capital of it than most.

Passages

Antifoundationalism
Difference
Legitimation
Marxism
Pluralism
Scepticism

TOUCH

Stuart Sim

Lyotard lays great store by the ability to be sensitive to events, to respond to them as they happen without imposing a theoretically derived structure on them. It is a case for him of being 'open to the "It happens that" rather than to the "What happens"', which demands that we become particularly skilled in 'the perception of small differences' (*P*, 18). The tendency among most of humanity, however, is to concentrate on the 'What happens' and to force it into some preconceived pattern, such that the experience loses its uniqueness and we miss the opportunities it provides for change.

As an example of that skill in action, he cites the art of Paul Cézanne, whose Montagne Sainte Victoire series of paintings reveal just such an 'acute sensitivity' (*P*, 20) to the landscape. What Cézanne manages to achieve in the series is to capture 'the birth of colors, like the dawn of a cloud on the horizon' (*P*, 19), indicating both an intensity of engagement with the landscape and a refusal to process it through existing aesthetic models. As one of the major figures in the development of post-impressionism Cézanne is very self-consciously breaking new ground, responding to the 'It happens that' and allowing it to shape his art. Lyotard plays on the various senses of the English word 'touch' to describe this condition, suggesting that it 'brings together perfectly the idea of an agonistic, loving contact between the flesh of the painter and what Merleau-Ponty called the flesh of the world and the connotation of a singular style' (*P*, 19). We could say that the landscape touches Cézanne's emotions and that he proves himself to be in touch with the play of differences in it as they unfold over time, adding his own particular touch to their artistic depiction. Touch comes to be equated with the kind of sensitivity that Lyotard wants us to display at all times to events.

Although he sees no direct correlation between the worlds of art and politics, Lyotard nevertheless invites us to consider whether touch plays a key role in the latter field too, pointing out that we have to learn how 'to "listen" here and there to the manifold contingency of data' (*P*, 21) in politics no less than in art. 'The stakes of politics', as he puts it, 'are definitely not to know something but to change something' (*P*, 21), and this is a matter yet again of possessing and exhibiting a finely honed sensitivity to unfolding events. Touch can be identified to a certain extent with svelteness, which calls for a similar kind of flexibility and openness on the part of the individual. To display touch is to manifest a receptivity that is necessary if we are to effect the changes that keep a society functioning in a dynamic manner, rather than being ruled by a restrictive metanarrative. Unfortunately, as Lyotard notes, we all too often take refuge instead in metanarrative thinking because of the insecurity that touches from the unknown can induce in us.

Passages

Aesthetics
Art
Event
Politics
Probity
Svelteness

UNKNOWN

Stuart Sim

Lyotard insists that we must acknowledge the fact of the unknown as a permanent feature of our existence, and that this ought to have a profound effect our worldview. It is the unknown that prevents any project of totalisation – such as that assumed by Marxism – from ever being successful, and such projects are a characteristic feature of the modern world, where grand narratives are obsessed with exerting domination. There is always something that lies beyond our capacity to know, as in the case of the sublime, for example, a topic that Lyotard is very much concerned with in his later career (most notably in *Lessons on the Analytic of the Sublime* ([1991b] 1994), his commentary on Immanuel Kant's *Critique of Judgement* ([1790] 2000)). Even science cannot claim to be able to conquer the unknown, with Lyotard arguing that in its current form it simply generates ever more of it: 'by concerning itself with such things as undecidables, the limits of precise control, conflicts characterized by incomplete information, "*fracta*," catastrophes, and pragmatic paradoxes . . . [i]t is producing not the known, but the unknown' (*PC*, 60). This is an expression of what he calls our 'desire for the unknown' (*PC*, 67). While most scientists would no doubt dispute this picture of their activities, recent scientific enquiry, especially in the field of physics, does seem to keep discovering new mysteries that current theories cannot encompass. Doubts are even beginning to be aired about whether a truly all-explanatory Grand Unified Theory (GUT), a long-standing goal of the physics community, will ever be achievable.

The notion of there being limits to human abilities is a recurrent theme in Lyotard, and is part of his reaction against the Enlightenment project and its seemingly boundless faith in human reason. That project, as realised in the form of modernity, is committed to achieving complete control over the environment through the use of a rationally directed technology, and is constantly trying to roll back the boundaries of the unknown. The point that a thinker like Lyotard is making is that no matter how much rolling back takes place there always will be a boundary ahead of us, and that it is an illusion that we can ever reach a state of total knowledge. In that respect, the sublime, which by definition transcends human reason, strikes a particularly damaging blow against Enlightenment pretensions, signalling where we hit the limit of our powers.

To acknowledge the ineradicability of the unknown is to admit that totalisation is a futile exercise, which ought to make us sceptical about all universalising theories: effectively, these cannot deliver on their promises. As Lyotard trenchantly observes, 'We have paid a high enough price for the nostalgia of the whole and the one, for the reconciliation of the concept and the sensible' (*PC*, 81–2). That nostalgia has even fed into our artistic practice, as in modernism, when what it should be facing up to is that there is a realm of the unpresentable and that it is bad faith to pretend otherwise. Yet again, the message is that there are barriers we cannot breach.

Passages

Enlightenment
Knowledge
Modernism
Postmodern Science
Sublime
Totality, Totalisation

UNPRESENTABLE

Stuart Sim

Lyotard's work exhibits a persistent concern with what transcends human understanding – the sublime or the unknown, for example – and the unpresentable is yet another aspect of this. The unpresentable emerges from the sublime in that phenomena like the infinite can be conceived but never experienced, therefore they lie beyond our ability to represent. While we may have an idea of such a thing as the infinitely great, 'we do not have the capacity to show an example of this' (*PC*, 78). Recognition of this lack on our part can be frustrating since it signals that we can never have a total understanding of our world. But whereas Lyotard wants us to acknowledge this as an inescapable part of being human, many thinkers and artists have instead sought to find ways to overcome it. Immanuel Kant devoted his *Critique of Judgement* ([1790] 2000) to this very exercise, and modern art in general, Lyotard contends, is engaged in a similar project:

I shall call modern the art which devotes 'its little technical expertise' . . . as Diderot used to say, to present the fact that the unpresentable exists. To make visible that there is something which can be conceived and which can neither be seen nor made visible: this is what is at stake in modern painting. (*PC*, 78)

This can be considered a more general observation about the arts in the modern period, with many authors having a similar objective in mind, as Lyotard notes is the case with Marcel Proust and James Joyce.

Lyotard dismisses the modernist attempt to present the unpresentable as being merely an instance of 'nostalgia of the whole and the one' (*PC*, 81), based on the illusion that there ever was, or could be, such a unity of experience. The sublime ought to disabuse us of such a belief, but modernism subtly encourages it by tapping into its audience's capacity for a comforting nostalgia. For Lyotard, such a response is a world away from what they should be feeling: 'the real sublime sentiment, which is an intrinsic combination of pleasure and pain' (*PC*, 81). Modernism makes the unpresentable seem less of a threat therefore, and that is to mislead us as to the real nature of existence.

To be postmodern is to go beyond that pointless desire for a totality of understanding, with Lyotard asking us to 'be witnesses to the unpresentable' (*PC*, 82) rather than pretending that we can somehow reconcile the gap between what we can conceive and what we can experience and represent. Postmodern artists will communicate no 'nostalgia for the unattainable', but will strive instead 'to impart a stronger sense of the unpresentable' (*PC*, 81) in their work, to make us aware that it should engender the full sublime sentiment of simultaneous pleasure and pain. We have to face up to the unpresentable as a fact of our existence, instead of regarding it as a sign of some kind of cultural fall from grace that can be assuaged relatively easily by pressing the right emotional buttons.

Passages

Aesthetics
Art
Literature
Modernism
Sublime
Unknown

WITTGENSTEIN, LUDWIG (1889–1951) – see 'dissensus', 'game theory, gaming', 'language games', 'little narrative', 'paralogy', 'phenomenology', 'pragmatics' and 'thought'

WRITING

Stuart Sim

In *Writing and Difference* (1967b [1978]) Jacques Derrida complained of the structuralist approach to literary criticism that it was based on the assumption that each work of an author was an expression, whether well or poorly realised, of some overall theme or concern that drove the author's writing career. For a structuralist critic, there was an essence to every author's work that shaped his or her output, meaning that the act of writing was to a large extent predetermined. Each time around a germ of the overall pattern to their particular oeuvre was present, and the author followed this through as best as he or she could. Derrida rejected this idea, insisting that writing was more akin to a voyage of discovery whose end-point could never be known in advance, a state of becoming rather than a predigested activity. To think otherwise was effectively to deny that there was real creativity involved in the writing process – an assessment which could be applied across the other arts.

Lyotard's view of writing takes a similarly poststructuralist stance: writing is, as he provocatively puts it, 'irresponsible, in the strict sense of the term, because it does not come in response to a question . . . Writing marches to its own beat and it has no debts' (*P*, 8). He goes on to claim that the author must take no account of the reader when writing, emphasising the poststructuralist dislike of anything that hints at predetermination. In a further thought-provoking aside in one of the interviews for *Just Gaming* ([1979] 1985), Lyotard suggests that writing philosophy and creative literature are not such different activities as they are traditionally considered to be:

[W]hat I write is not fiction. But I do wonder more and more: Is there a real difference between a theory and a fiction? After all, don't we have the right to present theoretical statements under the form of fictions, in the form of fictions? Not *under* the form, but *in* the form. (*JG*, 5)

While there is a long-standing tradition of utilising fiction to put across philosophical ideas (think of such well-known examples as Jean-Paul Sartre's *Nausea* ([1938] 1965)), there is a more subversive implication here that there is no ultimate truth-value for philosophy, that it is just another narrative which is either found interesting or not.

Lyotard does worry about manipulating the reader, however, and is aware that writing can be an exercise in power, of the author seeking to control the reader's response, which is not something he would wish to promote. At times he goes to extreme lengths to avoid falling into that trap, speaking of *Libidinal Economy* ([1974] 1993a) as being 'drawn up more in the spirit of the bottle tossed into the ocean than in that of a return of the effects of the statements to their author' (*JG*, 5). In a sense that is true of all of Lyotard's later philosophical writings, in that he does not want to be perceived as propagating yet another metanarrative. The author should be as careful as possible not to predetermine the linkages the reader goes on to make.

Passages

Aesthetics
Links, Linkages
Literature
Philosophy
Power

Bibliography

JEAN-FRANÇOIS LYOTARD

Main Published Works

(1948), 'Nés en 1925', *Les Tempes Modernes*, 3/32, pp. 2,052–7.

(1954), *La phénoménologie*, Paris: Presses Universitaires de France.

(1971), *Discours, figure*, Paris: Klinckseick.

(1973a), *Dérive à partir de Marx et Freud*, Paris: Union Générale d'Éditions.

(1973b), *Des dispositifs pulsionnels*, Paris: Union Générale d'Éditions.

(1974), *Économie libidinale*, Paris: Les Éditions de Minuit.

(1975), *Le mur du pacifique*, Paris: Christian Bourgois.

(1976), *Sur cinq peintures de René Guiffrey*, Paris: Galerie Stevenson and Palluel.

(1977a), *Instructions païennes*, Paris: Galilée.

(1977b), *Récits tremblants*, Paris: Galilée.

(1977c), *Rudiments païens: Genre dissertatif*, Paris: Union Générale d'Éditions.

(1977d), *Les transformateurs Duchamp*, Paris: Galilée.

(1979), *La condition postmoderne: Rapport sur le savoir*, Paris: Minuit.

(and Jean-Loup Thebaud)(1979), *Au juste*, Paris: Christian Bourgois.

(1980a), *La Partie de peinture*, Cannes: M. Candela.

(1980b), *Sur le constitution du temps par le couleur dans les oeuvres récentes d'Albert Aymé*, Paris: Éditions Traversière.

(1981), *Monory. Ciels: Nebuleuses et galaxies: Les confins d'un dandysme*, Paris: Galerie Maeght.

(1982a), *Monogrammes/Loin du doux*, Paris: Catalogue Baruchello, Galerie Le Dessin.

(1982b), *Le travail et l'écrit chez Daniel Buren: Une introduction à la philosophie des arts contemporains*, Limoges: NDLR.

(1983), *Le Différend*, Paris: Minuit.

(and Ruth Francken) (1983), *L'histoire de Ruth*, Paris: Le Castor Astral.

(1984a), *L'assassinat de l'expérience par le peinture: Monory*, Paris: Castor Astral.

(1984b), *Tombeau de l'intellectuel et autres papiers*, Paris: Galilée.

(ed.) (1985a), *Les Immateriaux. Vol. 1: Album. Inventaire*. Paris: Centre Georges Pompidou.

(1985b), 'Judicieux dans le différend', in Jacques Derrida et al., *La Faculté de juger*, Paris: Éditions de Minuit, pp. 195–236.

(1986a), *L'enthousiasme: La critique kantienne de l'histoire*, Paris: Galilée.

(1986b), *Le postmoderne expliqué aux enfants: Correspondance 1982–1985*, Paris: Galilée.

(1987), *Que peindre? Adami, Arakawa, Buren*, Paris: Éditions de la Différence.

(1988a), *La guerre des Algeriens: Écrits 1956–63*, Paris: Galilée.

(1988b), *Heidegger et 'les juifs'*, Paris: Galilée.

(1988c), *L'inhumain: Causeries sur le temps*, Paris: Galilée.

(1989), 'Le survivant', in Migel Abensour, ed., *Ontologie et politique: Actes du colloque Hannah Arendt*, Paris: Tierce, pp. 257–76.

(1990), *Pérégrinations: Loi, forme, événement*, Paris: Galilée.

(1991a), *La face des choses*, Le Havre: Catalogue Laponge.

(1991b), *Leçons sur l'analytique du sublime*, Paris: Galilée.

(1991c), *Lectures d'enfance*, Paris: Galilée.

(1992), *Sans appel: La geste d'Appel en quête d'un commentaire*, Paris: Galilée.

(1993a), *Moralités postmodernes*, Paris: Galilée.

(1993b), *Sam Francis: Lessons of Darkness – "Like the paintings of a blind man" (Sam Francis)*, Venice, CA: Lapis Press.

(and Eberhard Gruber) (1994), *Un trait d'union*, Sainte-Foy, QU: Éditions Le Griffon d'argile.

(1995), 'Libidinal economy in Sade and Klossowski', in David Allison, Mark S. Roberts and Allen S. Weiss, eds, *Sade and the Narrative of Transgression*, Cambridge: Cambridge University Press, pp. 62–75.

(1996a), 'Musique et postmodernité', *Surfaces*, VI:203, pp. 4–16.

(1996b), *Signé, Malraux*, Paris: Grasset et Fasquelle.

(1997a), *Flora Danica: La sécession du geste dans la peinture de Stig Brøgger*, Paris: Galilée.

(1997b), *Corinne Filippi: Photographie*, Reims: Les Éditions du Paysage.

(1997c), *Pastels/Pierre Skira: Parce que la couleur est un cas de la poussière*, Paris: Galerie Patrice Tregano.

(1998a), *Chambre sourde: L'anthiesthétique de Malraux*, Paris: Galilée.

(1998b), *La confession d'Augustin*, Paris: Galilée.

(2000), *Misère de la philosophie*, Paris: Galilée.

(and Christine Buci-Glucksmann) (2009), *Karel Appel, un geste de couleur (Karel Appel, a Gesture of Colour)*, trans. Vlad Ionescu and Peter Milne, Leuven: Leuven University Press.

Works in English by Jean-François Lyotard

(1984a), *Driftworks*, trans. Roger McKeon, Susan Hanson, Ann Knab, Richard Lockwood and Joseph Maier, New York: Columbia University Press.

(1984b), *The Postmodern Condition: A Report on Knowledge*, trans. Geoffrey Bennington and Brian Massumi, Manchester: Manchester University Press.

(and Jean-Loup Thébaud) (1985), *Just Gaming*, trans. Wlad Godzich, Manchester: Manchester University Press.

(1987), 'Judiciousness in dispute, or Kant after Marx', trans. Cecile Lindsay, in Murray Kreiger, ed., *The Aims of Representation: Subject/Text/History*, New York: Columbia University Press, pp. 23–67.

(1988a), *The Differend: Phrases in Dispute*, trans. Georges Van Den Abbeele, Manchester: Manchester University Press.

(1988b), *Peregrinations: Law, Form, Event*, New York: Columbia University Press.

(1989), *The Lyotard Reader*, ed. Andrew Benjamin, Oxford and Cambridge, MA: Blackwell.

(1990a), *Duchamp's Trans/Formers*, trans. I. McLeod, Venice, CA: Lapis Press.

(1990b), *Heidegger and "the jews"*, trans. Andreas Michel and Mark S. Roberts, Minneapolis: University of Minnesota Press.

(1990c), *Pacific Wall*, trans. Bruce Boone, Venice, CA: Lapis Press.

(1991a), *The Inhuman: Reflections on Time*, trans. Geoffrey Bennington and Rachel Bowlby, Oxford: Blackwell.

(1991b), *Phenomenology*, trans. Brian Beakley, Albany, NY: State University of New York Press.

(1993a), *Libidinal Economy*, trans. Iain Hamilton Grant, London: Athlone Press.

(1993b), *Political Writings*, trans. Bill Readings and Kevin Paul Geiman, London: UCL Press.

(1993c), *The Postmodern Explained to Children: Correspondence 1982–1985*, trans. Don Barry, Bernadette Maher, Julian Pefanis, Virginia Spate and Morgan Thomas, ed. Julian Pefanis and Morgan Thomas, Minneapolis: University of Minnesota Press.

(1993d), *Toward the Postmodern*, ed. Robert Harvey and Mark S. Roberts, Atlantic Highlands, NJ, and London: Humanities Press International.

(1994), *Lessons on the Analytic of the Sublime*, trans. Elizabeth Rottenberg, Stanford, CA: Stanford University Press.

(1997), *Postmodern Fables*, trans. Georges Van Den Abbeele, Minneapolis and London: University of Minnesota Press.

(1998), *The Assassination of Experience by Painting – Monory*, trans. Rachel Bowlby, London: Black Dog.

(1999), *Signed, Malraux*, trans. Robert Harvey, Minneapolis and London: University of Minnesota Press.

(and Eberhard Gruber) (1999), *The Hyphen: Between Judaism and Christianity*, trans. Pascale-Anne Brault and Michael Naas, Amherst, NY: Humanity Books.

(2000), *The Confession of Augustine*, trans. Richard Beardsworth, Stanford, CA: Stanford University Press.

(2001), *Soundproof Room: Malraux's Anti-Aesthetics*, trans. Robert Harvey, Stanford, CA: Stanford University Press.

(2006), *The Lyotard Reader and Guide*, ed. Keith Crome and James Williams, Edinburgh: Edinburgh University Press.

(2009a), *Enthusiasm: The Kantian Critique of History*, trans. Georges Van Den Abbeele, Stanford, CA: Stanford University Press.

(2009b), 'Music and postmodernity', trans. David Bennett, in David Bennett, ed., *Postmodernism, Music and Cultural Theory*, special issue of *New Formations*, 66 (Spring), pp. 37–45.

(2010), *Discourse, Figure*, trans. Antony Hudek, Minneapolis, MN, and London: University of Minnesota Press.

Critical Works

Pretty well all books discussing postmodernism will mention Lyotard at some point or other, and it would be unrealistic to include all of these here. What follows instead is a list of the major critical works specifically mentioning Lyotard in the title, and a selection of the more prominent studies of postmodernism as a general cultural phenomenon which will help to put Lyotard's work in context.

Adair, Gilbert (1990), *The Postmodernist Always Rings Twice: Reflections on Culture in the 90s*, London: Fourth Estate.

Altieri, Charles (1989), 'Judgement and justice under postmodern conditions; or how Lyotard helps us read Rawls as a postmodern thinker', in R. W. Dasenbrock, ed., *Redrawing the Lines*, Minneapolis: Minnesota University Press, pp. 61–91.

Anderson, Perry (1998), *The Origins of Postmodernity*, London: Verso.

Bauman, Zygmunt (1992), *Intimations of Postmodernity*, London: Routledge.

Benhabib, Seyla (1984), 'Epistemologies of postmodernism: A rejoinder to Jean-François Lyotard', *New German Critique*, 33, pp. 103–26.

Benjamin, Andrew, ed. (1992), *Judging Lyotard*, London and New York: Routledge.

Bennett, David (2009), 'Lyotard, post-politics and riotous music', in David Bennett, ed., *Postmodernism, Music and Cultural Theory*, special edition of *New Formations*, 66 (Spring), pp. 46–57.

Bennett, David (2010), 'Libidinal economy, prostitution and consumer culture', *Textual Practice*, 24:1, pp. 93–121.

Bennington, Geoffrey (1985), 'Lyotard: From discourse and figure to experimentation and event', *Paragraph*, 6, pp. 19–27.

Bennington, Geoffrey (1988), *Lyotard: Writing the Event*, Manchester: Manchester University Press.

Bennington, Geoffrey (2008), *Late Lyotard*, CreateSpace.

Bertens, Hans (1995), *The Idea of the Postmodern: A History*, London and New York: Routledge.

Best, Steven, and Douglas Kellner (1991), *Postmodern Theory: Critical Interrogations*, New York: Guilford Press.

Boyne, Roy, and Ali Rattansi, eds (1990), *Postmodernism and Society*, Basingstoke and London: Macmillan, now Basingstoke: Palgrave Macmillan.

Browning, Gary (2000), *Lyotard and the End of Grand Narratives*, Cardiff: University of Wales Press.

Callinicos, Alex (1989), *Against Postmodernism: A Marxist Perspective*, Cambridge: Polity Press and Blackwell.

Carroll, David (1987a), 'Narrative, heterogeneity, and the question of the political: Bakhtin and Lyotard', in Murray Krieger, ed., *The Aims of Representation: Subject/Text/History*, New York: Columbia University Press, pp. 69–106.

Carroll, David (1987b), *Paraesthetics: Foucault, Lyotard, Derrida*, London: Methuen.

Colebrook, Claire, and David Bennett (2009), 'The sonorous, the haptic and the intensive', in David Bennett, ed., *Postmodernism, Music and Cultural Theory*, special edition of *New Formations*, 66 (Spring), pp. 68–80.

Connor, Steven (1989), *Postmodernist Culture: An Introduction to Theories of the Contemporary*, Oxford and Cambridge, MA: Blackwell.

Crome, Keith (2004), *Lyotard and Greek Thought: Sophistry*, Basingstoke: Palgrave, Palgrave Macmillan.

Curtis, Neal (2001), *Against Autonomy: Lyotard, Judgement and Action*, Aldershot and Burlington, VT: Ashgate.

Dhillon, Pradeep, and Paul Standish, eds (2001), *Lyotard: Just Education*, London and New York: Routledge.

Diacritics (1984), 14:3, special issue on Lyotard.

Docherty, Thomas, ed. (1993), *Postmodernism: A Reader*, Hemel Hempstead: Harvester Wheatsheaf.

Featherstone, Mike (1991), *Consumer Culture and Postmodernism*, London: Sage.

Foster, Hal, ed. (1985), *Postmodern Culture*, London and Concord, MA: Pluto Press.

Gellner, Ernest (1992), *Postmodernism, Reason and Religion*, London and New York: Routledge.

Haber, Honi Fern (1994), *Beyond Postmodern Politics: Lyotard, Rorty, Foucault*, London and New York: Routledge.

Harvey, David (1990), *The Condition of Postmodernity: An Enquiry into the Origins of Cultural Change*, Cambridge, MA, and Oxford: Blackwell.

Hutcheon, Linda (1989), *The Politics of Postmodernism*, London: Routledge.

Ingram, David (1987), 'Legitimacy and the postmodern condition: The political thought of Jean-François Lyotard', *Praxis International*, 4:3, pp. 286–305.

Jameson, Fredric (1991), *Postmodernism, or, The Cultural Logic of Late Capitalism*, London and New York: Verso.

Jencks, Charles (1984), *The Language of Post-Modern Architecture*, 4th edn, London: Academy Editions.

Jencks, Charles (1986), *What Is Post-Modernism?*, London: Art and Design.

McRobbie, Angela (1994), *Postmodernism and Popular Culture*, London and New York: Routledge.

Malpas, Simon (2003), *Jean-François Lyotard*, London and New York: Routledge.

Naas, Michael (2007), 'Lyotard Archipelago', in Claire Nouvet, Zrinka Stahuljak and Ken Still, eds, *Minima Moralia: In the Wake of Jean-François Lyotard*, Stanford, CA: Stanford University Press, pp. 176–96.

Nicholson, Linda J., ed. (1990), *Feminism/Postmodernism*, New York and London: Routledge.

Norris, Christopher (1990), *What's Wrong with Postmodernism: Critical Theory and the Ends of Philosophy*, Hemel Hempstead: Harvester Wheatsheaf.

Nouvet, Claire, Zrinka Stahuljak and Kent Still (2007), *Minima Memoria: In the Wake of Jean-François Lyotard*, Stanford, CA: Stanford University Press.

Olson, Gary A. (1995), 'Resisting a discourse of mastery: a conversation with Jean-François Lyotard', *JAC*, 15:3 <www.jacweb.org/Archived_volumes/Text_articles/V15_13_Olson_Lyotard.htm>.

Pefanis, Julian (1991), *Heterology and the Postmodern: Bataille, Baudrillard, and Lyotard*, Durham, NC, and London: Duke University Press.

Raffel, Stanley (1992), *Habermas, Lyotard and the Concept of Justice*, Basingstoke: Macmillan, now Palgrave Macmillan.

Readings, Bill (1991), *Introducing Lyotard: Art and Politics*, London and New York: Routledge.

Readings, Bill (1992), 'Pagans, perverts or primitives? Experimental justice in the empire of capital', in Andrew Benjamin, ed., *Judging Lyotard*, London and New York: Routledge, pp. 168–91.

Robbins, Derek, ed. (2004), *Jean-François Lyotard*, I–II, London: Sage.

Rojek, Chris, and Bryan S. Turner, eds (1998), *The Politics of Jean-François Lyotard: Justice and Political Theory*, London and New York: Routledge.

Rorty, Richard (1985), 'Habermas and Lyotard on Postmodernity', in Richard J. Bernstein, ed., *Habermas and Modernity*, Cambridge: Polity Press, pp. 161–75.

Rose, Margaret (1991), *The Post-modern and the Post-industrial: A Critical Analysis*, Cambridge: Cambridge University Press.

Ross, Andrew, ed. (1989), *Universal Abandon?: The Politics of Postmodernism*, Edinburgh: Edinburgh University Press.

Sarup, Madan (1988), *An Introductory Guide to Post-structuralism and Post-modernism*, Hemel Hempstead: Harvester Wheatsheaf.

Silverman, Hugh J. (2002), *Lyotard: Philosophy, Politics and the Sublime*, New York: Routledge.

Sim, Stuart (1986), 'Lyotard and the politics of antifoundationalism', *Radical Philosophy*, 44, pp. 8–13.

Sim, Stuart (1996), *Jean-François Lyotard*, Hemel Hempstead: Prentice Hall.

Sim, Stuart (2001), *Lyotard and the Inhuman*, Cambridge: Icon Press.

Sim, Stuart (2002), *Irony and Crisis: A Critical History of Postmodern Thought*, Cambridge: Icon.

Sim, Stuart, ed. (2005), *The Routledge Companion to Postmodernism*, 2nd edn, London and New York: Routledge.

Smart, Barry (1992), *Modern Conditions: Postmodern Controversies*, London and New York: Routledge.

Soja, Edward W. (1989), *Postmodern Geographies: The Reassertion of Space in Critical Social Theory*, London: Verso.

Sokal, Alan, and Jean Bricmont (1998), *Intellectual Impostures: Postmodern Philosophers' Abuse of Science*, London: Profile Books.

Taylor, Victor E., and Charles E. Winquist, eds (1998), *Postmodernism: Critical Concepts*, I–IV, London: Routledge.

Taylor, Victor E., and Charles, E. Winquist (2000), *Encyclopedia of Postmodernism*, London: Routledge.

Taylor, Victor E., and Gregg Lambert, eds (2005), *Jean-François Lyotard:*

Critical Evaluations in Cultural Theory, London and New York: Routledge.

Van Den Abbeele, Georges (2004), 'Interview with Jean-François Lyotard', in Derek Robbins, ed., *Jean-François Lyotard*, vols I–III, London: SAGE, pp. 247–56 (originally published in *Diacritics*, 14:3 (1984), pp. 16–21).

Van Reijen, Willem, and Dick Veerman (1988), 'An interview with Jean-François Lyotard', *Theory, Culture and Society*, 5, pp. 277–309.

Watson, Stephen (1984), 'Jürgen Habermas and Jean-François Lyotard, postmodernism and the crisis of rationality', *Philosophy & Social Criticism*, 10:2, pp. 1–24.

Williams, James (1998), *Lyotard: Towards a Postmodern Philosophy*, Cambridge: Polity.

Williams, James (2000), *Lyotard and the Political*, London: Routledge.

Woods, Tim (1999), *Beginning Postmodernism*, Manchester and New York: Manchester University Press.

Woodward, Ashley (2005), 'Jean-François Lyotard', *The Internet Encyclopaedia of Philosophy*, <http://www.iep.utm.edu/lyotard/#H2> (accessed 30 May 2010).

Woodward, Ashley (2009), *Nihilism in Postmodernity: Lyotard, Baudrillard, Vattimo*, Aurora, CO: The Davies Group.

OTHER WORKS CITED

Adorno, Theodor W. ([1948] 1973), *Philosophy of New Music*, trans. Anne G. Mitchell and Wesley V. Bloomster, London: Sheed and Ward.

Adorno, Theodor W. ([1966], 1983), *Negative Dialectics*, trans. E. B. Ashton, New York: Continuum.

Althusser, Louis, et al. (1965), *Lire le Capital*, vols I–II, Paris: Maspero.

Althusser, Louis, and Étienne Balibar (1970), *Reading Capital*, trans. Ben Brewster, London: NLB.

Aristotle (1955), *On Sophistical Refutations. On Coming-to-be and Passing Away. On the Cosmos*, trans. E. S. Forster and D. J. Furley, Cambridge, MA: Loeb Classical Library.

Aristotle (2009), *The Nicomachean Ethics*, ed. Lesley Brown, trans. David Ross, Oxford: Oxford University Press.

Assiter, Alison (2003), *Revisiting Universalism*, New York: Palgrave Macmillan.

Auerbach, Erich ([1959] 1984), *Scenes from the Drama of European Literature*, trans. Ralph Mannheim, Minneapolis: Minnesota University Press.

Barrow, John D. (1998), *Impossibility: The Limits of Science and the Science of Limits*, Oxford: Oxford University Press.

Barry, Peter (2002), *Beginning Theory: An Introduction to Literary and Cultural Theory*, 2nd edn, Manchester: Manchester University Press.

Battersby, Christine (2007), *The Sublime, Terror and Human Difference*, London: Routledge.

Baudrillard, Jean ([1973] 1975), *The Mirror of Production*, trans. Mark Poster, St. Louis, MO: Telos Press.

Beiner, Ronald (1983), *Political Judgement*, London: Methuen.

Benhabib, Seyla (1990), 'Epistemologies of postmodernism: A rejoinder to Jean-François Lyotard', in Linda Nicholson, ed., *Feminism/Postmodernism*, New York and London: Routledge, pp. 107–33.

Benhabib, Seyla (1992), *Situating the Self: Gender, Community and Postmodernism in Contemporary Ethics*, London: Routledge.

Bhabha, Homi K. (2005), *The Location of Culture*, 2nd edn, London and New York: Routledge.

Bloom, Harold (1982), *Agon: Towards a Theory of Revisionism*, New York: Oxford University Press.

Bourriaud, Nicholas (2009), 'Altermodern', in Nicholas Bourriaud, ed., *Altermodern: Tate Triennial*, London: Tate Publishing, pp. 11–24.

Castoriadis, Cornelius (1973), *La société bureaucratique*, Paris: Union Générale d'Éditions.

Castoriadis, Cornelius (1988), *Political and Social Writings. Volume 1: 1946–1955. From the Critique of Bureaucracy to the Positive Content of Socialism*, trans. and ed. David Ames Curtis, Minneapolis: University of Minnesota Press.

Deleuze, Gilles, and Felix Guattari ([1972] 1983), *Anti-Oedipus*, trans. Robert Hurley, Mark Seem and Helen R. Lane, Minneapolis: University of Minnesota Press.

Deleuze, Gilles, and Felix Guattari ([1980] 1988), *A Thousand Plateaus: Capitalism and Schizophrenia*, trans. Brian Massumi, London: Athlone Press.

Derrida, Jacques ([1967a] 1976), *Of Grammatology*, trans. Gayatri Chakravorty Spivak, Baltimore, MD: Johns Hopkins University Press.

Derrida, Jacques ([1967] 1978), *Writing and Difference*, trans. Alan Bass, Chicago: University of Chicago Press.

Derrida, Jacques (1988), *The Ear of the Other: Otobiography, Transference, Translation*, trans. Peggy Kamuf, ed. Christie McDonald, Lincoln, NE, and London: University of Nebraska Press.

Derrida, Jacques, et al. (1985), *La Faculté de juger*, Paris: Éditions de Minuit.

Descartes, René ([1641] 1970), *Meditations on First Philosophy*, in

Philosophical Writings, trans. and ed. Elizabeth Anscombe and Peter Thomas Geach, London: Thomas Nelson.

Farías, Victor ([1987] 1991), *Heidegger and Nazism*, ed. Joseph Margolis and Tom Rockmore, Philadelphia: Temple University Press.

Foucault, Michel (1981–8), *The History of Sexuality*, I–III. I, *The History of Sexuality: An Introduction*, trans. Robert Hurley, Harmondsworth: Penguin, [1976] 1981; II, *The Use of Pleasure*, trans. Robert Hurley, Harmondsworth: Penguin, [1984] 1987; III, *The Care of the Self*, trans. Robert Hurley, Harmondsworth: Penguin, [1984] 1988.

Freud, Sigmund (1953–74), *Standard Edition of the Works of Sigmund Freud*, vols 1–24, ed. and trans. James Strachey, London: Hogarth Press.

Freud, Sigmund (1999), *The Interpretation of Dreams*, trans. J. Crick, ed. R. Robertson, Oxford: Oxford University Press.

Gasché, Rodolphe (2000), 'Saving the honor of thinking: On Jean-François Lyotard', *Parallax*, 6:4, pp. 127–45.

Habermas, Jürgen (1962), *Strukturwandel der Offentlichkeit*, Frankfurt: Suhrkamp.

Habermas, Jürgen (1976), *Legitimation Crisis*, trans. Thomas McCarthy, London: Heinemann.

Habermas, Jürgen (1981), 'Modernity versus postmodernity', *New German Critique*, 22, pp. 3–14.

Haraway, Donna J. (1990), 'A manifesto for cyborgs: Science, technology and socialist feminism in the 1980s', in Linda Nicholson, ed., *Feminism/Postmodernism*, London: Routledge, pp. 190–233.

Haraway, Donna J. (1991), *Simians, Cyborgs, and Women: The Reinvention of Nature*, New York: Routledge.

Hardt, Michael, and Antonio Negri (2000), *Empire*, Cambridge, MA: Harvard University Press.

Hartsock, Nancy C. M. (1998), *Feminist Standpoint Revisited and Other Essays*, Oxford: Westview Press, pp. 205–26.

Heidegger, Martin ([1927] 1962), *Being and Time*, trans. John Macquarrie and Edward Robinson, Oxford: Blackwell.

Hume, David ([1739–40] 1962), *A Treatise of Human Nature*, ed. D. G. C. Macnabb, Glasgow: Fontana/Collins.

Husserl, Edmund (1950), *Idées directrices pour une phénoménologie*, trans. Paul Ricoeur, Paris: Gallimard.

Husserl, Edmund ([1900–1] 1970), *Logical Investigations*, trans. J. N. Findlay, London: Routledge & Kegan Paul.

Hutchings, Kimberly (1996), *Kant, Critique and Politics*, London: Routledge.

Joyce, James ([1922] 2008), *Ulysses*, Oxford: Oxford University Press.

Kant, Immanuel ([1764] 1973), *Observations on the Feeling of the Beautiful and the Sublime*, trans. John T. Goldthwaite, Los Angeles: University of California Press.

Kant, Immanuel ([1781] 1999), *Critique of Pure Reason*, trans. and ed. Paul Guyer and Allen W. Wood, Cambridge: Cambridge University Press.

Kant, Immanuel ([1788] 1997), *Critique of Practical Reason*, trans. and ed. Mary Gregor, Cambridge: Cambridge University Press.

Kant, Immanuel ([1790] 2000), *Critique of the Power of Judgment*, trans. Paul Guyer and Eric Matthews, Cambridge: Cambridge University Press.

Kant, Immanuel (1951), *Critique of Judgment*, trans. J. H. Bernard, New York: Hafner Press.

Kuhn, Thomas (1970), *The Structure of Scientific Revolutions*, 2nd edn, Chicago: University of Chicago Press.

Laclau, Ernesto, and Chantal Mouffe (1985), *Hegemony and Socialist Strategy: Towards a Radical Democratic Politics*, London: Verso.

Liddell, Henry George, and Robert Scott (1995), *Greek-English Lexicon. With a Revised Supplement*, 9th edn, Oxford: Clarendon Press.

Marx, Karl, *Capital* ([1867, 1885, 1894] 1976, 1978, 1981), vols I–III, trans. Ben Fowkes, Harmondsworth: Penguin.

Nicholson, Linda J., ed. (1990), 'Introduction', *Feminism/Postmodernism*, New York and London: Routledge, pp. 1–16.

Orwell, George, *1984* (1949), London: Martin Secker and Warburg.

Pearce, Fred (2006), *The Last Generation: How Nature Will Take Its Revenge for Climate Change*, London: Eden Project.

Pierce, David, and Peter de Voogd, eds (1996), *Laurence Sterne in Modernism and Postmodernism*, Amsterdam and Atlanta: Editions Rodopi.

Quine, Willard van Orman (1964), *Word and Object*, Cambridge, MA: MIT Press.

Rorty, Richard (1980), *Philosophy and the Mirror of Nature*, Oxford: Blackwell.

Sartre, Jean-Paul ([1938] 1965), *Nausea*, trans. Robert Baldick, Harmondsworth: Penguin.

Sartre, Jean-Paul ([1943] 1958), *Being and Nothingness: An Essay on Phenomenological Ontology*, trans. Hazel E. Barnes, London: Methuen.

Sim, Stuart (2010), *The End of Modernity: What the Financial and Environmental Crisis Is Really Telling Us*, Edinburgh: Edinburgh University Press.

Souyri, Pierre (1982), *Révolution et contre-révolution en Chine: Des origines à 1949*, Paris: Christian Bourgois.

Stevens, Wallace (1997), *Collected Poetry and Prose*, ed. F. Kermode and J. Richardson, New York: Library of America.

Tett, Gillian (2009), *Fool's Gold: How Unrestrained Greed Corrupted a Dream, Shattered Global Markets and Unleashed a Catastrophe*, London: Little, Brown.

Thom, René ([1972] 1975), *Structural Stability and Morphogenesis: An Outline of a General Theory of Models*, trans. D. H. Fowler, Reading, MA: W. A. Benjamin.

Von Neumann, John, and Oskar Morgenstern (1944), *Theory of Games and Economic Behaviour*, Princeton: Princeton University Press.

Weber, Max (1921), *Gesammelte Politische Schriften*, Munich: Drei Masken.

Weber, Max (1948), *From Max Weber: Essays in Sociology*, ed. H. H. Gerth and C. Wright Mills, London: Routledge and Kegan Paul.

Weber, Samuel (2000), *The Legend of Freud*, Stanford, CA: Stanford University Press.

Wittgenstein, Ludwig ([1953] 1976), *Philosophical Investigations*, trans. G. E. M. Anscombe, Oxford: Blackwell.

Notes on Contributors

Bella Adams is a Lecturer in American Literature and Director of the American Studies Resource Centre at Liverpool John Moores University. Her publications include *Amy Tan* (2005) and *Asian American Literature* (2008). In addition to research and teaching interests in Asian America and US race relations, she is also researching antiracist pedagogies.

Pamela S. Anderson is Reader in Philosophy of Religion, University of Oxford, and Tutorial Fellow in Philosophy, Regent's Park College. She is the author of *Ricoeur and Kant: Philosophy of the Will* (1993) and *A Feminist Philosophy of Religion: The Rationality and Myths of Religious Belief* (1998), and co-author (with Jordan Bell) of *Kant and Theology: An Introduction* (2010). She has also edited *New Topics in Feminist Philosophy of Religion: Contestations and Transcendence Incarnate* (2009) and co-edited (with Beverley Clack) *Feminist Philosophy of Religion: Critical Readings* (2004). She is currently working on *Michèle Le Doeuff: A Woman Philosopher in Dialogue*.

David Bennett is Reader in English and Cultural Theory at the University of Melbourne and Visiting Faculty Member of the London Consortium. His many publications include a guest-edited special issue of *New Formations*, no. 66 (Spring 2009), entitled 'Postmodernism, Music and Cultural Theory', which includes his translation of Lyotard's 'Musique et Postmodernité' and his critique of Lyotard's political aesthetics; and 'Libidinal Economy, Prostitution and Consumer Culture', *Textual Practice*, 24:1 (February 2010), which includes a critique of Lyotard's *Libidinal Economy*.

Gary Browning has been Professor of Political Thought at Oxford Brookes University since 1997. His publications include *Hegel and the History of Political Philosophy* (1999), *Rethinking R. G. Collingwood: Philosophy, Politics and the Unity of Theory and Practice* (2004*)*, *Lyotard and the End of Grand Narratives* (2000), *Contemporary Social Theory* (with A. Halcli and F. Webster; 2000), *Critical and Post-Critical Political Economy* (2005), *The Political Art of Bob Dylan* (with D. Boucher; 2009) and *Global Theory From Kant to Hardt and Negri* (2011). He was the founding and General Editor of *Contemporary Political Theory* (2000–10).

Eleanor Byrne is a Lecturer in the Department of English, Manchester Metropolitan University. Her works include the books *Deconstructing Disney* (1999) and *Homi K. Bhabha* (2009; co-authored with M. McQuillan), and the book chapters 'Muriel Spark shot in Africa' (in M. McQuillan, ed., *Theorising Muriel Spark: Gender, Race, Deconstruction*, 2002), 'Postmodernism and the postcolonial world' (in Stuart Sim, ed., *Routledge Companion to Postmodernism*, 2005) and 'Unpacking Homi Bhabha's library' (in M. McQuillan, ed., *Deconstruction Reading Politics*, 2007).

Keith Crome is Senior Lecturer in Philosophy at Manchester Metropolitan University. His research interests are in twentieth-century French Philosophy and Ancient Greek Philosophy. He is Assistant Editor of the *Journal of the British Society for Phenomenology*, the author of *Lyotard and Greek Thought: Sophistry* (2004) and co-editor (with J. Williams) of *The Lyotard Reader and Guide* (2006). He is currently writing a comparative study of Merleau-Ponty and Lyotard's writings on art.

Neal Curtis is Associate Professor in the Department of Cultural Studies and Director of the Centre for Critical Theory at the University of Nottingham. He is the author of *Against Autonomy: Lyotard, Judgement and Action* (2001), *War and Social Theory: World, Value, Identity* (2006), and is currently working on a book entitled *On Sovereignty and Superheroes*.

Thomas Docherty is Chair Professor of English and of Comparative Literature in the University of Warwick, having previously held Chairs of English in Trinity College Dublin and in the University of Kent. He is the author of many books, including *Postmodernism* (1993), *After Theory* (1996), *Criticism and Modernity* (1999), *Alterities* (1996), *Aesthetic Democracy* (2006) and *The English Question; or, Academic Freedoms* (2008). He is currently completing a book about confession and writing, provisionally entitled 'I Confess', and is writing another about the state of the University as an institution, provisionally called 'The University of the Idea'.

Angélique du Toit is a lead academic in coaching at the University of Sunderland. She is widely published in the area of coaching, postmodernism and organisations, and her books include *Corporate Strategy: A Feminist Perspective* (2006) and a co-authored text (with Stuart Sim) on critical theory and coaching, *Rethinking Coaching: Critical Theory and the Economic Crisis* (2010); journal articles include 'Power and the tale: Storyselling' (2010), 'Making sense through coaching' (2007) and

'Fundamentalism in global management and organisational ideologies' (2007).

Anthony Gritten is head of the department of performing arts at Middlesex University. He has co-edited two volumes on *Music and Gesture* (2006) and published in the journals *Musicae Scientiae* (2001, 2005), *British Journal of Aesthetics* (2004) and *Dutch Journal of Music Theory* (2009), and in the collections *Phrase and Subject: Studies in Literature and Music* (2006), *In(ter)discipline: New Languages for Criticism* (2007), *Recorded Music: Philosophical and Critical Reflections* (2008), and *The Routledge Companion to Philosophy and Music* (in press).

Karen Langhelle holds a BA (Hons) from the University of Oslo, Norway, and an MA from Simon Fraser University, Canada. She is currently a PhD candidate in the Department of English at Royal Holloway College, University of London. Her research deals with poststructuralist readings of literary dialogue, and of the dialogue novel in particular.

Tony Purvis teaches in the School of Arts and Cultures at Newcastle University. He has published in the fields of media and cultural theory, television studies, contemporary American fiction and psychoanalysis. His publications include *Television Drama: Theories and Identities* (2005) and *Media and Cultural Studies* (2006). He is currently researching late twentieth-century dialogues which connect psychoanalysis and discourses of the secular with religion, faith and discourses of the sacred.

Derek Robbins is Professor of International Social Theory in the School of Humanities and Social Sciences at the University of East London. He is the author of *The Work of Pierre Bourdieu* (1991) and of *Bourdieu and Culture* (2000) and *On Bourdieu, Education and Society* (2006); the editor of two four-volume collections of articles on Bourdieu in the Sage Masters of Contemporary Social Thought series (2000 and 2005) and of a three-volume collection of articles on Lyotard in the same series (2004). He is now writing 'The Internationalization of French Social Thought 1950–2000'.

Roy Sellars is currently on leave from his position as Senior Lecturer in literature in the English department of the University of Southern Denmark, Kolding, and is working in the English department of the University of St Gallen, Switzerland. He first became interested in Lyotard while writing his thesis at Oxford University; since then he has published, edited and translated in the field of literature and philosophy, and is writing two monographs, one on John Milton and another on Theodor W. Adorno.

Stuart Sim retired as Professor of Critical Theory at the University of Sunderland in 2008, and is now Visiting Professor of Critical Theory and Long Eighteenth-Century English Literature in the Department of English, Northumbria University. He has published widely in the area of critical theory and continental philosophy, and among his books are *Jean-François Lyotard* (1996), *Contemporary Continental Philosophy: The New Scepticism* (2000), *Post-Marxism: An Intellectual History* (2000), *Lyotard and the Inhuman* (2001), *The Routledge Companion to Postmodernism* (ed., 2005) and *The End of Modernity: What the Financial and Environmental Crisis Is Really Telling Us* (2010).

Richard G. Smith is Senior Lecturer in Human Geography and Co-Director of the Centre for Urban Theory, at Swansea University. He is the editor of *The Baudrillard Dictionary* (2010) and co-editor of *Jean Baudrillard: Fatal Theories* (2009). His writings on globalisation and cities, published over the past decade in books and journals such as *Cities*, *Urban Geography*, *IJURR*, *Annals of the Association of American Geographers*, *Environment and Planning A* and *Progress in Human Geography*, have pioneered new network approaches. His current research concerns the poststructuralist city.

Lloyd Spencer is Senior Lecturer in the School of Media at Trinity and All Saints, a college of the University of Leeds. He is the author of *Introducing the Enlightenment* (2006), *Introducing Hegel* (2007) and a biographical study of Walter Benjamin. He has also collaborated on various photographic and other projects with the art critic and essayist John Berger.

Georges Van Den Abbeele is Dean of Social Sciences and Humanities at Northeastern University, Boston. He is the author of *Travel as Metaphor: From Montaigne to Rousseau* (1992) and the forthcoming *Retreat of the French Intellectual*, as well as the co-editor of *A World of Fables* (2003) and *French Civilization and Its Discontents* (2003). He has also translated the following works by Jean-François Lyotard: *The Differend* (1988), *Postmodern Fables* (1997) and *Enthusiasm* (2009).

Daniel Whistler is a Lecturer in Philosophy at the University of Liverpool, and holds a DPhil from the University of Oxford for a thesis on the interplay of religion and language in the philosophy of F. W.

J. Schelling. In addition to writing on Kant and German Idealism, he has published on continental philosophy of religion, and in this vein is co-editor of *After the Postsecular and the Postmodern: New Essays in Continental Philosophy of Religion* (2010) and *Moral Powers, Fragile Beliefs: Essays in Moral and Religious Philosophy* (2011).

Ashley Woodward is a member of the Melbourne School of Continental Philosophy and an editor for *Parrhesia: A Journal of Critical Philosophy*. He is the author of *Nihilism in Postmodernity: Lyotard, Baudrillard, Vattimo* (2009) and of various scholarly articles on Lyotard.